To Edith - the Mother of the
Granddaughters!

Never underestimate the reward for raising
daughters - called motherhood!

Rossana's Lessons on Motherhood

Rossana Lin

Merry Christmas!

For a childe is born and a son is given!

Love,
Dad & Mom

ISBN-10: 1986489620
ISBN-13: 978-1986489621

DEDICATION

"Listen, O daughter, consider and give ear: Forget your people and your father's house. The king is enthralled by your beauty... All glorious is the princess within her chamber, her gown is interwoven with gold. In embroidered garments she is led to the king; her virgin companions follow her and are brought to you. They are led in with joy and gladness; they enter the palace of the king. Your sons will take the place of your fathers; you will make them princes throughout the land. I will perpetuate your memory through all generations; therefore the nations will praise you for ever and ever."   -- Psalm 45: 10-17

There are rumors of another world and another identity waiting for many who have yet to lay claim to it. The question is whether we are living in our true identities as royalty, making decisions daily out of our inner abundance, or are trapped inside the prison of our minds, living like refugees with no resource or recourse. This book is dedicated to all the princesses out there who are yet to discover their true identities and are waiting to be set free. May you lay hold of your inheritance and discover your exciting destinies as a princess!

CONTENTS

FOREWARD I: MY WIFE

I don't think I had any idea when I asked Rossana to join me in a life of adventure that we would have three boys and raise them in the US and then in China. Looking back on the 23 years of marriage, I couldn't have asked for a better partner and a friend to experience such a wonderful life together.

We were very different people with different ideas about things. With our first child we disagreed about how to coach him to sleep through the night. I was the tough dad and she was the tender mom. We would read many books on parenting and seek after advice. From the first to the third boy, we learned to work together as a team.

She sacrificed her promising career to devote herself to mothering. She wanted to be there for our boys. During the preschool years, she would take them to school every day and bring them home. When they became older she would be there when they come home from school to process the day, listening to their frustrations or victories.

While I taught the kids how to ride the bicycle, they would run to her when they fell and got hurt. She would tenderly clean up the cut and take them to the bathroom to help them pick out their favorite Band-Aid. Whether it's giving them a bath or dressing them in the morning, she would always handle the boys with great love.

She believed in reading, taking the boys regularly to the library to check out books and read together at home. She built a great tradition of reading stories at bed time and just before saying good night, reading a passage from the Bible and praying with them. Rossana is gifted in music and passed this on to our children. Our family band has performed in many places and inspired many people that a family can have so much fun together.

Boys not only need listening ears, but they also need solid instructions. Rossana is always dispensing advice and helping them with homework. She didn't shelter them by protecting them from the world. She encouraged them to help others, to be friends with those that other moms would rather have their kids stay away from. Here lies her greatest gift, a compassionate heart. A truly great mother not only loves her own but also knows how to teach them to love others, especially those that seem undeserving.

We learned to take time out even when our kids were small to work on our marriage. Whether it's going out on a date night or simply taking a walk together, we knew a strong marriage is the foundation of a healthy family. Talking over our differences and working through conflicts are important parts of modeling what an intimate relationship looks like and how a man loves his wife and a woman respects her husband.

This is why after 23 years I am still madly in love with this woman. She is my best friend and a great mother.

David Lin, Rossana's Husband

FOREWARD II: HANDS

Everybody in my family carry strong hands. My Dad's hands, careful and precise, shaping my world view with loving pinches, nudging me in the right direction. And me, my hands are clumsy. I'm not sure I have control over them as they glide across sheets of paper. Caleb's hands which always finds the closest instrument. Calloused from the guitar and sore from typing stories that sing louder than his lonely melodies. Jonathan whose fingers have flipped through the pages of every book he could get his hands on, shaking the hands of every opportunity that he comes across, his hands reaching endlessly after his dreams.

But my Mom's hands, my Mom's hands, like the cover of a journal, soft and weathered from where the pen rests, and where her finger tips tell stories through a keyboard. Always writing, the sound of keys clicking like a lullaby, and the screen monitor watching over me with its warm gaze. The feeling of her stroking my back when I'm sad or worried, the feeling of knowing it's going to be alright. Their gentle touch as they see where I've been bruised. My Mom's hands so gentle, with the feeling of knowing it's going to be alright. My Mom's hands telling a story of her love for me, and the sound of her typing.

Stephen Lin, Rossana's Youngest Son

FOREWARD III: THE MOST BEAUTIFUL GIFT

Along life's journey, sometimes we are surprised with a gift that delights our soul. Rossana was such a gift to me. As we became friends and I stayed in her home, my soul was inspired and fed and encouraged. As she shared deep love and affection with her children and husband, I wanted to be more loving to mine. She talked about her ideals and passion and I found myself wanting to be more excellent in my own life. Seeing her generously extend her love, encouragement and inspiration to others around her inspired me to reach out more, to give more, to work harder. Her whole life was an unexpected gift to me.

That is what you will find in her book--a gift. Your heart will be inspired, your life will be enriched, your desire to extend love and grace to those around you will grow, your ideals will be affirmed. Rarely have a I met a woman so given to living life well and fully. I will forever be grateful that I met Rosanna and I know that you will feel the same way as you meet her in this wonderful book. Be encouraged, affirmed, inspired and know that her writing will be an unexpected gift to your heart, mind and soul. I highly recommend this book to you.

Sally Clarkson, Rossana's friend & mentor,
Author of "Mission of Motherhood"

FOREWARD IV: I AM A PRINCESS

I am a princess - one of Rossana's princesses. With Rossana, we have grown from single, independent young headstrong women to married women, blending identities and dreams with our spouses. Now, twenty years later, we have morphed into mothers establishing our identities not just within a dual spousal framework, but within a more complex family structure. Motherhood is dynamic, constantly challenging and sculpting a woman's personal and marital identity. Far from sentimental bliss, motherhood is so difficult to execute that there is no one universal memo or formula describing just how to do it correctly. There was no owner's manual attached to my son when I took him home from the hospital (and yes - I did look for one). If we are fortunate, we can look to our own mothers for advice because we know that her child turned out okay :-) More likely, we will look to our peers as resources to establish our bearings. Rossana has been that invaluable guide to engage the Princesses to aim high for their own children, and to remain relatively grounded while doing it. In an age where many parents can provide so much because they have the vision and the assets to dream at high levels, a constant tension has been to gauge how much parents should provide, rescue, and engineer. While Rossana's family has never been short on fantastic ideas, dream vacations, and creative projects, they eat regular meals, cover stains on their carpet with throw rugs, pretend they are super heroes, and have lifestyles that are not museum quality but relational quality. Rossana has modeled a course of mothering that has placed discovery of destiny in a context of community. She is not just a superb resource to give out advice, but a thirsty sponge. She is constantly being sparked by new ideas from others, seamlessly sharing wisdom and gaining wisdom simultaneously. She has amassed a breadth of information, and then engages her family to live it to become people of depth and character. Not all experiments have been good; but all have been profitable. Within her own family, they have become people who will stand at the end of the day, weathering storms that no longer shake their foundation. Her community, which loves her dearly, has stood by her extraordinary experiences and has helped provide a bit of stability for her while she goes out and saves the rest of the world, princesses included.

FOREWARD V: ROSSANA'S UNUSUAL CAREER

Everyone who sees Rossana is drawn into her strong magnetic field – her elegant attire, warm and genial smile, and sincerity of speech all reflect her excellent upbringing and education. Her being constantly radiates a special intellect, warmth, serenity, sunny cheerfulness, and wisdom.

When you mention the name Rossana, this name is familiar to many in parenting circles. She is the China Regional Chair for MIT's Education Council; She flies to many places to conduct etiquette training; She has published 3 books thus far, and all of them currently flying off the bookshelves… but if you mention career, she will very frankly tell you, I am a full time mother, a mother of 3 boys.

Many years ago, when the young and high-spirited Rossana entered the MIT campus, she must have never imagined that she will become a full time mother some day. At the time, she highly disdained women who aspired to an "MRS degree". After graduation, armed with unwavering passion into the world of business, as if she had always been made for this, she would have never imagined that one day she would give up all this that she is so good at. Several years later, the beginnings of a fast track business woman has emerged. However, after her first child arrived, to the astonishment of everyone who knew her, she put away all her glowing accomplishments, retreating into the home to become wife and mother. Now, looking back, Rossana puts it bluntly, this is a turning point that she would have never predicted for herself. The decision was enormously difficult, but was very firm. She said, this is what her family needed, and what she must do at the time. Because of this one choice, her life completely changed.

Not long ago Rossana bumped into a college classmate in an airport. The past 10 years made the path of two people with the same starting point diverge in completely different directions. One became a full-time mother, another became a thrice divorced entrepreneur. The admiring gaze of her classmate further cemented Rossana's belief that she did not make a wrong choice. From her point of view, she cannot tolerate a life with a successful career yet with defective family life.

After nearly 20 years as a full-time mother, Rossana's "workplace" has only become wider and wider. Not only has the scope of her work expanded beyond her own home, but has even been wider than the traditional working woman. Even though she continues to define her role as a full-time mother, family only occupies a part of her "workplace". Her performance in this area is undoubtedly excellent. Last year, her eldest son received an early admission letter to MIT and other top schools on his own merit, finally deciding to become his mother's fellow alumnus. Before checking in to college, he took a gap year where he wrote over 50 songs, a symphony, while arranging the publication of his trilogy novels. Her 11th grader second son not only excels in academics and personal character, but is also an outstanding athlete who has currently set his careers sights on biology, as he dreams of a future helping to solve the problem of the global energy and food crisis. Her youngest son is still small, but has a sunny and independent personality. As for her husband, according to his secretary, he is a man who always books the latest departure flights and earliest return flights when traveling away from home on business. And according to Rossana, is her best friend between whom no secrets are kept from each other.

Rossana has set up a warm environment in her home full of diverse elements that demonstrate the breadth and width of the family's interests. Her home is like a large library, with books stacked everywhere. These books not only include those in vogue today, but also include classics from various cultures past and present. Besides books, she has subscribed to large numbers of magazines from within China and abroad, with content ranging from science & technology, to sports, architecture, business, economics, geography and news. Rossana has the habit of sharing a good book to read with her whole family during fruit time after dinner, where there is much animated discussion and enjoyment.

Rossana's home is like a small music hall, with piano, violin, double bass, guitar, electric guitar, drums, and bass. Every weekend, the entire house reverberates with various melodies as if a live concert was going on. Rossana was strictly trained in classical piano since early childhood, but now music is an indispensable part of her relaxation. Her favorite music ranges from modern, rock, and jazz, to classical. Yet her love of music is not merely restricted to listening. Under her leadership, her sons all have their own instrument of choice. Instead of showing off her own talent, she and her musically talented husband spend more time playing simple melodies with their kids, allowing music to be the common game that the entire family enjoys to play.

Besides books and music, the entire family enjoys watching and playing tennis, soccer, badminton, basketball, swimming, skiing, and skating together. These times of physical exercise are also favorite family times.

As for the parts of the "workplace" outside of her home, Rossana uses this analogy: it's like having many pots cooking on the stove at the same time. What does this mean? It means that there are way too many things that she needs to do, is doing, and is planning on doing.

The words most frequently rolling off Rossana's tongue are "sharing" and "serving". Therefore, everything big and small that she does revolve around these two words. Among them, things related to education occupy most of her time. For several months out of the year, her "title" is the MIT Education Council China Regional Chair, where she hosts guests from her alma mater, helps recruit and train fellow alumni in interviewing, conducts interviews, writes reports, and sees applicants. All these are done as a volunteer. In a typical day, she likes to share all kinds of experiences and lessons with people. When she sees problems that surface in Chinese education and topics bewildering Chinese parents, she busies herself writing, speaking, and sharing her life, her education, her work, and her parenting experiences. For example, she will observe problems around her, and then use her own network of relationships to form teams to collaborate and solve these problems. Or she is bringing in InvenTeams from MIT into China, finding school leaders to communicate and collaborate with to make invention a part of school culture and increase the competitiveness of Chinese schools. She says that education is too important for children. And because she knows this too deeply, she is constantly involuntarily being drawn to this big magnet, wanting to do more for more people. Each summer, her entire family of 5 would set out for Gansu, where they volunteer as English teachers. This activity has been taking place for several years now.

Besides education, she is a promoter and example of families serving together. On weekends, she would invite families to her home to share enriching content that include parenting, business, family band, etc. Her firm belief is that to change someone or some family, there needs to be life on life contact. She hopes that through this kind of contact, to freely share whatever has benefitted her before. Even more surprisingly, as a foreigner, she has also been elected a member of her community's Home Owner's Committee, helping to attend to a Committee that has fracture as a result of previous conflicts. To protect the environment in the community from breaking down, to make sure building additions go through proper permitting process, a sense of service and justice compelled Rossana to volunteer herself. She said, these things need someone to take the lead and bear the responsibility for. If no one attends to them, the environment in the entire community will be affected, and will then impact children who live there and are growing up there. This is our home, and I need to take a part.

Rossana's family of 5 has now been in Beijing for 8 years. I hear that the decision to move the entire family over was made by her husband and her together. Their lives in America has been one of ease. However, because of common beliefs on wholeheartedly serving the world, they decided to move to a place that could use their help and that they can help change through their hard work. In the end, it was a coincidence that they decided on Beijing. Rossana revealed that before they came, to make sure that there was no way back, they sold their house and cars in America. Imagine, a woman who leaves the work and living space that she is so familiar with to arrive in a completely strange city, how confused she must be? But because there is a sense of mission to serve society, Rossana's journey has been easy, light, clear, and colorful. She unwittingly began to possess a wide "workplace", one that gets wider and wider with each passing day.

Excerpted from the December, 2011 issue of China Home Education, interviewed by reporter Xiao Yun

MOTHERHOOD IS MY GREATEST CAREER

I've had many careers since graduating from college, and have successfully started and managed two thriving businesses. However, the greatest, most frustrating and challenging, and yet the most rewarding career of all, has to be my lifelong career as a mother. There is no other career that reveals my innermost weaknesses most directly, yet rewards me with the most unconditional of acceptance, affirmation of who I am deep inside, and love, than my career as a mother. I love meeting and getting to know all kinds of interesting people from work and my community. Yet I have never met anyone else more interesting, exasperating, brutally honest, or gracious and forgiving than my family. My own children will not disguise their assessment of me with soothing words out of politeness, but will tell me if I'm taking out my anger or embarrassment on them instead of what I say is the real reason of wanting to discipline them. Yet in the face of owning up to my own inadequacies, there are no others on earth more loving, resilient, and willing to overlook my offenses than my family.

For me personally, I chose to stay home for a period of time when my children were young. It was a long and difficult road, and perhaps the toughest challenge in my entire life, tougher than any careers I've previously had. I discovered that all the skills that I prided myself on before in my working life worked against me. I was a high achiever very focused on tangible and measurable results. In the workplace, I had constant feedback from my boss and coworkers, plus a regular paycheck and bonuses to reward my results. However, the home was where being patient, sacrificial, hidden, taken for granted, and forgiving were the valued characteristics. At work, if I worked hard enough and mastered enough skills, I will eventually finish a task at hand and accomplish something tangible. At home, it seemed that the mundane daily tasks are never done and I can never finish what I set out to do. My children don't always turn out the way I want them to, especially when I'm trying new methods of training after reading a parenting book. On top of that, I was constantly interrupted by the seemingly insignificant, constantly having my own needs usurped by those of my children. Growing up, I did not have little baby cousins or sisters that I needed to help take care of, and I had no patience for little kids. When faced with having to take care of a little life whose basic survival depended on my competence, I was at a loss. For the first time in my adult life, I was dependent upon another person, my husband, to feed me and provide for my basic living needs. Growing up, mother had always reminded me that men are not to be relied upon and that it's best to work and rely upon myself so that I won't have to be forced to be at his mercy. Everything within me was screaming against my decision to stay home for my young children. Yet looking back, it was during that period of struggle that I grew up the most, and changed from a self-centered young girl bent on gratifying her own wishes and desires to a mature woman capable of caring for and nurturing others. In the process, with each additional child, my heart was enlarged. I was dethroned from my position as the center of my universe. In this process and struggle to find success, fulfillment, and contentment in my career as a mother, I have learned many valuable lessons about myself and about motherhood, which I would like to share with you.

I find that my generation of women, while being liberated from the home to the workforce, has few skills or training on coping with motherhood. Recently, the process of raising daughters has shifted from a focus on her homemaking skills to her academic and professional skills. I increasingly find new mothers emerging from the hospital delivery room to dark periods postpartum when they are feeling unsupported and inadequate for the job, especially if their ideas of child raising differ from those of the previous generation. I'd like to give you some practical tips as well as inspiration and encouragement based upon my own struggles that it is more than possible, and that motherhood is the greatest career of all, whether you work outside the home or not. If I, having entered motherhood with so little resources and training, can succeed, then you can, too.

When you're entering into a battle, you must have a clear objective and battle plan, as well as having taken stock of your ammunition in terms of troops, supplies, and strategy. This is no less for the battle for your child's future. You must not enter motherhood without a clear understanding of your call, your mission, and the costs involved. But once you have that lofty vision, or the theory, if you will, you must have a very concrete battle plan, without which you can never execute the steps to fulfill your vision. You also need to quickly learn about yourself: your strengths, weaknesses, interests, fears, and doubts, because they will all play into how you will execute your battle plan. Here are some concrete ideas to consider as you develop a career development plan for motherhood:

1. Switch mindsets: the qualities that help you succeed at work will work against you in the home. For example, being competitive and results oriented is great for business but disastrous for relationship building. Instead, substitute nurturing (unconditional love and acceptance), self-sacrifice, and filling your home with joy and gratitude, no matter the current circumstance. This is a lifetime lesson for me. Sometimes I get mad and resentful when my efforts are not acknowledged and instead I get rewarded by being taken for granted. However, I need to constantly surrender my need for control but seek to love, give, affirm, guide, and rejoice at every little bit of progress, no matter how relatively insignificant.

2. Seek mentoring: Since mothering is such a sacred task, and most of us Asian high achievers grew up knowing only how to get A's in school, and we sometimes have no clue what constitutes good mothering, it's important to seek help. Seek out older moms you know around your community and ask her lots of questions, as well as permission to spend some time with her to see how she mothers her child. My MIT brainwashing comes into play here: since our school motto is "Mens et Manus", or mind and hand. I'm only interested in theory in as far as I can integrate it into my daily living. It's good to know that apples are nutritious but even more important that I love its taste. Look for practical tips of what other mothers do that you'd like to imitate and make your own. Then come up with your own style of mothering that suits your talents and personality.

3. Seek support and cheerleaders: Sometimes it's just tough to find something to cheer about when you can't seem to even keep the house organized. As soon as one task is done, another two more are lined up waiting to be done. There seems no end in sight. You need to seek to develop a support system so that you have other mothers like you who are there to cry with you and cheer you on in your small daily victories.

4. Set goals: small, realistic, and measurable: It's one thing to desire quality time but another to feel that you've had quality time. But if you set a goal that this week you will take a 20 minute walk three times around the neighborhood with your child, then that's something that's tangible, measurable, and rewardable. I remember that some of my funnest times with my son are on walks because

we'd encounter so many insects and little critters that we can either catch and inspect, or just watch them make their way through the grass to their home under the ground. Other worthy goals to consider are: learn and cook a new recipe a week. Being the ultra organization freak that I am, I plan my menus a week ahead and stick it on my fridge for my family to see. This will ensure "no surprises" as well as allow room for protest and revision. It's also good for shopping, saving me frequent side trips to the grocery store and freeing up my time to hang out with my kids. Another worthy goal is to learn a new activity with your children each week: it could be a magic trick you learn off the internet, a science experiment with household foods, a craft project, or explore the art museum together on a Saturday morning.

5. Seek ways to reward yourself: When you've checked off your list of manageable and measurable goals, go get a Caramel Macchiato from Starbucks or that pair of earring that you've been eyeing. Or ask your husband to watch your kid while you sip something bubbly in the bubble bath. It doesn't need to cost an arm and a leg, as long as you understand that it's a reward. Remember, you have to love your job to stay committed to it, so you have to seek ways to measure your progress and reward them!

6. Seek to involve your kids in chores. Having ayis (Chinese slang for maid) is both a blessing and a curse. If we rely on household help to do all our household chores, we deprive our children of some of the best opportunities to be trained in responsibility and good personal organizational habits. We make it a point to make sure that our ayi does not do the dinner dishes, make our kids' beds, clean their rooms, or clean up after them. Neither does she come in on the weekends when we are home with them. This will still give us some chores leftover to do together. My kids' fondest memories of our family time together is cooking breakfast together on Saturday mornings, as we can get creative and messy in inventing new ways to cook eggs or pancakes. Also, kids always love to help with the dishes afterwards because of the soap bubbles that we can play with.

7. Self-care: affirm yourself , accept your non-strengths, and learn from your failures: This is where self-knowledge is of paramount importance. If you don't know who you are about, what your life's about, then it's hard to know what to celebrate and what to accept. Motherhood is the toughest job in that you're having to constantly

look at yourself in the mirror. If being indecisive is a weakness you are ashamed of, you can bet that it will show up in one of your kids to annoy you. Unless you've accepted that about yourself, you can't find it in yourself to accept that in your child, who will see right through you no matter how many hundred "I Love You's" you say.

8. Life-long learner's posture: remain humble: The more secure a person is, the more willing she is to admit that she doesn't know or that she blew it. As a result, the more that person will learn. We never had any formal education on how to be an excellent mother, and there is no ISO9000 standard list of traits to check off on the "standard" mother. The key is to constantly seek to learn and improve yourself, just like you would in your other professional career. The tougher thing here is that those qualities are often intangible and unmeasurable (i.e. being more patient, grateful, gracious, and forgiving). Having all the mechanisms above in place such as mentors, cheerleaders, goal setting, and reward systems in place for yourself will help you maintain that life-long posture of learning.

9. Remember that marriage comes first, before your children: This is so easy to know and so hard to put into practice, as the children's needs are constantly screaming in your face, while your husband's might not be noticeable at all, often until it's too late. Make efforts to carve out a regular time for yourselves, and seek creative ways to speak his love language, whether it's sending regular text messages of love and encouragement to his cell phone, spending time with him giving him a message, or giving him little gifts to remind him that you remembered him. Plan into your budget for babysitters and carve out times for nights out. Or be creative and go meet your husband for a business lunch. Because men are visual creatures, take care to dress well and not let your weight gain spin out of control. Take care to eat well, exercise, and dress up nice when you are around your husband.

10. Beware that your children don't become your idol or source of affirmation: Often it's easy to have our children become the center of our universe and let their well-being become the measurement of our success as mothers, whether that well-being is measured in health, grades at school, manner, or performance at swimming or piano. We need to constantly remind ourselves that our children are ours to steward for a short time before we launch them off like a kite into the big blue sky. They will ultimately be responsible for

how they choose to live their lives, not you. Develop the habit early on to constantly reminding yourself to let them go into the Creator's hands. That way, when you hear that your neighbor's kid is such a math genius while yours is still struggling with addition, you won't feel a pang of guilt or self-condemnation, because you know your mission is about molding your child for the long marathon of life and not the next Math Contest or piano recital. Your choice to stay at home is to develop a relationship with your children so that you will be the first person they choose to go to to mull over an important decision or to confide a secret or to confess something they feel bad about. It's not about beating out the next kid in the midterm exam or having him be the next violin prodigy. And it's definitely not about him having to go to a famous school because you are well educated and if your kid doesn't get in it reflects poorly on either your own IQ or mothering.

11. Keep your own interests and passions; stay current on your profession; keep in touch with a group of friends and supporters in your career as a mother. Make sure you don't lose yourself to your motherhood, as high a calling as that is. You need to remind yourself about who you are and what else you're called to be. Keep up with your interests, be it dancing, music, or reading. Stay current with your field, be it through reading or attending conferences. Seek to ask your husband about his job and understand what he's facing at work, as best as you can. Develop hobbies yourself or with your mate so that when the kids are grown and out of the home you won't catch yourself facing a stranger in your husband because you've forgotten how to enjoy each other's company apart from the kids.

Being a mother is the toughest and most rewarding career of all. This year, through this column on motherhood, I invite you to journey with me as we explore practical ways to work out our calling as mothers in our homes, so that it becomes a warm and safe haven for our family members.

PREFACE

These days there is a way to certify every skill under the sun, whether it's piano, swimming, or even etiquette! Some skills require you to attend school for many years, and a title of PhD is an honor bestowed upon people who invest large amounts of money, brain power, and energy to master a certain subject. There are so many topics and skills that are worthy of a PhD level research and study, yet I believe that the toughest subject of all is one that we all must face someday – parenthood. Yet that is precisely the one subject that there is no preparation or certification for. Ironically, just as there are certain things in life where failure to prepare is of little consequence to life (such as ballet or piano), failure to prepare for parenthood can impact one's life, and many grown adults never fully recover from the impact of bad parenting throughout their childhoods.

With the new advances that women have gained in the workplace, opportunities abound for women to go far in careers never before imaginable by our mothers and grandmothers. However, we are also faced with a dizzying array of bewildering choices that our ancestors never had to make. While there is lots of rhetoric extolling the virtues of motherhood, there is always a subtle underlying pressure amongst women of our generation that belittles motherhood as a "substandard" profession. I often hear from my own mother that any village woman with less than an elementary school education can do what a mother does, as the tasks associated with child rearing are mostly menial, but that it's important not to waste my education but to have a successful career, as if being a successful mother does not really count as a successful career.

For those of us high achievers who have been told to just get a good education, there is little in the way of preparation for us to become parents. I stumbled into parenthood without any training or knowledge of what the job entails, but my thought was: "How tough can changing a few diapers and holding a cute little baby in your arms all day really be?" Surely it can't be as demanding as my fluid dynamics class! But motherhood ended up being tougher than anything I've had to learn before, and required my 110% to just keep up, let alone master! It's tough to be a good mother, and there are no metrics out there for me to measure how I'm doing, no awards to win to affirm that I'm on the right track, and no standard set of tools that I can pull off the shelf if something is broken.

This book is an attempt to share some of the lessons I've learned along my journey of learning to be a mother. It's not as systematic as calculus, but I've attempted to categorize this demanding career into four areas, in line with the four major types of relationships that a mother will need to face and manage. My hope is that some of what I've learned will be of help to other women facing the daunting task of raising another little life, and that motherhood will be the most rewarding of all careers for you, as it has been for me.

SECTION I

IDENTITY RESHAPED:

BECOMING A WHOLEHEARTED

&

GROWING MOM

1.1 FULL TIME OR PART TIME?

The first Christmas after my son was born, my sister gave me a Christmas present that gave me a good laugh. It was entitled "The Mother's Guilt Book", written on the premise that no matter what a mother did, guilt was her constant companion. There is no issue that is more hotly debated or guilt producing than around the decision of whether to be a full time mother or a part time mother. For those who can afford to live on one income, there is a "chip on the shoulder", a bracing against others looking down at the mothers who have lost touch with mainstream society and no longer have marketable skills. Full time mothers such as I used to be feel guilty that perhaps they have wasted their hard earned education and are not utilizing their talent and professional training more fully. On the other side of the issue are the part time mothers, or those who work because of their need to work, or their need to utilize their talents, training, or to feel a greater sense of significance through their work. While there is a defensiveness on both sides, and sometimes a judgmentalness against those on the other side of the issue, in our moments of total honesty, there is also a longing to be on the other side. Full time mothers, while knowing how noble their calling is to shape the souls of the next generation, struggle with the feeling that they are performing menial and repetitive tasks day in and day out without any recognition or reward for any tangible or outstanding achievement to their job. In the meantime, working mothers struggle with guilt at not being able to spend more time with the children that they love and left behind in another's care. Let's face it, no matter what decision we ultimately make, guilt will be right there.

So which side of the issue do I stand on? Well, I believe that we need to break the lie that you can have it all, because there ain't no free lunch. There is a cost to every decision you make, but there is also a benefit to that decision as well. The question is never which choice is absolutely correct, but how you choose to face the choice you make that determines the outcome. Please allow me to share four stories to help us understand the key to dealing with our ever present guilt.

Christie and Diana were both pharmacists before they had their first baby. Both worked in large hospitals in Los Angeles as managers in the hospital pharmaceutical staff. Both were delighted to have their first baby girls, and both continued to work shortly after their babies' arrival. However, this is where the similarities ended. Christie loved her job, and looked after her employees as if they were her own family members. She felt that her work is making a significant impact in the lives of others and the patients that she serves, helping to make their lives better. At the same time, she loved her four kids dearly. While her mother took care of her kids during the day, Christie also realized that her mother is older and has less energy to run around with the kids like younger women would. Whenever she came home, she would leave work behind and bring a happy smile as she walked in the door, acting like her kids are the best thing to happen to her all day. At home, she will take over and release her mother to rest, watch TV in her room, or to go visit other elderly friends in the neighborhood. Her mother kept "working hours" and kept a busy schedule off hours with dance lessons with her friends, flower arrangement classes, and choir. Christie enjoyed cooking with the kids, but occasionally when she's too tired to cook or clean, does not mind the occasional fast food, disposable plates and cups, or take-out food. The focus is on being with her kids and enjoying family time. Christie's husband also works long hours at another hospital, but both have the same practice of leaving work at work and being fully present with the kids when they come home. They also serve the community together in many projects, whether it's bake sales to raise money for orphans or car washes to raise money for troubled youth education programs. Today, all the kids are happy, healthy, and successful young adults, continuing to serve the community around them.

Diana also works as a manager in a major hospital pharmacy. However, she was pressured to return to work by her mother and her husband. Having been through the war and believing that men are not trustworthy, her mother insisted that Diana return to work immediately so as not to lose her job skills or marketability in the work force, and so that she would not need to depend on a man for her living. Diana's husband grew up poor and does not feel that they could survive on his income alone. Besides, he wanted to be able to afford the many nice things that he desired to own. Even though Diana didn't care about having material things, and she all she wanted was to be at home with her children, she did not argue, but went back to work like a good daughter and wife. However, she missed her children terribly and became resentful at her husband. Even though she never voiced her own opinions, her resentment seeped through at home, when she would sometimes speak to him with contempt. She belittled him for his lackluster accomplishments and for his work selling real estate. She sometimes spoke unkindly and disrespectfully to her mother, who looked after her kids for her, and constantly put down her mother's way of raising her kids. The home life suffered as a result because Diana was unhappy and characterized by negativity and a critical spirit, and had no trouble in expressing this unhappiness. She continued to feel guilty and resentful and then feel bad about feeling resentful and negative. Her continual efforts to suppress her own negative feelings would lead to occasional blow ups, which would shock everyone. Diana was not a cheerful person to be around, and the kids grew afraid of her and tried to avoid being with her as much as possible, which made her feel even more guilty and resentful.

Jane and Jackie were both psychologists. Jane was a professor of psychology in a large and reputable university in Southern California, while Jackie was a clinical psychologist who counseled troubled teens referred by the state government. Both decided to quit their jobs to become full time mothers when their baby boys arrived. Jane and her husband made the decision for Jane to stay at home full time to be with the baby while her husband John worked. They agreed that even though John only earned a Master's degree while Jane earned a PhD and was a professor, that it was important for her to be with the kids in the early years of growth. To help Jane make the transition from being a busy and well respected professor to a full time mother, John offered to transfer $1000 of his salary each month into Jane's bank account for her to spend on whatever she wanted. Even though this was very small compared to her usual salary, it was a touching gesture on John's part to acknowledge that Jane's work at home was just as important and worthy of compensation. Jane never spent this money on herself, of course, but often used it to purchase bigger items such as a car seat or furniture for the family, but having this money in her own separate account and seeing new deposits each month really helped her to feel appreciated. Even though she didn't go to work, Jane wore make-up and wore neat and cheerful clothes around the house. She started exercising regularly and soon lost the weight she gained during pregnancy, and felt great about herself. Jane plunged herself fully into home making, and enjoyed being with her son. Soon she and John began making plans to have another child because they enjoyed raising kids so much. Both their children are in high school and are active leaders in their school. They both adore their mother and think that she is really cool for someone her age.

Jackie became a full time mother because the government was having budget cuts and decided to lay her off along with her maternity leave. She did not find any suitable jobs because she was overqualified as a PhD. Even though her husband Todd was supportive of whatever decisions she made for her career, Jackie found it very difficult to be at home, feeling that she was wasting her education and becoming anxious that she was being replaced by younger and more energetic competitors in her field. She experienced mild postpartum depression, but never fully took care of herself to recover fully. She felt that her friends looked down on her for not working and her former coworkers avoided her. She walked around her house all day in a torn large size T-shirt, hair unkempt, and never took the time to lose the weight that she gained during pregnancy. Her son did not sleep well and she was tired all the time, so sometimes she and Todd would eat fast food, take-out food, or use paper plates to save time cleaning and washing up. Todd and Jane stopped communicating as Todd worked later and later and traveled more with his promotion at work. Jane felt alone and resentful for not getting any help from Todd, and nagged him for being a workaholic when he was home. They became like strangers who lived together in the same house. Their son became shy and withdrawn, and spent most of his free time alone playing computer games.

As you read the real stories of these four women (all names have been changed to protect their identities), do you see any similarities? Contrasts? What do you think were the key factors that led to each women's outcome? What can you learn from each women? I believe that each women had a choice, and had the ability to choose how to live with that choice, whether it's with gladness or with regrets. Even though we can't always choose our circumstances, we can choose our attitudes, and I believe that happiness is a choice. Two of those women played the role of the victim, and allowed their resentment of others to rob them of their ability to be happy, when they could have taken responsibility for communicating their needs, boundaries, and desires rather than allow their repressed feelings of resentment to rob their families of joy. The other two had similar circumstances but chose to be grateful for what they had, and to express that gratitude to those around them. Whether you are a full time mother or a part time mother, the power and choice lies with you whether you want to make motherhood one of the most joyful and fulfilling experiences that enrich you for the rest of your life, or one that makes you feel trapped with no way out and drains you of energy and drive to realize your dreams and goals. Which will you choose?

For Your Growth

1. This week, as you go about your day, try to monitor your feelings, and instances when you feel guilt. Do you see a pattern of the types of events or situations evoke this sense of guilt? Think through these situations and check with a trusted friend to assess whether these feelings are legitimate, and if you should be doing something to correct a bad situation, or if the guilt is not legitimate and should be dismissed.

2. Do the same with the feeling of regret. Is there something you can do to address the regret? Or should you choose to let it go and move on with your life? Picture an empty balloon, fill it with that regret that you are feeling, and release it into the air. Picture that regret flying away. Now say goodbye and determine not to go back to think about it.

3. Whether you are a full time mother or a part time mother, take a few minutes to write down 5 things you are grateful for in your spouse, and if someone else is caring for your child as you work, your child's caretaker. Take some time to verbalize your appreciation to them.

1.2 MASTERING EMOTIONS

There's a popular saying that says: "If Mama ain't happy, then ain't nobody happy". I couldn't agree with that more! A mother is the emotional barometer in her home – she sets the emotional atmosphere of the home like no one else does.

One of the gifts given to women is that we are rich in emotions, and some are particularly good at expressing them. However, one lesson I've been learning my whole life is how to master my emotions, instead of letting them dictate my actions. When I was a young girl, I suppressed emotions and tried to distance myself from them, wanting to deny that part of myself and be just like a rational boy. I allowed myself to only feel and express anger, which is a more male and aggressive emotion, as I distrusted all the other "feminine" emotions that would make me seem weak. Later, I learned to own and embrace the whole range of emotions as my own, but can't seem to control them, as my actions would instinctively flow out of my emotions. The movie "Fireproof" gives insight into the proper place of emotions.

In the movie, a couple on the brink of divorce no longer feel any more love toward each other. The husband's father gives him a book of dares challenging him to actions that are loving when the emotions are no longer there. There is a classic line in the movie where the father has a heart to heart talk with his son, and encourages him to not be led by his feelings, but to lead his heart, for that defines true leadership. As people created with a mind to think and a will to make rational decisions, we are called to lead our emotions, not to be led by them. This does not mean that we are not allowed to feel them or should deny that they're there, but to let the higher functions of the mind and will to control them. So many times I have felt dry and dead inside towards either my husband or kids, but have had to chose to lay aside my feelings and continue my loving actions to serve them, because that is what I had committed to do when I made a promise at my wedding. Oftentimes, my feelings of love would follow, after I made the choice to do the right and loving thing, instead of waiting for the feeling to come before acting.

When I was living in Los Angeles, a friend called me up all the way from Boston, asking for advice. She told me that she had just locked herself inside her bedroom, with her son knocking hard on the door asking to be let in. However, she was so angry at him that she was afraid that she would hurt him. She locked herself in to prevent herself from doing something foolish, but confided in me that she was ashamed that she sometimes didn't like her son at all, even hated him sometimes. Before she had her child, she was confident that she would always love her child unconditionally, no matter what. However, after her child was born, she was horrified to discover that sometimes she didn't feel any love for her child at all, and felt that something was wrong with her, because all mothers are supposed to be able to love their children unconditionally. She was shocked when I admitted to her that it's perfectly normal to feel that way, and that I sometimes felt the same way towards my own children, especially when they do something that makes me feel like my life is out of control or that I'm incompetent as a mother. However, during those times I just needed to acknowledge that my own love had run dry, accept myself and what I felt was legitimate, and make a choice to perform actions or say words that seem loving rather than acting or saying things according to how I truly felt, in order to honor the commitment I made to them. Often times I am amazed to discover that the responses I receive in return was enough to re-fuel my love for my family.

In the earlier part of our marriage, I used to pray that my husband would cherish me and verbalize his appreciation to me more. I didn't want to ask for it, but felt that he should know that this is my deep desire. After repeatedly dropping him hints and not seeing any change, I confided in an older friend that I felt that I had married the wrong man. This friend told me, "Honey, you have a perfect right to say that before you married him, but after you said those vows, whether or not you like it, he IS Mr. right, and you will have to treat him like he's Mr. right, no matter how you feel at the moment." I began to examine myself and discovered that I was not being appreciative of him. In fact, I was withholding my love until I could see him giving me the appreciation that I wanted first before returning my love. That's when I realized that my love was quite conditional. I decided that the only person in the world that I can change is myself, and determined to be a more grateful person, and to express that gratitude to people around me. I discovered that as I changed, my husband changed as well, because my attitude affected his reactions towards me. When I was joyful and appreciative, he was able to see me in a different light and appreciate me back, because his emotional bank was full.

When my son Caleb was in grade 3, his teacher told me that his ability to express himself was extremely poor, especially now that the class was learning to write. Because he was my first child, I was really worried that he would be a poor student, but underneath that worry, I was afraid to admit to myself that it would reflect that I was a poor mother. Initially, my worry led me to fretting and to forcing him to sit down to practice writing. He must have sensed my worry and anxiety, because the more I pushed him, the more he resisted, which led me to be even more frustrated and anxious. Luckily, my husband David came along and lightened up the atmosphere, and had us all writing and sharing with each other the funny stories that we wrote. Caleb began to catch his enthusiasm and soon started to like writing. This affected my attitude towards this "chore" to "fix my son's writing problem". I started looking forward to reading his stories, and was truly amazed at how creative he can be. Caleb loved writing so much that at age 14 he completed a 90,000 word novel, which has now evolved to 150,000+ words at the age of 15.

By the time we faced our second son Jonathan's pre-school teacher, who told us that he had a speech problem and might be mentally and developmentally slow, I was ready to lead my emotions. I didn't get angry at the teacher, but calmly went to his classroom to observe him with other kids, and discovered that he was slower to develop emotionally and socially, as he was very shy and didn't engage people easily. However, once he took some time to observe others and decide on a friend, he will remain loyal to that friend for the long term. On the other hand, his speech problem was actually because his mind worked so fast that his mouth was unable to keep up, which led him to slur his speech instead of taking his time to communicate his thoughts slowly. In keeping an open mind, I enlisted his teacher as an ally in investigating this problem and we came to similar conclusions as a result of asking more open minded questions. If I had been anxious, I would have been unable to separate the two issues and would have agreed with the teacher's assessment of him, treating him like a problem child needing to be fixed, secretly being ashamed of him. Later, when his second grade teacher urged us to have him skip a grade because he was too quick to learn and often bored in class, I was able to befriend the teacher and firmly and calmly insist that he remain in the grade to allow him time to develop emotionally and socially with his peers while working with her to provide him with extra puzzles and games to keep him mentally engaged. As a result, Jonathan had a normal and happy childhood, in a large part because I had learned the earlier lessons to keep my emotions in submission to my will.

By the time I experienced similar problems with Stephen and his low scores in English in his Chinese bilingual class, I was not surprised or anxious, knowing that boys are slower to develop than girls, especially in verbal ability. Having gone through this twice with my older two boys, I was ready to handle Stephen's low performance in English with the long view in mind.

There are many more examples of how choosing my heart to lead my emotions has set a positive atmosphere in my home, helping it to be a place of unconditional love, acceptance, and warmth, making it a place that everyone likes to dwell in. However, this goes against our natural tendencies as more emotional creatures, and our emotions need to constantly be led and trained. I would like to share some tips that have helped me to train my emotions to affect the atmosphere in my home for the positive:

1. The Serenity Prayer by Reinhold Niebuhr has reminded me on many occasions to apply this to myself, my spouse, and my children in reining in my runaway emotions:

    "God grant me the serenity
    To accept the things I cannot change;
    Courage to change the things I can;
    And wisdom to know the difference."

2. Avoid Comparing. This is such a deadly trap where no one wins. In the U.S., the way that real estate agents determine how much an owner of a house should sell his house for is using the method of "comparables", where they find data on similar houses sold in the area in the past year and take an average of the final selling price in

order to determine the listing price of this house. This may work for something as simple as a house with a few variables such as square footage or age, but would never work for people who are created unique and differ so much with one another. Rather than comparing with others and worrying about where we fall short, seek to affirm what is special and unique about you, your spouse, your child, and your family. Often being thankful for our uniqueness will lead us to feel better about ourselves, because the way we view our world has changed.

3. Seek to study, understand, and accept your child as you study, understand and accept yourself. Our children are often like our mirrors. They reflect our strengths, which make us proud, or our weaknesses, which make us frustrated, ashamed, or exasperated. For example, I am very frustrated with myself for not being able to hold my boundaries with people to say no, and have trouble accepting my weaknesses. When I see my son struggling with the same problem, I have trouble loving and accepting him. By coming to accept that weakness within myself, I am better able to accept it when I see it in my son, and am even able to laugh about it with him.

4. Open the gift instead of fixing the problem. People are created as gifts to be opened, not problems to be fixed. When we approach our children with an expectation of discovering something delightful, we will find it. By the same token, when we approach them expecting problems to solve, we will find them as well. Opening gifts will make us happy, while solving problems will make us tired and frustrated.

5. Learn to wait. Cultivate the discipline of patience by habitually allowing others to go first, whether it's at home waiting to eat a meal or in public waiting in line at the market. This discipline is especially handy when something happens that makes you angry or impatient. Cultivate a habit of inserting a wedge of time, or waiting, until your emotions have cooled, so that you can deal with the matter calmly and rationally, whether the matter is disciplining a child that has done something to make you angry, or something your spouse did or said that was particularly insensitive or inconsiderate. You will find that after waiting for your emotions to

35

cool down, you will be able to be more effective in communicating your needs and expectations rather than reacting out of your righteous anger or hurt.

6.   Cease striving and looking for results. In this performance driven and results oriented world, it is easy to forget that the process of arriving at your goal or result is often more enjoyable than attaining it. Learn to do things slowly so that you can enjoy the process rather than always striving to arrive at the results and doing something only if it will give you results. Do something for the pure enjoyment of it rather than the tangible material benefit it can bring you. For example, cooking a meal can be a very enjoyable activity, but when rushed for the purpose of eating it for nutrition only or consumption, it can become a tiresome chore. The same thing for washing the dishes, which can be a bothersome task, or something you look forward to doing together with your spouse to have some quality time to discuss what's in your hearts.

7.   Live richly. There are two ways to become rich: increase your income or decrease your desires. I think that the easier way is to monitor and contain your desires so that you will always feel content and wealthy, secure in the knowledge that you have all you need to live well. I am constantly asking myself the question: "Is this a need or a desire?" Often I discover that most of the things I want are desires, not necessary for living. When I cultivate an attitude of contentment, I find that I infect my children with the same attitude.

8.   Give until it hurts. This is true of not only our money and material things, but also of our time and ourselves in terms of emotional energy and service to others. When we live a lifestyle of giving, first to our family members and then to others around us, we will find that we live in increasing freedom from the tyranny of materialism and so much of the empty vanities that enslave so many around us.

9.   Humor is a great gift to be used daily. One of the best gifts that my husband has given me is his ability to see humor in every situation. When he is staring at his own weakness, rather than be embarrassed, he can laugh at himself and make the situation lighter

rather than take himself too seriously. This has greatly increased the ability of the whole family to deal with serious setbacks or circumstances, always looking for the funny side in each situation.

A mother sets the atmosphere in her home, making it a warm and welcoming place, or a place of tension and anxiety. Her decision to choose to master her emotions will enable her to make her house into a home, not only for her own spouse and children, but also for their friends who will long to rest their tired souls in this place of comfort and warmth.

For Your Growth
1. This week, be sure to apply at least 7 of the above suggestions for at least an hour.

2. How will you apply these suggestions effectively in your daily life? For example, if you want to avoid comparing, you can make a list of positive traits that you admire or affirm in yourself, then read and memorize specific items on the list each day to remind yourself to stop comparing with others. Every time you feel the urge to compare, recite these traits out loud to yourself and give thanks for these traits. You can also find some creative ways to manage your emotions (especially negative or explosive ones), instead of letting them rule over you.

1.3 THE DANGER OF BEING PERFECT

Ever since I graduated from college, I had a recurring dream. In the dream, I was back at college taking classes at MIT. We had a policy where we could register for classes we were interested in taking and if the class was too difficult or uninteresting, we had the option of dropping the class by a certain date without any penalties. In the dream, I would have signed up for a senior level class that I forgot to attend and drop. Then when the time came for the final exam week, I received a list of my exams and classroom locations. That's when I would realize to my horror that I had forgotten to drop that class and would have to finish studying for an entire semester's worth of material on my own and go to take that final exam, because the deadline to drop that class had long passed. I would re-live my anxiety as I frantically studied, and the dream would end with me entering the exam room unprepared and facing certain failure of the class. Other variations of the dream had me packing for trips and missing the plane. These dreams began when my first child was born, and their frequency has decreased significantly over the years, but they used to be like a barometer of my inner world, as they occurred with regularity to haunt and remind me of the anxiety within my heart.

That "One Bottle" Saga
When my first child was born, all of my weaknesses and issues from my family of origin roared to the surface with a vengeance, refusing to be hidden no more. The ugliest one was my perfectionism. The anxiety caused by my perfectionism was further exacerbated by my having no knowledge whatsoever of how to take care of a newborn. The first day I brought my baby home from the hospital, I also brought home a lot of literature given to me by my doctor on caring for an infant. Among them was a brochure called a "stool guide", with colorful pictures and descriptions of various states of baby poop. I remembered with each diaper change, I would hold up my baby's diaper against the brochure to compare and stare hard at the poo in the pictures and in the diaper. Like a scientist, I studied the brochure closely to assess if the poo was diarrhea, jaundice, dehydrated, or normal. When I read that mother's milk was best, I determined that my baby would not drink one drop of baby formula, but get all his nutritional needs from me. I also read that if the baby drank too exclusively from one breast, the

breast sizes would become unevenly sized. Upon learning this, I kept detailed charts of how much time my baby took to drink from each side, and analyzed the data to make sure that he got exactly equal time on each breast. I wanted to get everything just right, and I wanted to earn an "A" in motherhood and raise the perfect baby. Any mother would laugh to think that all these generations of mothers had trouble raising their kids and had uneven breast development without this obsessive focus on doing things "just right"! All this obsession just pushed my husband out of the parenting loop, because I had to do everything myself to ensure that they were done right. This meant that I pushed myself to the point of exhaustion while my husband felt frustrated at being excluded. He pleaded with me repeatedly to give him a chance to feed the baby from a bottle, so that he can also enjoy new parenthood while at the same time help to offload me so that I can get more prolonged periods of rest. I refused.

One sunny day, my husband was frustrated with my stubbornness, and while I wasn't watching, took the baby from my arms, and gently pushed me out the door to urge me to take a walk. In the meantime, he locked the door and started preparing baby formula to feed the baby. I was enraged, and banged on the door, but to no avail. He was determined to show me that feeding the baby one bottle a day would not harm him. By the time he let me back in the house, the baby was full from milk from the bottle, and I was livid. The next day, I decided that I would not allow him to "ruin" the health of my child, packed up my bags, and checked into a hotel, ready to take the next flight to Vancouver to my parents' home, so that I can bring up the child the right way – my way. I was haunted by anxiety from the thought that now my baby wasn't perfect. Fortunately, my distraught husband brought two other friends to intercept me at the hotel lobby, and persuaded me to go home with the baby. I saw how ludicrous it was that I was willing to make my child grow up without his father over a bottle of milk, and decided to face down my own anxiety at my imperfect parenting. My baby Caleb has grown up to be a healthy grown adult, and adores his Dad, who continued to feed him a bottle of baby formula milk every day since then. ·

Growing Up with Chaos and My Coping Mechanism
I grew up with chaos in my family of origin. When I was 5, Canadian immigration law had changed, and my parents had to report to Canada to

live there for two years in order to earn their permanent residence permit. My sisters and I were shipped off to various relatives and friends, and my world disappeared for two years. When I saw my parents and sisters again, I didn't recognize them, and was afraid of my father. After that, we would move around a lot, finally all moving to Canada, where shortly thereafter my father had a business failure and we were all driven out of our home. Living with this kind of uncertainty and chaos meant that I had to come up with ways to make sense of my world, or in psychological terms, "coping mechanisms". The more chaotic and unpredictable my world got, the more perfectionistic I became in an effort to gain a sense of control over my own little corner of the world. If my environment wasn't neat and organized, anxiety would rise up within me. Disorganization was intolerable to me.

Whenever I felt stressed or anxious, I would clean and organize. One period of time I was having arguments with my mother, and she would call me at the office. My boss jokingly told me that he always knew when I had a fight with my mother because the next day when he arrived at the office, his desk would be perfectly clean, with papers piled together neatly without even one corner out of place.

When I carried my perfectionism into my home, the results were disastrous. A messy home and especially a messy kitchen brought on large amounts of anxiety, and anxiety robbed me and my home of joy, spontaneity, and freedom. My obsession to wash every dish after each meal became a point of conflict between David and me. With motherhood, perfectionism reared its ugly head, and I now had a new enemy. I need to slay the ugly monster called perfectionism before it robs me and my home of happiness. The war was declared, and steps needed to be taken to conquer perfectionism in my home.

Dish Therapy

It started with dish therapy. I would deliberately leave the dishes in the sink overnight without washing them. The first few times, I was unable to sleep, and would wake up in the middle of the night, sneak over to the kitchen when no one was watching to finish them. With practice, I can overcome higher and higher levels of anxiety. Just like alcoholics with alcohol, I know that perfectionism will always be a weakness of mine, and that in times of high stress and anxiety I still resort to scrubbing down the kitchen or reorganizing my closets. However, by naming my weakness and enlisting the help of my family members, perfectionism and anxiety no longer control me, but I control them.

Beginning with "Good Enough"

My family is helping to learn to live with "good enough" instead of perfection. I discovered that a little messiness actually helps me to accept and get used to the fact that the world is not perfect, and neither am I, and that it's OK. It started with our camping trips, where we would go to bed without a shower, dirty from being in the beautiful outdoors for a whole day. Those experiences enabled us to make trips together as a family to live in an orphanage in Mexico on long three day weekends to serve the poor and disadvantaged, where "good enough" was a special treat for those kid who had to grow up living without what I considered necessities. My hard work really began to pay off when I started training my own children to do chores, because those dishes were never scrubbed completely clean, and my son would always forget to clean that pot on the stove. But because I was able to live with "good enough", I was able to let them learn at their own pace, improve from their own mistakes, praise them for every effort made and every result produced, and begin to slowly entrust them to do more of the chores better and better as time went on. Living with "good enough" helped me to share the load of household chores with my family, teaching them responsibility while freeing up more of my time to enjoy other meaningful activities with them.

I still have not yet reached perfection, and probably never will. Occasionally I will break down and go back to re-do the dishes that my children did not wash completely clean, but most of the time, I'm proud to say, I am learning to tame my perfectionism, enjoying and celebrating each small victory day by day.

For Your Growth

1. How do you know when you are anxious? What will you do to manage or decrease this anxiety?

2. Do you have tendencies towards perfectionism? How does that make you unable to accept yourself and others? If you have perfectionistic tendencies, how will you deal with it to keep it from impacting your kids as you parent them?

1.4 I AM JUST A MAN

We all love to hear my husband David tell us stories of when he was small. Once, after he watched the movie "Superman", he wanted very much to be just like him. He took a bath towel, tied it around his neck, climbed up high upon his dining room table, closed his eyes, and bravely jumped off. However, he was disappointed to discover that he was just an ordinary person. Not only could he not fly, he got injured after he jumped.

After we hear his story, we always laughed at how naïve he was. However, I often find that I am disappointed by my ordinariness. I find that this "superman" lie continues to hurt parents, as a voice of criticism and shame continues to linger in our minds. The effects of this lie manifests itself in the following ways:

1. When others express their opinions to us about our parenting style of methods, we are filled with self-recrimination, and even anger. Once, after I confided to my husband about my disappointment with my inability to discipline my children, he tiredly told me: "how can you mishandle things this way?" Immediately, my heart filled with a sense of failure, causing me to be unable to sleep well all night. The next day, after I quieted myself down, a voice whispered in my mind: "He is just a man". These words gave me freedom, because I realized that I had elevated my husband's words to the same level as God, letting his every single word pull me along on an emotional roller coaster ride. He can't and shouldn't shoulder the weight of being my god or superman. No matter how important someone is in my life, be he my husband, parent, boss, or teacher, I should never let his words be everything. We are all just ordinary and imperfect people who will disappoint. We need to accept their imperfections as well as our own.

2. We are always harder on ourselves than others. Being a perfectionist, I have high expectations of myself and am often disappointed in myself. Yesterday, I was discussing with a friend about the lie that "as long as you work hard enough, you can always beat out others." The truth is that some people score higher on that math or English test because they are naturally smarter than we are, not because they worked so hard. I am reminded of the movie "Amadeus". Salieri was a very hard working and earnest musician of his time. However, he knew that in comparison to Mozart, he was rather ordinary. One scene in the movie

depicts Salieri performing a composition that he had spent a long time working on in front of an appreciative audience which gave him a polite applause. However, along came Mozart, who, with a few simple changes to Salieri's original tune, turned the song from an ordinary piece into an even more beautiful and elegant song, amazing everyone present, and making Salieri awkward. At the end of the movie, Salieri's jealousy and self-recrimination ultimately lands him in the insane asylum. In the final poignant scene, Salieri finally accepts his own ordinariness and forgives himself. It was ironic that he was only able to gain true freedom by accepting and forgive himself after he had made himself "lose his mind".

I have great admiration for earnest parents who work so hard to study and learn about parenting. During my children's parent teacher conferences, the teacher would invite the parents of the #1 student to come share the secrets of their successful parenting. However, I often find that the parents had no clue what to say, because their child could just be genetically very smart and not require them to do much. A wise friend reminded me: "God is the most perfect of parents, and even He raised rebellious children". As parents, we can only try our best, but ultimately, the choices are still made by our children for themselves, not us. The best starting point is to accept yourself and give yourself the freedom to fail. This way, you will not need to use your child's performance to validate or "score" yourself. Only then will you be free to devote yourself to discovering and studying your child, accepting him (no matter how "ordinary"), admiring him, and truly enjoying him. Only then, no matter how others define or criticize your child, he will still be your "most beloved" child.

For Your Growth

Think about which areas of parenting or your personality you have a hard time accepting yourself. Write it down here and determine that you are willing to accept and love yourself even if those areas never change. Share this with either your spouse (if you feel safe), or a good friend that you trust, so that they can extend that acceptance to you, and remind you to accept that in yourself.

1.5 THE GIFT OF TEARS

When Caleb was about 8 months old, a friend introduced me to a book entitled "Solve Your Child's Sleep Problem" by a Dr. Richard Ferber, who was a psychologist from Harvard who specialized in sleep problems in children. I was troubled because Caleb still was unable to sleep through the night. Each time he woke up, he had to be rocked back to sleep, and then 3-4 hours later, he would wake up and would need to be rocked back to sleep again. This made me exhausted, as I was unable to sleep without interruption for even one night. This book was much needed and was very scientific and easy to understand and implement. Dr. Ferber described that every person has an attachment object when he sleeps, whether it's a particular pillow for adults, or for children, a blanket, stuffed animal or toy, being rocked, or Mom or Dad. Caleb his means that without that particular object, the child is unable to fall sleep. The trick of getting K to sleep by himself and fall back to sleep when his sleep cycle awakes him temporarily is to transfer his attachment to an object that is in his bed. It sounded easy and hopeful. So after reading the book together, David and I chose a soft and fluffy blanket, and determined to implement the re-attachment training plan step by logical step. Except that the process involved baby crying, and leaving him to cry for 5, 10, 15, … minutes before returning to pat him down and then leaving again. Even though I was prepared ahead of time for the crying, when I heard it, I started to waver. On the first day, after we got to waiting for 15 minutes, I couldn't hold it anymore, gave up, and went to go pick up my baby. However, this left me exhausted the next day, so we decided to try again. David got my permission to keep me from giving in again, and would block me when I tried to go back into baby's room to pick him up. He kept a stopwatch and showed it to me as I waited anxiously for him to stop. Finally, I couldn't stand the crying any longer, and decided to break my promise to go pick up the baby. David, as promised, tried to block me in the hallway to his room. I started punching him with my fist, demanding to go past him. When I saw that he was not going to budge, and continued to hear my baby's cries getting louder and louder and sounding more desperate, I collapsed on the ground and started crying myself, feeling more desperate than my son. At that moment, I hated my husband. I don't remember how long the crying continued, but miraculously, it seemed, the crying sputtered to a stop. David collapsed beside me on the ground, exhausted. He ended up with bruises all over, while I struggled to pull myself back together. I found to my surprise that Caleb was able to comfort himself back to sleep. He didn't suffer any emotional trauma from this crying, and is able to re-attach to his blanket, which he slept with until he was well past 4 years old and the blanket was all ripped and tattered.

This incident exposed my strange attitude and reaction to crying. I had no tolerance for negative emotions in my children, because I had no tolerance for negative emotions in myself, and pushed it down as soon as I felt it surface in me. Growing up as the eldest of three daughters, in a family that favored boys over girls, my mother raised us up to believe that we were better than boys. I rejected my feminine side, acted like a boy, and wanted to be regarded like a man. Therefore, tears were unacceptable. However, when I became a mother, a tender side of me that I never knew existed came out, and a cry of distress from my baby brought forth all kinds of feelings of helplessness, distress, and anxiety. I had to silence these feelings at any cost, because I couldn't tolerate them in myself. My inner demons had surfaced, and now I had to fight them to gain the right to raise my child in a world where ALL emotions, positive or negative, were accepted and allowed free expression.

What this meant for me personally, though, was that I needed to go through a period of inner healing, where I gave myself permission to feel and embrace these negative emotions that are fully a part of myself. I went through a "weepy" period where I cried easily, because I had so many years of pent-up emotions waiting to be released. I was lucky to have around me a group of supportive friends who did not question my sanity, but wept with me and embraced me in that vulnerable time when I had in a way opened up some wounds from the past, allowed some of that pus underneath the surface to come out, and experience true healing, free of past unresolved hurts or unmet needs. Only when I was able to face my own negative feelings was I able to face and accept them in my spouse and in my children.

Crushed Spice Smells Fragrant

As Caleb and Jonathan got a little older, my father began pressuring me about when to take over his business. After all, I was the one to help him to build his business into an international business with multiple millions of dollars of revenue. Also, as the eldest daughter, it was my duty to take over the family business. My family and relatives thought that David would be the lucky one getting a free ride. However, my parents, especially my mother, looked down upon David, and thought that I married beneath me. I knew that if I did what was expected of me as the eldest daughter, it would mean that my husband would never be able to come out from under the shadow of my parents to become the leader of my house, which would mean that my children will not be able to grow up respecting their father or regarding him as the hero. I wasn't sure if my marriage would survive if I said yes to my father. After a period of agonizing struggle, I knew that I needed to invest into my marriage and my kids, and communicate my decision to my parents. I wrote a long letter to my father, explaining how much I loved them and have always wanted to be a good daughter, and yet how I could not live up to that duty because I owed it to my children to raise them under the strong leadership of my husband. Needless to say, it was the first time that I saw, heard, and felt such a deep, deep disappointment in me from my father. His silence ripped me apart inside.

I entered a period of insecurity, wondering if I will ever have any job skills needed to re-enter the work force. It was during one of those times when I was feeling low that I was at a church service. The speaker challenged everyone there to give their best to God, whether it's their talents, abilities, time, or money. I felt lost, because I had nothing to give. At the back of the church, I knelt on the ground and cried. "God, I have nothing good to offer you – I'm just a washed up middle aged housewife!". It was then that I heard a voice inside me, asking me what I had left to offer. I said, "All I have left in me are my tears and my brokenness". The voice inside said, "I will take it and make something beautiful out of it." I cried and cried. Never before have I ever felt so accepted, so affirmed of my own self-worth. Finally, I experienced what I had grown up longing for: the acceptance that came with no strings attached. The speaker came by and saw me crying. He whispered in my ear: "Crushed spice smells fragrant." I knew that I would be OK. Somehow, someday, not only will my past training, including my love of music, people skills, and ability to speak in public be put to use, but also my tears and my brokenness. Looking back, my greatest and deepest impact on others has been those tears and that brokenness. The other skills and abilities are mere by-products to support the main thing.

Gift of Tears

Are there areas of tears or brokenness that are hidden in you? I have personally experienced the crushing that produces a sweet fragrance. I know that when you offer up your tears, God can also make something beautiful out of it!

Now I have personal experience of embracing my tears, and experiencing the wonderful healing effect of tears, I no longer fear them. Before embracing my tears, I would fret when my children cry, and would hesitate in disciplining them. However, I gained a new sense of peace and confidence after this encounter. When my kids cry, I know that tears are an agent of healing, and that they bring comfort in times of distress. They are nature's powerful mechanism for self comfort! When I can escape the grip of fear and anxiety that tears create in me, I can now give my children the gift of training and discipline they need to grow up to be responsible adults who are able to delay gratifying their petty personal desires for a greater goal, or to put aside their immediate needs to care for the needs of others. I have befriended tears, and in the process, given my children the gift to be fully human.

For Your Growth

1. What is the attitude of your family of origin towards tears? How has that affect how you react to your own tears? Others' tears? Your child's tears?

2. What is your reaction when your child cries? Are you able to think clearly when that happens? Which part of your reaction is natural instinct, and which part is influenced by the way you grew up?

3. Are there hurts and wounds from the past that you need to put to rest in order to restore a more healthy balance to your reaction to tears?

4. Has your child's tears been a hindrance to you in disciplining and training him/her? If the answer is yes, how will you start to overcome your own internal resistance to the training that they need?

1.6 BEFRIENDING ANGER

One sunny morning, I was driving my children to the market, and saw Caleb hard at work drawing up a chart. On the left are a lot of X's, and on the right is one check mark. Curious, I asked him what he was working on against the car window. He told me that it's a checklist of my behavior, and on the left side are the bad behaviors, and the right side are the good behaviors. "The reason for so many X's is because this morning Daddy and you had a fight, and you took your bad feelings out on me and yelled at me for something that was not my responsibility. This led to more bad behaviors because you didn't handle your anger properly. However, I still gave you a check because last night you snuggled me while you read to me and made me feel really loved." I was speechless for a moment, and realizing that he saw right through me, decided to eat humble pie and apologize for my childish behavior.

Anger was another negative emotion that was not tolerated in my home. However, I saw that my mother would often hurl very elaborate, hurtful, and belittling insults to in effect express that anger and cut people down. My father, on the other hand, is the ultimate Mr. Nice Guy who never got angry, but would occasionally explode at some little thing, surprising and scaring all of us into silence. Since it was not ladylike to get angry, my sisters and I developed ways to cover up or redirect our negative emotions, and ended up expressing those emotions in private at each other. I, as big sister, would become very bossy and critical of my little sisters, and frequently "spaced out" to cut myself off from my emotions, thus rendering me unable to feel those negative emotions, but also the positive ones such as joy and excitement, thus earning me the nickname of "Spock" in high school (Spock is a character in Star Trek who is from a planet of creatures that have no emotions, and act out of pure logic). As I grew older, I began to develop some unhealthy ways of my own to deal with my anger.

Denial
I do not like anger. I do not like conflicts. I'm a very peace loving person, and conflicts make me extremely uncomfortable. So at the first sign of awareness of anger, my first immediate response is to deny that it exists. This kind of tendency at denial makes me disconnected with my inner

world, so that by the time that anger can no longer be pushed down, it will be totally out of control. This kind of avoidance of anger also wreaked havoc in my marriage, as when David would ask me what was wrong, I would tell him:" Nothing", when in fact I was unhappy but couldn't give myself permission to verbalize them. I became passive aggressive like my father, and began to develop coping mechanism that allowed me to escape my negative feelings, but also left me unable to connect with my husband in intimacy. Being used to juggling multiple projects and interests and many, many friendships at the same time, I used these activities and commitments, as well as my workaholic tendencies, to escape from dealing with my anger instead of just verbalizing them to my husband. This left him hurt and bewildered, and led to even more attempts at confrontation that would further drive me into escapism.

Distortion

When I refused to acknowledge my anger, resentment would begin to brew and brew within me. Sometimes, a careless word spoken by my husband out of impatience could have immediately been addressed and dealt with on the spot, but because of my tendency to deny and bury the feeling, I would end up turning and enlarging this incident over and over in my mind until it evolved into crisis proportions. I would wonder what he meant by those words, what his intentions were, and attribute reasons that weren't there. For example, when he makes a comment that I'm cooking the same dish too many times, and that he was tired of it, I start wondering if he's growing tired of me, and become insecure about his friendships with other women. Instead of trying to clarify what he meant, I would stew over it until it blows up in his face.

Displacement

Since I would not give myself permission to get angry at home or at work, I "leak" by displacing this anger elsewhere. For example, if I felt unappreciated by my boss at work, I might go to the department store after work to return an item, find the store clerk unhelpful, and end up on a manhunt to get the store clerk fired. At some point, the expression of fear on the clerk's face might awaken me to the fact that the force with which I was handling a perceived wrong is not proportional to the deed done, but then find myself unable to stop myself. I see a lot of this kind of anger displacement on the streets of Beijing. It is also this kind of displacement that my son was trying to call out in me.

As I began to notice these disturbing behaviors within me, I became angry. However, I didn't know how to understand, explain, or process my anger, so I got mad at God that my life was so out of control. I had become the kind of angry person that I avoided! I distinctly remember one particular church service, where people all around me were singing songs with exuberant joy, but somehow this just made me angry. I went to the back of the church to sulk, and was determined not to be "fake". Inside, I prayed: "God, I'm just not going fake happiness, I'm so angry at you!" As I sat there sulking, I saw a picture of a big big teddy bear like person embracing me. At first I just yelled at him, but then I started punching him, and then used every single one of my arms and legs to punch and kick him with all my strength. The person continued to embrace me, a smile on his face, his body like giant sponge pads. He said, "Come on, give me all you got. I can handle your anger. It's totally OK for you to be angry with me!" Just like that image, I let him have the full force of my pent up anger, built up over all these years, yet suppressed with no permission for release. I continued punching and kicking in my mind until the church service ended. I didn't hear a single word of what the preacher said, but I just felt an enormous sense of release. I felt like I had just finished a wrestling match and won, and now I was totally spent. However, I also felt a new sense of freedom and release. From the depths of my being, I "knew" and understood that it was OK for me to be angry. Now I just need help to find new and healthy ways to process and handle my anger.

I went to a counselor for some therapy and help. My first lesson is to find ways to get in touch with that anger before it rages out of control, to name it, and then once it has been correctly identified, to deal with it correctly. My therapist suggested that my husband and I make two signs out of cardboard and popsicle sticks, one yellow, one red. If we are starting to feel anger rising, we will hold up the yellow sign as a warning to let the other person know that something has triggered anger but we are still not able to name, understand, or articulate it yet. If we have already gotten so angry that we cannot behave rationally, we can hold up the red sign to ask for a "time-out", much like "time-out"s are called in the middle of an athletic match. This time-out enables us to win some time and space for us to cool down so that we can process the anger in a more rational way that will not hurt the other person who hurt you.

These two signs helped us a great deal, giving us concrete ways of asking for help with our anger. Many times, it was just a matter of using the yellow sign to ask the other person to help clarify and apologize for a perceived hurt that was never intended. Other times, it helped me to dig deeper to ask about the need underneath the hurt and to ask if I was reasonable in expecting the other person to be able to meet that need.

The biggest personal breakthrough for me was that I was given permission to be angry. This in turn gave me freedom to give my children permission to be angry. Anger is a legitimate emotion created to help us correct a situation that is wrong or unfair. However, how we go about dealing with that situation requires wisdom and love. I am still trying to correct bad habits from of old, but now my whole family knows and understands the fight before me, and we are learning to do this together. And that makes all the difference in the world.

For Your Growth

1. Have you grown up with permission to be angry? How have you usually expressed this anger"
2. What are some ways that are typical of how you process and handle anger?
3. Has this worked for your marriage? In what ways can you improve this to make your marriage even more harmonious?
4. If you discover that anger is an area you need more help on, read "Anger, The Other Side of Love" with your spouse. It would be even better if you can find another couple or two to read through this book together and discuss ways you can improve anger management in your homes.

1.7 SELF-CARE

Lately I've been hearing many commercials from a clever car company in Shanghai advocating the importance of maintenance to the long-term health of a car. When car owners take the trouble to take their cars in for regular check-ups, tune-ups, and oil changes, chances for a major repair are reduced. This same principal that applies to all major machines and appliances also applies to human beings and our relationships. When children are born, we are so diligent to take them in for regular physical check-ups to make sure that they are developing normally and to catch any diseases early. They get vaccinated against possible bacteria that might make them very sick later. After the onset of adulthood, somehow check-ups and prevention is dropped in the optimism and confidence of youth and peak health. This can be very deceptive, as we develop lifelong habits that can be very hard to break later in middle age. Habits such as healthy eating and regular exercise. Habits such as maintaining important relationships such as the ones with our loved ones in other cities or with our spouses. Habits such as self-care.

When I worked in IT, I regularly went for training to update my technical skills, and had to keep up with all the latest developments in the IT community through reading industry news and periodicals. Others working in sales and marketing keep an extensive list of relationships that they need to maintain. Scientists and doctors go to conferences and conventions to share their research and findings with each other to make further advances in scientific breakthroughs. Whatever career you choose, even if you are a plumber or dentist or painter, you will need to keep up with the latest products, people, and techniques to your field in order to stay current and ahead of the competition. Motherhood is one of the most demanding careers of all, as it not only involves the mental and physical, but also the emotional, social, and spiritual. However, just like there is a sad lack of training for parents, there is also a sad lack of help and accountability for self-care and improvement for mothers.

As mothers, we get into automatic giving mode. We are well known for our selflessness and sacrifice. Many do so until they burn out and die an early death. The other day my friend was telling me about her mother-in-law, who was the perfect and sacrificial wife and mother. She never missed cooking a flawless meal for her family throughout the many years that her children were at home, and served her husband until he died. My friend's husband held her up to be the model of a faultless mother, ever dutiful and always there to serve her family. However, growing up, he rarely saw his mother laugh, and he never characterized her or his home as a place of warmth or joy. He rarely saw any affection exchanged between his parents, although his home ran like clockwork and was always spotlessly clean. It wasn't until his father passed away that she stopped cooking, and everyone else realized that she hated cooking, and was merely doing it out of her sense of duty. This made the family feel even more guilty. As a result, they put her even more on a pedestal as an incredible and longsuffering woman. China's long history is full of women like that, who are models of Confucian women's morality, some who would remain single for the rest of their lives even when their husbands died young. However, the ingredient that I often find missing in these virtuous women is joy that bubbles forth from within. Would you rather be in a perfect home without a thing out of place yet devoid of laughter and warmth or a home that is slightly messy but where you feel the freedom to let down your guard, laugh, be yourself, make the occasional mistake, and have your soul loved and nurtured? Would you prefer to grow up in a perfect home where no one ever makes mistakes, or in a not so perfect but life giving home?

My husband keeps reminding me to eat well and exercise because he wants me to live long and healthy so that we can see our grandchildren grow up, and help many more people in the long term. In our house, when we are sometimes both tired after a long day, we give ourselves the grace to eat the occasional unhealthy fast food meal rather than get further stressed by having to cook a healthy and organic home cooked meal. To us, it is more important to have laughter, freedom, and enjoyment of each other's company than to get everything just perfect.

Just as regular maintenance cannot happen without advanced planning, accountability, and regular evaluation, so self-care will not automatically happen. However, without regular and well planned self-care to help yourself refuel, you will not have the strength to truly love and enjoy your family. Just as planning activities that are restful or rejuvenating vary from person to person, so the same applies to self-care. I would like to suggest some general categories for mothers to consider how they can begin to formulate a plan for self-care that will help them to be better and more loving wives and mothers in the long run.

☐ Mental: When we care for our minds it means that we are constantly learning & improving in our knowledge. I am always excited to read about the latest scientific breakthroughs and innovations, and like to keep up with reading related periodicals and books. I also like to read a wide variety of books and periodicals related to people, businesses, and other bestsellers. These readings, in addition to having conversations with fascinating people who are excited about their lives and what they do, nourish my mind and keep it active. My son Jonathan and I like to work on math games and puzzles together, and our whole family enjoys finding and reading good jokes together. One complaint that I hear from husbands when marriages break down is that their wives get so preoccupied with the day to day operations of the home and on raising the children that they stop being enjoyable, engaging, and interesting people. One of the things you can do to keep yourself interesting is to keep nourishing your mind with new knowledge and information so that you would be fun to engage in discussion and your husband and children will want to seek you out for your thoughts and opinions on various topics or issues.

☐ Emotional: When I was a teenager, I would take refuge in music when I needed to fill my emotional tank. Tchaikovsky and Beethoven's piano sonatas were favorite pieces to express my anger, sorrow, or joy. Reading books, especially inspirational biographies or stories of exciting adventures gave me fresh motivation to live my life fully and meaningfully. The English word for fun is recreation, which literally means to re-create, or make anew. Setting aside regular times to fill your emotional tank or process toxic negative emotions is essential for your own well-being as well as your family's. This can take the form of having regular chats with friends over a cup of tea, or immersing yourself in good art, music, or literature. Whatever it is that does the trick for you, make sure to have enough time of your own for this. Your family will be thankful that you do, because you will be a more joyful, pleasant, and loving person to be around.

☐ Physical: Maintenance of your body involves regular exercise, healthy eating habits, care for your skin, and dressing well as a reflection of your self-respect and your wish for others to respect you. Caring for your body ensure that you will be able to endure for the long run, and be around to watch your grandchildren grow up, and that your golden years will be productive ones rather than a healthcare burden to your children. I remember growing up in my younger days when I would regularly pull all-nighters (staying up all night without sleeping) or go for long periods of time without eating or going to the bathroom, especially when I was busy working. Somewhere along the way a friend and mentor observed that I did not cherish or value myself very much, and often abused my own body as a result. She suggested that I stand in front of the mirror every morning to look at myself, say to myself: "I am fearfully and wonderfully made. I love this body, and will take good care of it the way it deserves to be cared for. I choose to bless and honor this body today." By consciously doing this over a period of time, I found that I cherished my body more and made sure to give it the attention it needs to help keep it healthy and rested. This has meant that so far I have been fortunate to avoid major illnesses and to recover very quickly when I do get sick with a cold. As a result, I have more energy for my family, to be fully present and engaged, especially for a household of energetic boys who are all very physically active.

☐ Social: One of the best advice an older female friend gave me before getting married was that it was essential that I develop a close circle of women friends outside of my family or work, because I can't expect my husband, children, or my parents and sisters to meet all of my social needs. Having this circle of friends freed me to release my husband from the unrealistic expectation that he has to meet all of my needs, and prevents me from sinking into discouragements whenever I feel disappointed with him when he is unable to meet my needs. It was also important that I choose friends who will support me and my marriage, and will keep me accountable to my own personal goals and aspirations. A real friend will give me permission to vent my frustrations with my husband yet remind me of my commitment to him so that I will work on changing myself rather than expecting him to change. Or that I am too hard on my child because I am comparing with others and that is not fair for him. Or that I need to stop coming up with excuses and start going to sleep on time. Friendships can also be interest based. For example, I love to play classical piano even though my family will only play popular music or other modern genres with me. When the itch comes, I will schedule to meet with a friend who plays violin or cello and we will just get together to play our favorite classical pieces. Back in the U.S. I was also part of a reading club where each of our small circle of friends took turns to choose a book for us all to read and then get together to share our thoughts about the book. Other times I met with friends who liked to put together beautiful photo album scrapbooks and we would get together to share about our photos, the fun stories behind them, and to trade advice on how to better decorate each page. Similarly, I also encourage my husband to meet with his group of male friends to share about the challenges that they face at work, at home, or trade tips in a particular hobby. My husband David plays tennis with friends and likes to meet with other friends who are interested in photography or the latest technical gadgets. He also has an informal network of "techie" friends who can help each other find the best and most reliable deals on purchasing computer parts and equipment. I find that when we allocate part of our social needs onto people other than our family members, we can often come to each other with our cups fuller, looking to give, share, and inspire rather than looking to be filled and served.

☐ Spiritual: Finally, what most fulfills me and allows me to give joyfully, fully, and willingly to others is caring for my spirit. When I know who I am, why I'm here, and am secure in my spirit, then I can give freely out of that sense of security, of being loved and accepted unconditionally by my Creator, and of perfect freedom to be who I am in expressing my love to others. I do this through regular readings of authors with the same belief as mine who share certain teachings and insights, through worshipping through listening to or playing music, or through prayer and contemplation of Scripture and truths.

Our mental, emotional, social, and spiritual needs can also be met through mentors and mentoring others. This is a topic I will discuss in more detail later in the book. The business of self-care is the business of prevention. Preventing a fire is a lot easier and less costly than fighting a fire. Likewise, preventing illness is a lot easier and less painful than having to treat or live with an illness. In order for us to be the best wives and mothers to our families, we should proactively and intentionally plan to care for ourselves so that we will bring benefit to our loved ones for the long haul.

For Your Growth

1. Take a look at your current use of time. Is there any room in there for self care? What can you replace?

2. What area do you need to most practice self care? Starting this week, start with allocating one hour a week to self care. Tell a friend about it, so that s/he can check up on you to ask you about how it went, and how to improve upon it the following weeks. Enlist your spouse to support you in carving out the time to care for yourself.

1.8 SHOWERS OF BLESSING

It was a dark and wet night, on a rare rainy day in the always sunny Southern California. My baby was just a few months old, and my husband was travelling on business for a week. I had endured a few days with baby glued to my side. Even when I was in the shower, I would strap him to a car seat and put him in front of my glass shower door so that he could see me. I remembered a few times when he would wake up and start crying for me, and I would be in the shower with a full head of soap bubbles, feeling guilty and desperate to finish so that I can get out of the shower to attend to his cry. I felt mounting frustration and helplessness, being the only person who can help my baby. By the end of the week, I had grown resentful of him, and of my husband, who dared to leave me all alone with a helpless baby 24/7.

An auntie came by to drop off some chicken soup, and to ask me how I was doing. I expressed my frustration at my situation. I was no good at mothering – I didn't know how to do anything, and I didn't have any help. I felt resentful at times at my baby for taking away all my freedom and space, and felt guilty for feeling that way. Basically, I was a mess – how did I get to this place? The auntie smiled a patient smile and patted me on the head. "Just let him cry a little! It will be good exercise for his lungs!" I was shocked at her cruelty. She told me that I needed to carve out some sacred spaces for myself, without any demands being placed on me. I needed to cultivate the habit of nurturing myself first before I have anything with which to nurture others. All kinds of questions ran through my head. When? Where? How?

"When do you feel most resentful?" she asked.

I knew immediately – it was when I felt the most helpless – in the shower. She suggested that I begin with the shower. The evening before my husband returned from his trip, I put baby in the hallway in his car seat with a little toy, and hopped into the shower. Needless to say, I caught myself fighting all kinds of conflicting feelings, and it was not an enjoyable feeling. When I came out, he was still happily rattling his toy. Relief. I can do this – just got to keep going.

When my husband returned, I shared about my struggle to carve out my own sacred space, where no emergency or crisis can get to me. He pledged his support.

That was the beginning of this joyful journey to discover and protect my own sacred space, beginning with the shower. I can't tell you how many times I've burst out into songs of spontaneous praise, or had insights and revelations of beauty in that shower stall. I found other places and ways to reward myself. There's my rocking chair, where I would feed baby and slowly savor a good book. And that special frozen yogurt place that has my favorite flavor of frozen yogurt – I reserved a cup for myself whenever I set a small goal and reached it, as a way to celebrate with myself. Whenever I succeeded in overcoming a baby related anxiety, I would make a date with myself to stop by for that cup, with chocolate fudge on top.

Motherhood became more enjoyable and less guilt inducing for me. When I was diligent to fill my own cup, I am then able to fill those of my family.

For Your Growth

1. Do you have a time or place where you can dedicate to recharging your batteries? Is this a regular thing? Is it adequate?

2. If not, set a goal to find a time and place this week to start experimenting on ways to carve out a sacred space for yourself. It could be going to sit in a secluded place, gardening, visiting a museum or café, or just shutting yourself in a closet to paint, play your favorite musical instrument, or just to listen to your favorite music. Be specific about blocking out that time and space and communicate this need to your family members to enlist their support.

1.9 SURPRISED BY GRACE

Have you ever experienced a string of lucky coincidences that takes you by surprise? Yesterday was one of such days.

Lately, my husband and I have been way too busy, not just from work, but also serving others, entertaining friends, and all kinds draining work related to helping and counseling others. My husband just recovered from a bout of illness, and we just headed for a short vacation in Hangzhou. This trip was hastily put together, without much plans or expectations. Our only wish was to distance ourselves from the hundred and one small interruptions of home life to gain some perspective and rest.

We woke up Saturday morning with plans to slowly walk to a hotel 20 minutes away to rent some bikes, and then to stroll around West Lake. On the way, we met several friendly locals who introduced us to local specialties and history. At the beginning, we were not used to such friendly strangers, constantly worrying that someone was trying to scam us. However, when we discovered that Hangzhou natives were truly hospitable and friendly people who love to introduce us two outsiders to their culture and answer our questions, we became excited. We saw a garden by the side of the road, and when we discovered that it's a shortcut to get to our destination, decided to go in. To our utter surprise and delight, what opened up before us was a treasure that was beautiful beyond words. It was such an unexpected gift, and our hearts were not prepared to receive it! Unexpectedly, God had arranged a new surprise at each step, each more delightful than the previous! How can there be such a beautiful place in China! No wonder Hangzhou produced so many poets! We originally wanted to walk quickly through the garden to get to our real destination, but couldn't bear to leave. Halfway through, we took a side detour off the main road, and couldn't believe that it was even more beautiful than before! Partway through, we suddenly heard three older people yelling after us: "Little brother, little brother, did you lose your camera lens cover?" We are often called big brother or big sister, but never little brother, and this made my husband enormously happy. Upon closer inspection, we discovered that David did indeed lose his camera lens cover. These three helpful elderly people gave us detailed instructions on where it is, and after we followed their instructions, immediately found the cover. The day passed in such a fashion, as if each detail was finely arranged for us, right down to the timing of the drizzle. In that fine drizzle, I experienced the haunting Oriental beauty, which was especially poignant when we watched the outdoor spectacle how "West Lake Impressions" choreographed by world famous director Zhang Yimou. Western beauty is typically open and sunny, yet Eastern beauty has a subtle shade of underlying sadness that is more difficult to capture and express, and felt even more beautiful for its elusiveness.

A verse in Romans says that "His kindness leads us to repentance". After a whole day of these coincidences, I truly felt undeserving. Before, when I heard other people say that they are undeserving, I always felt that they are either lacking in self-esteem or faking it. However, I truly experienced what this kind of undeserving means. When grace keeps coming at us, not because I fought for my right or worked so hard to earn it, our bodies and spirits are renewed. On the way home, I heard over the phone that Caleb took his brothers to eat their favorite noodles and Jonathan cleaned the house on his own initiative to enable us to celebrate Mother's Day immediately upon our return, I felt my heart overflow! Even though I am undeserving, but I willingly receive my portion of grace, and am happy to share this grace with my family and friends!

When we want to teach our children gratitude, have we taken the time to receive these little graces our selves and to express our gratitude to our children to show them what it looks like? If our own cups are not filled, it will be hard for us to show others how to fill theirs. So take some time to look around you, count your blessings, and express your gratitude for them.

For Your Growth

1. Find a quiet place to spend 1-2 hours looking over old photos of you and your spouse. As you look, write down a list of 15-20 things that you are grateful for in your spouse. Write another list of 15-20 things you are grateful for in your life.

2. Set a time aside to go on a date with your spouse, and then share this list with him. You might even want to bring along some of these photos that brought back some of those old memories. Look him in the eyes to express this thanks.

1.10 HOMEMAKING IN TODAY'S BUSY WORLD

What Are Your Big Rocks?

I remember when my children were small and I was at home full time with them. At the end of the day, my husband would come home from work and ask me: "So what did you do all day?" to which my mind will blank out and I will not be able to tell him one thing that was worthy of reporting. My reply would typically be that I don't remember. He would often give me a puzzled look and tell me that if this is what he told his boss that he would soon be fired. I remembered feeling so unappreciated, because I know that I was extremely busy all day long, but yet could not articulate or quantify what I did with my time at home, because our home looked the same when my husband returned as when he left it. Out of his heart to help me, he asked me if it would help me to have a "Mission Statement" in line with my career objective as well as monthly, quarterly, or annual goals statements to help me focus and stay on track in my new career as a full time mother and homemaker. The idea was great, but it was hard to make that shift from the corporate mindset to the home front, especially when the tasks accomplished are insignificant, frequently and regularly interrupted, highly repetitive, and of no importance. It was as if I had suddenly been demoted from a high level manager to a low level maid and factory worker. And did it make sense to sit down with the cleaning lady at the office to map out a Mission Statement and annual goals when what she did day in and day out was the same set of never changing tasks?

I started thinking about a book of Jewish proverbs and the Jewish ideal of a wife and mother. The picture painted in the very last chapter of the Jewish book of proverbs signify how much the Jews think of her, enough to use her to close up the entire book. This woman was amazing: she had many children, ran a busy household with many maids and staff, ran a thriving business selling cloth, made and repaired her own clothes, and was a wise money manager. It was the modern equivalent of being a wife, mother, CEO, COO (Chief Operating Officer), and CFO (Chief Financial Officer) all wrapped up into one. With her as a model to aspire to, I knew that I needed a plan to get there. In my journey of becoming my family's CDE (Chief Domestic Engineer), I have come across some very practical organizational tips that have helped me to run my household more smoothly. Things took a different turn after we arrived in Beijing and I discovered that all the tasks that used to take up so much of my time can now be taken over by a maid. That left me digging deeper to search for the meaning of my role as a mother, but it was not too difficult, because the Jewish woman also managed her household staff efficiently and effectively.

Before we begin, I had to survey the land, or my domain. Just last week, I kept a tally of a list of requests for things I needed to do in a typical week, to see how I can better organize myself. Here's what I came up with:

Children need:

- New batteries for a watch
- Re-stringing of a badminton racket with a broken string.
- New and bigger sized thermal underwear.
- A pair or ripped up pants to be repaired.
- A new pair of glasses to replace an old pair that was damaged on the basketball court.
- A pair of shoes fell apart at the front and either needs repair or replacement. In light of the fact that they were purchased two months ago, I made two trips to get them repaired, but they fell apart again after the second repair. So a new pair needs to get purchased.
- New water bottles for sports are needed to keep everyone's drinking utensils separate: everyone is sick.
- Parent teacher conference is coming up next week, but the school has not yet announced the time. I need to be on standby.
- A son's Saturday tennis game needs to be rescheduled around another soccer game, band practice, meeting with another family, lunch with out of town guests, and visitors for dinner.

Husband needs me to:

- Research our next family vacation options in light of our budget and time availability. I need to come up with 2-3 options to present to the family for decision.
- Send a card and gift for a family member whose birthday is coming up.
- Check our monthly expenses to see if we can reduce it by 1-2% to give away.
- Help him find certain items that were misplaced due to a recent bathroom repair.

- Monitor the expiration dates on various passports to renew the ones that are expiring, along with our visas and residence permits.
- Shop around and get quotes for certain car repair items because a recent maintenance session at the 4S shop turned up some major parts that needed to be replaced, and we think they are overcharging. We need to get a second and third opinion, and decide on purchasing original factory parts vs. generic parts for less.

My maid reported the following decisions for me to make:

- The dryer was broken, but the repair man came and told her that nothing was wrong and left. I need to be here to talk to him and tell him what I think is wrong and needs to be repaired. He wouldn't listen to the maid.
- The dog kept scratching her ears and need a visit to the vet for medical attention.
- The dog dug a hole in the backyard fence and escaped. After finding him, we need to fill up the hole to prevent future incidents.
- A worker shows up to repair the window without any tools. I need to loan him the tool so that he does not need to reschedule his appointment.

Friends need the following attention:

- A family visiting from America need a place to stay and would like some time to talk and catch up with us.
- A couple had a fight and the wife needs to talk to me about how to best handle the conflict.
- A friend's son is having trouble with school and needs me to talk to him to find out how he can be helped. He won't talk to his mother, who is too emotional and upset.
- A friend is looking for a job and is asking me to ask my friends for help.

So, if I were to categorize, prioritize, and organize my seemingly random and unrelated list of requests and demands in the running of my household, how would I go about it proactively so that I am not merely a fulfillment agent fielding requests as they come in chronologically? Where does my Mission Statement and monthly goals fit into this list?

The First Step: Home Organization

There are various categories of items to keep organized: time, money, things, and relationships. One can easily tell the values of an individual and a family not by merely listening to what they say but by looking at how they spend their time and money, as well as what kinds of things and relationships they own and maintain. Rather than letting the tides of societal whims and trends dictate and force you to allocate these as you react to external pressures when they come up, I suggest that you proactively follow the VIM model of organizing these things. The first letter is V, or vision. Set aside some time to sit down with your spouse and come up with a big picture of what you would like your family to look like, what kinds of values you want to live out. If corporations which merely produce goods and services take the time to define a Mission Statement and set out measurable goals as well as lay out a plan to attain these goals, then how much more a family unit that shapes and impacts lives for all eternity? For example, Google's Mission Statement is to organize the world's information and make it accessible and useful: a very ambitious goal. A family might not have a Mission Statement, but have a set of values of goals. For example, even though David and I both worked in IT, we developed a passion early on in our marriage for youth and for higher education. We have continually invested time, money, and developed relationships with people that worked with youth and higher education. Another family might have a passion for writing, literature, and want to seek to impact the world through their thinking, while another family might enjoy making music together and making the world a better place through their love of music. What are your dreams for how you will impact the world for the better as a family? Once you have defined your values and goals, then intentionally develop a plan to allocate your resources to realizing this plan. This is where the next steps, I (Intention) and M (Means) come in. When we receive a request for our time or resources, we evaluate whether or not we should say yes or no depending on whether or not it aligns with what we and our family are about. Without the intentionality and the means to reach these goals, defining them is mere wishful thinking. For example, if you want to be a family that wants to understand and impact the poor, especially those that are orphaned or imprisoned, then you will sit down together as a family to figure out a plan that allocates your time and resources to realize that goal and make that impact.

Many years ago, David came home one day after taking a "Seven Habits of Highly Effective People" class and excitedly showed me a graphic analogy that we still use to keep each other accountable today. After he set out a large jar and several big rocks as well as a pile of small pebbles, he asked me to figure out a strategy to put in all of the rocks. Through trial and error, I found that the consistent way to fit all the rocks into the jar was to put the big rocks in first and then to fit the rest of the smaller pebbles around it. So it is with our lives. When we determine which are the big rocks in our lives, or the non-negotiables, then the rest of the tasks and demands will have to fit around these non-negotiables. However, if I attend to the small and urgent requests first, many times I will discover that they have squeezed out the big and important tasks that are needed for my long term well being. What are these non-negotiables for you and your family? When you have taken some time to think through your family values and distinctives, it will be easier to map out some non-negotiables.

This month, carve out some time for you and your spouse to brain storm, reflect, and dream some big dreams. Take into account your past experiences, passions, interests, gifts, relationships, and even lessons learned through failures or hurts. Write them down separately and discuss them together. When you have some agreement on a possible Mission Statement or family values, then we can roll up our sleeves to get down to the nitty gritty matter of organizing our lives around these Big Rocks.

Managing Your Time, Money, Things, and Relationships

Hopefully by the time you read this article you and your spouse have had some time to reflect on what you want your family to be about, and what kind of legacy you want to leave the world. As a mother, your role in managing your home to transform it from a "house" to a "home" cannot be emphasized enough. This is why there is that well used cliché that says that it takes a woman's touch to make a house a home. This article helps you to develop the "I" and M" part of the VIM plan to reach your vision.

Time

The most important category to organize is your time. As mother, I am the Lin Family Calendar Master. Here are some major non-negotiables that I have managed to carve out time for in our family calendar throughout the years:

- Time to plan: One chunk of time that we often neglect to set aside is the time to plan, reflect, and evaluate. Each week, I set aside time to review and plan the budget and family finances, the weekly menu, draw up a shopping list, and map out my schedule. David and I would take some time at the beginning of each week (usually Sunday evenings before a new work week begins) to discuss our upcoming week and ask each other how we can be a better spouse to each other and a better parent. Each suggestion for improvement is to be preceded by three compliments. Each year, we set aside time individually and as a family to draw up goals for the year: academic, social, physical, and spiritual. Part of this time is first spent in reviewing how well we did with last year's goals, and how we want to adjust our new goals accordingly. For example, we made a decision coming to China that we will develop relationships with local Chinese friends instead of stay enclosed in foreign circles. This required a deliberate and intentional set of actions to say no to the many invitations we receive on a regular basis from our foreign friends and neighbors. Without a clearly stated intention, it will be very easy to get drawn away from our good intention. We consistently see other foreign friends who arrive with the best of intentions but never carry through because there are too many distractions along the way.

- Time to learn: Since one of our major family values is being in a posture of life-long learners, a major non-negotiable is time set aside for study and self-improvement. We always have a list of books or topics we want to learn, individually or together, and this list is constantly revised and updated. Time is allocated in our schedules for self-study. The topic can be serious (for example, we might want to read up more on China's modern history, time management, design theory, or renewable energy), related to the quality of life (for example, we wanted to learn new recipes that use organic vegetables and whole grains), or plain fun (we are always on the look-out for more new games, magic tricks, and hobbies. For example, we have taken rock climbing, skiing, and even dance classes together as a family).

- Time with each other: We take Mother Teresa's words to heart: "Together, we can make something beautiful". The question we are constantly asking each other is: "Is this something that must be done away from the family, or is there a way I can do this together with my family?" This means that on weeks when everyone is very busy with his own studies, interests, work, or volunteer activities, I as the master Lin Family Calendar Keeper block out time for us to spend with each other. Often we take out a deck of playing cards and play card games, or make music together. However, there are times when things at home get so distracting that we have to schedule time outside of our home, whether it's going ice skating, to the movies, or to visit a friend's home. We also make sure that my husband and I have regular times together with each other apart from the kids, and that we each have regular time alone with each child doing something that fills his love tank. Once a year, my husband and I plan 1-2 overnight trips away from our kids, just to be with each other. These times away from our kids communicate to them how much we value time with each other and how important our marriage is to each other. Rather than making them feel insecure, these trips away actually help them to feel more secure because we usually come back more in love, more relaxed, and therefore better and more loving parents.

- Time to serve: One of the non-negotiables in our family is serving others. We intentionally plan and block out times to serve together as a family, whether it's as simple as hosting visitors, spending time helping another family who is new to Beijing get around the city, or helping someone struggling with his English.
- Time to rest and rejuvenate: One day a week, we block out a minimum of 3-4 hours of time to do something that is restful of rejuvenating. This usually involves physical activity such as playing tennis or biking. Once a year, we will plan a longer time away, whether it's a ski trip, and camping trip, or a visit to another city.

The list above applies to our family, but I hope will serve to start you and your spouse thinking about the big rocks in your family. Once you are able to identify and agree on what they are, then it's time to get out your calendars and start scheduling them in!

Money

Many wise elders would tell me that you can tell what is most important to someone by looking at where he spends his money, for where your treasure is, there your heart will be. Over the years, my husband and I have occasionally experienced pangs of regret or envy because many of our peers and coworkers spend a lot of time and money managing financial investments, often through stocks, real estate, and mutual funds. We would often see people constantly checking a particular stock price or buying a brand new car because they made money investing in stocks. However, we had made a decision early on in our marriage that instead of managing a large and complex financial investment portfolio, that we would invest the same time and care managing our giving portfolio. Rather than just giving out cash, we monitor our "giving investment" to make sure that our money is invested in line with our values and is effectively used. For example, since we value higher education, we usually allocate part of our income towards funding tuitions or living expenses of someone involved in serving students through an NGO. We prefer giving to individuals rather than institutions, and will include the people we give financially to in our circle of friendship and care, through letters, emails, phone calls, and gifts. We monitor and evaluate the performance of our investments with the same degree of care as we would manage our stocks and real estate, and make adjustments accordingly. For example, our giving portfolio is divided into Disasters and Emergencies (such as the Sichuan Earthquake or helping a personal friend pay off an emergency medical bill), Poverty Relief and Development, Education, helping people not from our own language and culture, and other major areas of interest to our family.

The reason that we are able to develop a Giving Portfolio at all is wise and diligent budgeting. I highly recommend that every couple take a course through Crown Financial, which teaches financial management principles for the individual as well as for a business. A couple preparing to get married will gain a significant advantage for their married life if they can take this course in preparation for their lives together. Crown Financial even has courses for young children. As a result of courses like these, we have always involved our children in our budgeting process and money management. Our children know how much income we have and what our allocation is for each category such as groceries and entertainment, or car maintenance, electricity bill, and school tuition. When we have a spending or giving decision, we usually make it together as a family over an Excel Spreadsheet of our actual budget numbers. For example, when we are planning vacations, we usually look at how well we've done in living within the budget limits we've set for each category, how much we want to allocate to that vacation, whether or not we've lived up to our giving goals, and then decide on where to go. If, for example, a trip back to the U.S. exceeds our budget, but we all really want to do it this summer, then we will discuss which areas to cut or how to generate additional income to cover the difference. For example, my eldest son Caleb wanted a new tennis racket, which is not budgeted in the family budget. We agreed that we would eat out two less meals a month to help pay for half of that racket while he saves up for the other half through tutoring English and helping his brother do his chores for a month in exchange for part of his brother's allowance.

When the financial figures are open to every member of the family, even our youngest 7 year old son, everyone wins, because everyone acquires a critical life management skill -- the wise use of money.

Maybe you are already operating a well-planned budget, but if you are not, the best way to start is by keeping track of every yuan of your expenses for 6 -12 months. This should give you enough time to catch the major and non-weekly expenses such as major purchases (i.e. seasonal clothing, appliance, or furniture), home repair, car maintenance, tuition, gifts and vacations. Once you have a list of expenses, you can start to categorize each budget item to suit your household. Some example categories include Car (gas, toll, tax, repairs, maintenance, insurance), Home (repairs & maintenance, decoration, major purchase), Clothing, Entertainment, Groceries, Transportation (i.e. taxis), Education (i.e. piano classes, summer camp), Medical, Travel, Gifts, Utilities (i.e. electricity, water, & natural gas), and Giving.

Once you have a monthly average for each category, then you can calculate your expenses against your income and see how you want to adjust it. If you decide that you really need to control your spending in the clothing category, a very good method is the envelope method, where you take out the allocated monthly allowance for that category and put it in an envelope. When the money from that envelope is gone before the month is over, you will not be able to spend on that category. This is a good way to begin adhering to a set budget.

Be patient with the process. It's a lot of work up front to develop new processes and new habits, but once in place, you will have a much better control over your money, instead of your finances being master over you.

Things

The overriding principal we use in our family towards things is that we would rather spend the time and money up front to buy something of superior quality (this does not equate name brand) for the best deal in order to save ourselves the energy in repairing or replacing an item of inferior quality later. Once we have acquired an item, we invest the time and money to maintain, clean and organize our things so that an item will last as long as possible. An example of this is our couch. When we first moved into our new home 16 years ago, we decided to invest the money in buying an expensive leather couch rather than a cheaper cloth one because of its durability and easiness to clean. Throughout these 16 years, this couch has been subject to our kids jumping up and down on it, moving and flipping it over and over to build their forts, and being moved to different cities and countries, and is still being used today. I have accumulated a large number of bins and dividers to sort and categorize our things: everything from toys and stationary items to books, CD, or gardening tools. The initial work of sorting and organizing pays off in that it is usually easy to locate an item later on because everyone knows where it is and how to find it. There are also plenty of designated cabinets and storage spaces for seasonal items such as clothing, humidifiers, Christmas tree, seasonal decorations, coats, and blankets.

Relationships

Besides your spouse, your children are your most treasured relationships. It takes a lifetime to master the art of relating to your children. The only thing I want to mention here is that many parents have a will drawn up in the event of death or something that disables us from caring for or making decisions for our children. This will usually involves financial arrangements and directives on what to do with our possessions such as our house and car. In Western culture there is the custom of designating godparents. In China we might call godparents "gan die" or "gan ma". The intent of having godparents is that our children have a set of elders who know enough of our family values and how my husband and I desire to bring up our children if something were ever to happen to us that we trust that they will make similar decisions for them on our behalf. While grandparents, aunts and uncles might be able to help us make sound financial decisions for our children, we have already talked to a couple who know us well who have agreed to be our children's godparents to help them in their upbringing and spiritual guidance if we were unable to.

Just as in every other family where there is a division of labor and roles, I have taken on the area of maintaining relationships with others on behalf of the family. This means that I keep track of all the special dates such as birthdays and anniversaries of my extended family and close friends and send the appropriate gifts or greetings when the time comes. I also coordinate all the communications on behalf of the family, meaning that when visitors come, I take care to coordinate hosting or getting together, and communicate news about our family to our large circle of friends, neighbors, coworkers and former business associates. This means that when it comes time to allocate time and money, I need to make space for maintaining these relationships, which means that I usually plan my calendar and budget alongside my address book to remind me which upcoming events need personal attention or action item. Just as the marriage needs to be maintained and managed with intentionality and planning, so do the circles of relationships around our family.

For Your Growth

1. Hopefully you have had the time to sit down with your spouse after reading the first chapter to write down some core values of your household. If not, make a date this week to do just that.
2. The book "Purpose Driven Life" talks about SHAPE (Gifts, Heart, Abilities, Personality, and Experience). Take some time to reflect and write down your SHAPE. First, give thanks for all these special gifts that you've been given, and try to see how that has contributed to your ability to be a good mother.
3. Next, set some concrete and measurable goals, plus the accompanying consequences for not meeting those goals, or rewards for meeting these goals. Set at least one goal for each category:
    a. Time for learning, family, serving, and rest. Block out blocks of time and schedule it in your calendar.
    b. Money
    c. Things
    d. Relationships
4. Share these goals with a friend and ask for help to keep you on track.

1.11 A SERENDIPITOUS ENCOUNTER

The following story is based upon people I know, but the names and facts have been altered and scrambled to protect their identities.

I was on a business trip one fall day, when I ran into an old friend at the airport. Back in college, we were like battle buddies, Zoe and I. In a school where the majority of students were men, we women stuck closer than sisters because we were fewer in number, and especially because those in our little group were Asian. We went through freshman orientation together, had the same crush on that same handsome guy in first year biology class, along with the 10-20 other Asian girls who went to class early to stake out a seat close to him. We worked into the late night on tricky physics problems, and ate instant noodles and ice cream together while dreaming of our future. Zoe and I headed several student clubs separately and jointly, and often worked together on posters and strategies to attract more student involvement. We giggled with each other when new boyfriends came along, and cried with each other when we broke up with those boyfriends. There were several of us in this little group, but after graduation we all went our separate ways to pursue our dreams.

We giggled with excitement like little girls, gave each other a big long hug, and went arm in arm to find a café to go catch up on the last decade of life. She found out that I had become a full time mother and put aside my career to be with my boys. I found out that she had just divorced husband #3 after she caught him cheating on her, and was now a big hotshot venture capitalist in Silicon Valley. We looked wistfully at one another with a slight twinge of envy and admiration. "Wow! Big hot shot career woman, running with the big boys in Silicon Valley! What an exciting life!" I told her. "You're the one I envy! A home full of people who adore you for who you are, a warm place to come home to, and all I have is a house full of cats, who are better than the men in my life!" We sighed and laughed at each other. I guess the grass is always greener on the other side. . .

The conversation moved on to catching up on mutual friends. What happened to Cindy, who was the big student government officer, the lone Asian women to win the election? Well, when she broke up with her genius boyfriend, he committed suicide and she had to drop out of school to get away from the unbearable attention and pain, and many years later, finally completed her MBA at Harvard, preferring to remain alone, below the radar, and out of touch with friends. Then there was Tanya, who fought long and hard with her parents to study architecture instead of medicine, and finally had the courage to come out to declare herself a lesbian. Last we heard she had become a partner in an architecture firm but had developed quite a career on the weekends as a stand-up comedian, seeking to find life's answers in and through laughter. Then there is another student leader who went on to Stanford Business School, married her classmate, had a child, got divorced, and became a single mother. She keeps busy running the company she founded, which had won all kinds of awards for industry excellence, and divides the rest of her time between raising her son alone and other charitable activities. What about Rachel? Last I heard, she went through a nasty and bitter divorce with husband number 2, who had gone to court to sue her for alimony and won. To get him out of her life, she gave him her life savings, the house, and the car. The consolation was that she ended up switching jobs to get away further from him and ended up co-founding a company with other classmates that became one of the 10 hottest IPOs last year. There was Betty, who became chief surgeon at one of the most prestigious teaching hospitals in the country and delayed getting married until 42, and is currently struggling with trying to have a baby, expending all kinds of money and time on the latest infertility treatments. Then there is my friend Janet and me, who have decided to focus on the home and delay working until the kids are older. Janet continued to work part time and is a manager at a software company while I became a full time mother and had a bunch of kids, and we are both in the process of catching up to our classmates who are miles ahead of us, but are dealing with other regrets and heartaches.

I started thinking of Dan Folgelberg's song "Same Auld Lang Syne", which was one of my favorite songs in high school:

Met my old lover in a grocery store
The snow was falling Christmas Eve
Stole behind her in the frozen foods
and I touched her on the sleeve
She didn't recognize the face at first

but then her eyes flew open wide
Tried to hug me and she spilled her purse
and we laughed until we cried
Took her groceries to the checkout stand
The food was totaled up and bagged
stood there lost in our embarrassment
as the conversation dragged
Went to have ourselves a drink or two
but couldn't find an open bar
Bought a six-pack at the liquor store
and we drank it in her car
We drank a toast to innocence, we drank a toast to now
Tried to reach beyond the emptiness but neither one knew how
She said she'd married her an architect
Kept her warm and safe and dry
She said she'd like to say she loved the man
but she didn't want to lie
I said the years had been a friend to her
and that her eyes were still as blue
But in those eyes I wasn't sure if I saw doubt or gratitude
She said she saw me in the record store
and that I must be doing well
I said the audience was heavenly
but the traveling was hell
We drank a toast to innocence we drank a toast to time
We're living in our eloquence, another old lang syne
The beers were empty and our tongues grew tired
and running out of things to say
She gave a kiss to me as I got out
and I watched her drive away
Just for a moment I was back in school
And felt that old familiar pain
And as I turned to make my way back home
the snow turned into rain

Whenever I used to hear this song in the past, I would feel a twinge of sadness. Life is full of regrets. Every decision has a price. I look at the major decisions I've made, and am at total peace at where I am. In the

76

meantime, I also rejoice at my friends' victories and cry with them over their heartaches. There is no free lunch. Whoever said that the modern woman can have it all is a big liar.

It's true what the Chinese proverb says that each home has a book that is difficult to read, but what the writer of this proverb and Dan Folgelberg neglected to say is that hidden within each book and each song is a story of redemption whose melody gets harder and harder to ignore. When we look back, we can choose to look at all the hardships, pitfalls, and wrong decisions, link them together to form the main storyline, or search for those hidden gems of grace and redemption that have been waiting there all along, waiting to be discovered. When we find them and choose to make that the main melody, we find that within each book is a beautiful story waiting to unfold. When I broke up with my first boyfriend, I remember sitting with my father in the car, telling him that my life is over. No one wants used goods. My father told me that there's a Taiwanese proverb that says "One blade of grass, one drop of dew". Even if I am the humblest blade of grass on earth, there will always be a drop of dew to nourish me. Years later, I would find myself sitting in another car with my father. This time it was he who admitted to me that David is a better husband and father than he ever was. It's true that our lives are full of wrong decisions and occasions for regrets, but they don't have to define us. We can choose to look for the grace notes that accompany them, and see that the power of redemption is louder than the hardships, and that there is always enough dew every morning when we wake up. What Dan Folgelberg did not sing about is that the rain came down, and nourished the whole earth, which sprung up with life giving green grass and beautiful flowers to adorn the earth.

My life is not yet over. Just like Zoe, we have chosen to make peace with our past, knowing that there is redemption and grace. It's not what I've been given that defines me, but how I choose to write my last chapter. My book is not yet complete, but having made peace with my past, I can face my future with anticipation and joy, knowing that there is a drop of dew along every step. St. Paul said it well:

"For I am already being poured out like a drink offering, and the time has come for my departure. I have fought the good fight, I have finished the race. I have kept the faith. Now there is in store for me the crown of righteousness."

This is my goal. At the end of my life, I want to finish well, having fought the good fight and finished the race, leaving no regrets. Those wrong turns that caused tears of pain, may they in turn be poured out like a drink offering and provide nourishment to some dry and thirsty soul, because God never wastes a single tear.

There is no free lunch. There is a cost to every decision. We live with the choices we make, but we always have a choice to make joy and redemption the main melody and story line, not sadness and regret.

For Your Growth

1. Reflect over your past. What are some of the regrets that you have? How could you have decided differently?
2. Now write out those regrets on pieces of paper, and make a conscious decision to rip them up and put them in the trash. Make a decision to leave them behind.
3. Think about where you ended up. What are some of the things about your present circumstance that you are thankful for? What are those hidden gems of "grace notes"?
4. Write down these items on a piece of paper. Determine to let these items become the dominant theme of your life.
5. From this point forward, in light of the fact that there is a price for everything, what would you like to put at the top of that list of priorities? How can you adjust your life accordingly to reflect this list? Write down at least three concrete action items that tou can take to move towards that direction.

SECTION II

THE PROPER ORDER:

WHOLEHEARTED MOM

PUTS

HUSBAND BEFORE KIDS

2.1 MARRIAGE ALWAYS COMES FIRST

These stories are true, but the names have been changed to protect their identities:

John and Jane were college sweethearts, just like us. All over the MIT campus, whenever I saw John, Jane was sure to be nearby. They were everywhere together, and were the envy of all our friends. Jane was pretty and smart. She finished MIT in 3 years and was admitted into Harvard Medical School before we reached 4th year. John was a talented architect and had an air of an artist who appreciated beauty, starting with Jane. We all thought that they would always be happy together. Years later, my husband and I met them in Los Angeles as they were getting ready to get divorced. They had a daughter named Lily, who was super smart and pretty like her mother. Shocked, my husband and I spent a lot of time with John and Jane, trying to help them see if they could work things out. Jane was upset that John was not ambitious enough, and wasn't successful enough to impress her demanding father. John was upset that Jane's standards were too high, and that her perfectionism drove her to be a constant source of nagging and stress. Jane felt that it would be better for Lily's sake for them to live apart for awhile, so that Lily can have the best conditions to achieve more in life than her father John, who had switched careers from architecture to banking in order to make more money to impress Jane's parents. Lily had all the advantages that life can offer her: an IQ that was off the charts, enrollment into the best private school money can buy her, and access to the best private tutors and coaches to help her excel in school, which she did with flying colors. However, last year when we visited John, who was happily remarried and had built another family, and asked him how Lily was doing, he told me that as much as he and Jane tried to provide the best of conditions for Lily's education, she was hospitalized 3 times last year at the age of 14 for anorexia nervosa, a psychological disease in which she was literally starving herself to death. The root of anorexia has to do with control. When one's life is chaotic and out of control, the only thing that a person feels she can control is her own body. Anorexia is perfectionism carried to the ultimate degree, where a person never feels thin enough or good enough. Despite the best of all conditions for Lily's education, the divorce was literally killing Lily.

David and Cindy were another couple that we had befriended later in China. They too had a daughter, Stella, who was pretty and smart. Both David and Cindy graduated from the best schools in China and the U.S., and returned to China to start his own business. David was young, handsome, and very successful, which inevitably led to him giving in to one of the many invitations to begin an extramarital affair. Cindy had previously poured herself into Stella's education, providing the best conditions to help her learn both Chinese and English, as well as piano, swimming, and ballet lessons with the best instructors in China. However, after the affair was discovered by Cindy, David and Cindy decided that they would take the time needed to repair their much damaged marriage, and make that a top priority over everything else. During the two years that it took for this couple to work on rebuilding their marriage, Stella did not receive the attention she usually did on her education and homework, but her personality took a decisive change for the brighter. She gained a big sense of self confidence, and became more willing to take risks and make bold decisions. She turned down an offer from a boy who was interested in dating her because in her mind, he was too self-absorbed and didn't have enough respect for girls. She felt that she deserved better and decided to wait rather than give in to the first boy that came along. She also excelled in school and rose to the top of her class. Today, she is a self-assured and happy young lady who knows what she wants out of life and is pursuing it with all her energy and optimism.

What made the difference in the lives of these two equally privileged young ladies? It was the outcome of their parents' marriages. The former killed off Lily's soul, while the latter transformed Stella and gave her energy for life.

Without a happy marriage, there can be no happy child, because the marriage of the parents is the classroom for the future marriage of the children in that home. A home full of marital conflicts will not be able to bring feelings of security to the children. On the other hand, a harmonious marriage brings confidence to the children, so that they do not need to grow up feeling somehow responsible for the happiness of the parents and bearing this unhealthy burden. Therefore, parents who want their children to be happy should work hard on their own marriages, putting a higher priority on the marriage relationship over the parent child relationship, even honoring of grandparents. Furthermore, the marriage should never be sacrificed for the sake of the children's education. New parents often neglect this. Often when they do realize this, they have discovered that their spouse has become a roommate who is a stranger. Just like all other relationships, a marriage needs to be nurtured and cultivated in order to remain vibrant and healthy. The pressures of a fast paced city life pushes all romance out of a relationship if there is no concerted effort to keep it alive. In the absence of time and attention, a marriage will wilt and die a slow death without both partners being aware of it. The myth that a "good" couple will naturally have a good marriage is a lie. A good marriage takes a lot of hard work.

When we first got married at the age of 22, all our MIT classmates were making bets to see how long our marriage would last before we got divorced. The longest bet was 3 years. This is because we were both so young, proud, selfish, and strong willed. We had terrible fights about the smallest things, and lacked maturity and character to humbly work things through. Knowing that our marriage had an inauspicious beginning forced us to work hard on our maintaining our marriage. It took us over 3 years of weekly counseling sessions to work on our own character and family of origin issues. There were lots of tears, times of discouragement and even despair, and times of just willing myself to go on without any feelings of love for the other person. It wasn't easy, but it was worth it. Here are some tips that we learned along the way that provided the right "vitamins" for our marriage to make it what it is today:

The book "Love and Respect" is so true! The reason that John and Jane's marriage failed despite the best of intentions and lots of effort on both parts was that Jane did not respect John or his abilities, even though he switched careers to make her happy and proud of him. Jane did everything at home to free up John to pursue success in his career, but John never saw all the sacrifices she made for him, even turning down Harvard Medical school to wait for him to graduate and then enrolling in a less prestigious medical school to be next to John when he went to business school in the Midwest. This was the ultimate reason for their divorce. For modern women who are very successful in their careers, this will probably be the toughest lesson to learn. Once I learned to unconditionally respect my husband, he was willing to learn to unconditionally love and cherish me. For new mothers who are tired from sleepless nights and endless rounds of diapers, it might be tempting to get upset at their spouses for not doing enough. Restrain yourself from that temptation, and get into the habit of looking at him, speaking of him, and treating him with respect and admiration.

Love bank: Psychologist Willard Harley makes the analogy that our hearts are like a bank. Love expressed and received is the equivalent of a deposit while fights or criticism is the equivalent of a withdrawal. We need to make regular deposits into each other's bank accounts so that when bad things happen, we have a positive reserve of love and understanding from which to withdraw. When there is plenty of deposit in our love banks, big things become small, small things become nothing. However, when there is a negative balance in our love banks, even little things can trigger a big explosion.

Time: A relationship cannot develop without enough time together. This is why most long distance marriages end up falling apart. Without adequate time, a relationship cannot grow or deepen in intimacy, because there is no time to communicate, share our deepest needs or feelings. The relationship stagnates and finds itself unable to breakthrough shallow grounds into physical, emotional, and spiritual oneness. In our marriage, we have cultivated the habit of daily communication, regular dates, and annual outings with our spouse.

✓ Daily Communication: Even if it's a short text message to tell the other "I love you, I'm thinking about you", "you're my best friend and soul mate", "I'm thankful for you in my life", or "you're the best thing that happened to me!", or a couple simple exchanges of loving words face to face over household matters, it's important to cultivate the simple habit of checking in every day with your spouse.

✓ Regular Dates: These dates can be very creative. For example, we will meet each other over lunchtime during work days to eat or have a drink, or swap with another couple so that when we go on a date, they watch our child, and when they go on a date, we watch their child. However, one dating rule that we follow closely is that we don't talk about our kids, but spend the time to give our best friend our time, love, and undivided attention, because we deeply believe that our spouse should be our best friend and there is nothing we cannot share with our spouse.

✓ Annual Outings: Each year, we will also plan a weekend getaway where we spend time by ourselves overnight without the kids. If budget is low, we don't need to travel out of town, but can check into a local hotel in the city, as long as we have that extended time to be together. Our kids enjoy these periods of independence each year and we always return better and happier for our kids.

Love languages: "The Five Love Languages" is an excellent book to help us understand how to better love our spouses so that we can maximize each loving action or word as we make deposits into our spouse's love bank. Expressing our love in the wrong love language can mean that our expression is not received effectively and can be frustrating for the person expressing the love. However, knowing how to best express love to your spouse will bring many happy returns. Before I learned about love languages, I was always using my primary love language, acts of service, to love my husband, and was so hurt that those actions didn't get noticed or appreciated by him. He was always upset that I could not give him the quality time he needed from me, because that was his primary love language. After we learned to adjust ourselves, he would help me wash the dishes before asking me to sit down with him to talk or have a cup of tea, while I would put down the dishes or the chores to sit down on the couch with him before finishing up the chores. That difference in order made a huge difference in our marriage, as each of us felt 100% more loved after we made these adjustments!

Communication is a must to cultivate love and understanding in marriage. Understanding gender differences will help us to communicate with our spouse more effectively. "Men are from Mars, Women are from Venus" is a great book to help us understand those gender differences, particularly in communication. Most communication is done at the facts and opinions level. We must learn to communicate more deeply, at the feelings, expectations, and needs level to share more transparently of our deepest selves. We must also learn to hear with the intention of understanding and encouraging the other rather than with the mindset to solve problems.

Protecting your marriage with boundaries: One of the best things we can do is to protect the boundaries of our marriage. To protect our marriage, we often need to say no to the requests or demands of others around us. Earlier on in our marriage, my mother often ask me to go home without consulting with my husband. When I insisted on waiting until after I've discussed with my husband before making plans to return home, she was upset and said some insulting words to me in her anger. I told my mother that if she can't speak respectfully about my husband that I will need to hang up the phone. I followed through several times when she did not stop. However, because my mother loved me very much, each time after I hung up with her, we would inevitably reconcile. However, she slowly changed her habit. Now, whenever she asked me, she would always wait for me to finish discussing with my husband first, and respect our decision. My husband would often praise me to his mother. If my mother in law has opinions about me, he would always remind her to please respect his wife. In the process of managing our marriage relationship, we need to balance honoring our parents with respecting our spouse. I deeply believe that ultimately, our parents love us, and are able to handle our "training" of them to respect the boundaries that we set around our marriage. If we are unable to protect the boundaries around our marriage and allow our parents to invade those boundaries regularly, we will compromise the unity and feeling of intimacy in our marriage. When one spouse's filial piety brings about distance in the marriage, the other spouse often then turns his/her attention to work or to the children. This is our mother-in-law / daughter-in-law problems perpetuate from generation to generation – because many wives cannot find fulfillment in their marriage. Therefore I propose that the best gift that you can give to your children is to cultivate a good marriage, so that they will not need to grow up feeling responsible for your happiness, and that you can give to them the freedom to build their own happy marriages.

Resume sex life as soon as possible. Mothers, make yourselves attractive for your spouse every day, as an act of respect for yourself and your marriage. Just because you are no longer working or are not seeing any guests does not mean that you can look sloppy for your spouse, who probably sees professional and attractively dressed women at work all day long. Remember how much you primped and maintained yourselves in order to present yourself at your best to him when you were dating your spouse? Why should that change now that you are married? Should you do less for your best friend and soul mate, who is a male and is stimulated visually? Also, get your child to sleep by himself as soon as possible, not because you are selfish or cruel, but because your marriage is of more importance than sleeping with your child. When he is nursing, it is understandable and convenient to have the cradle next to your bed. However, there is no reason to continue to make your child a higher priority than your husband when there is no more physiological reason for your child to sleep in the same room as you. The old saying that men give love to get sex and women give sex to get love has a big ring of truth. Men have a physical need for sex. If he's not getting it at home, you are opening the door for him to look elsewhere to fulfill that legitimate need. If you love your spouse and want your marriage to flourish, then plan on having sex with him regularly. Don't wait until things are broken down to repair it. Cars need regular maintenance and change of oil. How much more critical is a marriage in comparison?

On my blog "Who Is First In Your Heart? ", I wrote: "Not long after Caleb was born, I saw my husband feeling very sad one day. He said that not only did he not gain a son, but he lost his best friend to a new boy in the home. He said that it's become a world for two, without any more room for him. I remember being so angry at the time, thinking that he is such a selfish and small hearted man for competing against a helpless little child. However, as I look back today, what he said reminded me that children are gifts entrusted to our care for a short time by God, not our possessions. Someday, they will leave our homes to face the world on their own and build their own families. Only our spouses will be with us for the rest of our lives. This realization helped me to reallocate my time and energies. A happy marriage is the motivation and engine for life, with happy children as a byproduct, not the main goal. Yes, when children are little, they are totally dependent upon us, needing huge amounts of time and energy from us, but we need to intentionally carve out the space to cultivate and maintain our marriage. The marriage begins to fall into danger when we realize in the midst of our busyness of caring for our kids that our love for our spouse has grown cold. When we finally get around to rescuing the marriage, we are often too tired and discouraged to put in the ever increasing effort needed, so continue to focus on our children, in an ever worsening vicious cycle. One reader commented that for her, it's already too late. My feeling is that it's never too late. Once there is a realization of a need for a change of course, then corrective action can be taken. Feelings come and go, but we can lead our feelings to follow us in the direction of our will and our convictions. Take that first step, make that first deposit into the love bank without any expectations of instant change, speak that first word, and your feelings will follow.

Managing your marriage, just like managing a company or learning to be a parent, is a lifelong learning process. To succeed, you should be constantly upgrading your skills, pursuing help from older mentors, walking along this journey with other companions with similar values who want to work on improving their marriages, and encouraging one another along the way. Our marriage beat the odds. So can yours.

There's an American saying that "The road to hell is paved with good intentions". When you married your spouse, you had lots of good intentions, but that is never good enough. There needs to be a concrete plan to follow through on those good intentions. What are yours?

For Your Growth

1. When was the last time you made an intentional deposit in the love bank of your husband? Write down at least one deposit you will make this week.

2. In what way have you disrespected your husband? How can you change that this week?

3. If you have not read "The Five Love Languages", read it together with your spouse and communicate with each other your primary love languages. Then make a date this week to practice loving each other according to the other person's love language.

2.2 SOWING AND REAPING

"If I speak in the tongues of men or of angels, but do not have love, I am only a resounding gong or a clanging cymbal. If I have the gift of prophecy and can fathom all mysteries and all knowledge, and if I have a faith that can move mountains, but do not have love, I am nothing. If I give all I possess to the poor and give over my body to hardship that I may boast, but do not have love, I gain nothing.

Love is patient, love is kind. It does not envy, it does not boast, it is not proud. It does not dishonor others, it is not self-seeking, it is not easily angered, it keeps no record of wrongs. Love does not delight in evil but rejoices with the truth. It always protects, always trusts, always hopes, always perseveres. Love never fails."

This morning, as I once again read this very familiar passage, I was especially touched. I always hear this passage whenever I attend weddings. After awhile, I would stop thinking about it. However, today, this passage continues to appear in my mind. I remember when I was dating, I kept wanting him to use more passionate or obvious ways to express to me and the world how much he loved me. I also remembered how I looked down on old married couples who were no longer expressive of their love or passion for one another, thinking that I would never allow myself to fall into that predicament. Then, when I walked into my marriage with this kind of idealism and expectation, and felt the sting of disappointment when I can't see it expressed, I felt deceived. Then, I always used the second paragraph as a yardstick to measure him, feeling that he's too this or not enough that. When I compare him against others, I felt that he's not as this or too that compared to others, as I kept hoping that he would change to finally become the knight in shining armor that I was hoping for. Then, the love between us felt as if it had died, because my unfulfilled expectations slowly turned our love into coldness, despising, and even hate. However, in order to keep the promise we made to one another, we gritted our teeth and kept plodding on , trying to rediscover that feeling of love again. Love is not a feeling, but a promise. This promise is the marriage vow between one man and one women, one husband and one wife for one lifetime.

Sometimes all we have left is this promise to keep us going in tilling the soil of our marriage. Although we know that the only person in the world that we can change is ourselves, and that we need to accept the other person, how difficult that is to live out! It's only when I set out to change myself that I discover that I need to back up to begin with accepting, loving, and treasuring myself. As a big sister in the family, I have developed the habit of ignoring my own needs to look after other people's needs first. This led me to a starting point of not accepting myself, instead asking others to accept, love, and treasure me. And so, little by little, I began to accept myself, and as a result, him. Unbeknownst to me, 22 year crept by, and I discovered that I changed, and he did, too.

Tomorrow, we will leave for an out of town trip together to use the weekend to celebrate our 22th wedding anniversary. This morning, when I read this passage, I felt deeply that if he had made some flowery promise, done some heroic deeds, or made some huge sacrifice, but has no love as described in the second paragraph, wouldn't it all be for nothing? The youthful expectations of love is so childish! Now, when I see him, I only have overflowing gratitude. Grateful that he's not a con man with sweet words, but is a honest man with few words; grateful that when we teach parenting classes, he says little, but does the most; grateful that when I'm feeling down, he will tell joke to cheer me up; grateful that all the things I can't stand about him are now blessing and protection for me; grateful for all the effort he put into our marriage, all the time he put in, all the sacrifices he made for the family, all the things he did for me ... too much! Why did I not see it before? I realized that what I'm sowing now is perhaps all the seeds down when I gritted my teeth, putting one foot in front of the other, to water, weed, and cultivate my marriage. Now, I can't imagine life without him for one day, because not only is he my best friend, most intimate partner, but is also a coworker with a common purpose. Now, we often discover that the other will finish our sentence for us if we start it. This must be what unity of body, soul, and spirit looks like!

The purpose of writing this blog is not to show off what great people we are, because when we first got married, our classmates from college were all betting that our marriage won't last beyond three years. How well can putting together two super proud and selfish people end? The reason for writing this blog is to encourage those of you who are feeling discouraged and disappointed in your marriage right now not to give up hope, but to keep working at it, keep sowing good seeds, keep using the kind of love described in the passage above to love the other. You will be like me to be surprised one day to discover that you have falling in love with your lover all over again, and this kind of love is deeper, stronger, and more realistic than the starry eyed romantic kind of infatuation from before.

Love is not a feeling. Love is a promise. Love never fails.

For Your Growth

1. Make a list of 15 traits in your spouse that you are grateful for. Make an appointment to sit down with him to communicate how grateful you are for him.

2.3 KEEPING THE FLAMES ALIVE

CB

Agent R approached D in the parking lot as he got out of his office on a sunny Friday afternoon. Dressed in a sexy little black dress, she walked up to him and asked in a seductive voice: "Ready for some adventure?"

He was the chief officer in charge of a top research facility, where they were working on a number of top secret military projects for the government. He eyed her suspiciously and contemplated the offer. Before he had time to reply, two men emerged from the shadows behind him, blindfolded him, tied him up, and pushed him into the back of her car, as it sped away into the twilight to a mystery location where she planned a romantic evening by a seaside resort.

She was a spy assigned from a rival company to see if she could coax some research secrets out of him. That evening she will turn on her charms and ply him with every trick she knows to see if she will accomplish her mission, from the soft music playing in their hotel room, dim lights, rose petals in the bubble bath, champagne chilling in a bucket of ice by the bath, to a romantic stroll by the beach and violins playing at the intimate French restaurant by the ocean. He would coyly play along to see how far she would go to woo him, as he held himself off at a distance. He was looking forward to an evening of cat and mouse, as they each try to play the other to see who will give in first.

CB

No, this is not some excerpt from some cheap romance novel, but a well-planned romantic getaway for my husband's birthday, where we concocted a plot to spice up our evening away. Of course, we had the help of a couple of other "actor" friends who participated in our fantasy, but only the sneak preview at the beginning ☺ Some people think that romance just happens spontaneously by chance, but from my observations of good marriages that have not just endured the test of time, but have thrived through the good times and bad, I am convinced that it takes a great deal of forethought, intentionality, planning, logistics, creativity, and budgeting to keep that flame of romance burning, especially after the kids arrive.

Motherhood can become an idol, an end in itself. I have seen many marriages crash and burn or die a slow death after the arrival of the first child, as the mother or both parents become absorbed with the child to the exclusion of everyone else around them, even their own spouse. Sex life comes to a standstill as both parents collapse in exhaustion after expending all their energies on work and on trying to be the best parents in the world to raise the best, brightest, healthiest, and happiest child to grace this world. The spouse becomes a stranger or a coworker in the task of raising the child, and the marriage takes a distant second, sometimes even third after family obligations to the parents and in-laws. Slowly those first exciting moments of falling madly in love with that beautiful or handsome person that used to take up all your mind space fade away into the background, replaced by diapers, baby formula, weekend classes, and homework every evening. Most people forgot that the marriage is the centerpiece of a family, and that without a living and thriving marriage, the child becomes elevated to the level of an idol that needs to live his/her life to fulfill the dreams, investments and hopes of their parents and grandparents. This kind of expectation is too much for any little child to bear, and he will be crushed under the weight, never having the freedom to enjoy simply being a child. It's time to re-evaluate your priorities as a mother and put cultivating your marriage back on top of your list of priorities, starting with restoring the romance back into your marriage.

I once heard a speaker at a marriage conference advise us to block out regular times in our schedules for sex. There was wide snickering and embarrassment in the audience, because we all felt that it would stifle our feelings if those times were so planned and mechanical. However, life in the big cities is busy, with many competing demands for our time constantly screaming at us. Without intentionally blocking out the time for each other, those demands will win every time, no matter how great our intentions or feelings for our spouse. Even a car needs regular scheduled maintenance to make sure that we prolong its life and keep the machinery in good shape before breakdown happens and incurs an even greater cost in repair. If a simple machine needs this maintenance, how about the most important relationship in your life? I can see some of you throw up your hands in despair, roll your eyes, and say, but I'm just not a young and starry eyed teenager anymore. There are too many cares in my life for me to fly freely like that, as I am weighed down with all kinds of responsibilities. All the more you need to intentionally allocate the time, energy, budget, and planning to keep your marriage alive and free, because you will discover that it will be a source of strength to you when you need to draw upon it.

So, how do you go about cultivating romance with a busy and active child and a sagging body that just does not seem to be as attractive as it used to be, no matter how much make up your put in strategic places and cover those wrinkles with colorful clothing? First, start by calling each other all those silly little endearments that used to make people around you blush, instead of referring to each other as "Mommy" or "Daddy". That is not your primary identity. It's still "Honey", "Sweety pie" (or please put in those terms in Chinese here for the reader ☺) or those silly names that you make up for each other when you were dating. You are a lover before you are a parent. It's OK if your children are embarrassed by it for a time, or if they tell you when you are so embarrassing they want to throw up, like my kids would use to say to us. They will get used to turning their heads away and will some day treat their spouses the same way you are treating your spouse. In fact, when they think of those "embarrassing" moments as adults it might even make them smile.

Next, birthdays and wedding anniversaries are the best opportunities to celebrate and plan a getaway. My husband and I make it a point to plan an overnight trip each year, away from the kids, just the two of us. And the rule of engagement when we are on our "dates" or getaways is that we are not allowed to talk about the kids or "family business". These "dates" can be as simple as one of you meeting the other at his office for lunch, or as elaborate as a weekend getaway to a resort. The point is to make the dates regular and frequent while the getaways can be once a year or couple of years when the kids are small. As the person with more talent for details and planning in our marriage, I have taken on the task of planning these surprises for my husband. It's always fun to ask around for ideas and advice, as those helping me also get to relish the idea of helping an old married couple stay freshly in love, and it feeds ideas into other people's heads for planning their own getaways. When I look at old couples walking hand in hand, looking in love, it always inspires me, so I know that a goal to remain madly in love as a married person is a noble one, not a strange one. Because as a woman I need to feed my imagination to get into a romantic frame of mind, I try to plan a story line or theme around a particular getaway, whereas men usually don't need so many preliminaries. Sometimes you need to enlist accomplices to help you with your mission.

The last time I planned a romantic getaway in the U.S. was for David's birthday. Knowing how busy he is at work and how often he travels, I called up his boss two months in advance to ask for an afternoon off for him. I also asked him if he could help me by booking an appointment with David on behalf of a client, and sending him to meet this client in a particular hotel known for its breathtaking view from the rooms at the top. Next I asked another mother whose kids played with my kids, and arranged a kid swap. When I was away getting ready for my getaway, she would feed them lunch, take them to play somewhere fun, and babysit them while I spent time with David. I had to call the hotel in advance to arrange for a room with a view, negotiate a good rate, and ask for whatever specials they may have for honeymooners. This means that I have to allocate budget and plan well in advance so that David's "surprise" can happen without him ever being aware of what was being planned. At the same time, I told him that we would go out to dinner at his favorite restaurant that evening to celebrate his birthday with the kids, which meant that we would need to end our afternoon tryst in time for me to go pick up the kids, get them and myself cleaned up in time to meet him at the restaurant after work.

On the morning of the planned tryst, I went ahead to the hotel room to make sure that the room was prepared with soft music and rose petals scattered in strategic places, as well as arrange with the hotel staff to have champagne on ice and some light snacks ready and waiting by 1pm. I had all the wardrobe planned and purchased ahead of time, including a new dress in the style and color he liked and other "accessories". At around noon, I get a phone call from him. He was pretty upset at his boss, who had just rearranged his schedule the last minute and sent him off to see a prospective new client without qualifying him or telling David the background on this potential big client. He felt that his boss wasn't trusting him enough to consult him to see if he is the right person to be assigned to this client, and felt unprepared because he didn't have time to do research in advance on this unknown XYZ client, which he had never heard of in his life. I had to smother a laugh as I tried to calm him down. I told him that I thought that the client was in the entertainment industry, right? He kept going, complaining in his frustration. Then I interrupted and asked: "Did he send you to this hotel and this room number?" Silence. I talked loudly into the phone to see what happened to him. "Oh, I almost swerved off the road and fell into the ditch. Bye." I guess the realization dawned on him that his new client was me. I love surprises! He had a wonderful and memorable birthday, and we were more in love than ever, despite all the weight I had gained and not been able to lose after having all those children!

As you could see from my example, this little tryst would never have happened on its own. It required advanced planning, coordination, and budgeting. I have continued to take on the responsibility for planning these "outings" for us, and David has enjoyed pitching in his own ideas, often surprising me with little touching gestures of love and consideration when I least expect it. This past summer he took me for a getaway to Yangshuo, the most romantic place in China, for our 20th anniversary celebration. It was an unforgettable time, not because it was so expensive (it was tagged onto the end of a business meeting he had there, and only costed us my plane ticket), but because of the thought and planning he put into it, complete with 99 red roses and a singer dedicating a love song to us at a restaurant we happened to "drop into" in Yangshuo.

I hope I have planted enough seeds of ideas into your head to plan your own little adventures with your husband, the first love of your life. Here are some suggestions that I've tried and works in China:

☐ The Financial crisis provides a great opportunity for cheap deals at 5 star hotels (or others) in the city. Just about every hotel has a weekend getaway special for room rates that include free breakfast. Buffets that normally cost well over RMB 200 each on weekends are sharply discounted to under RMB 90. Shop around for a good deal and plan a trip across town to that hotel and pretend you are tourists honeymooning in your city. And the plane ticket is free.

☐ Find other couples who have kids your age who would be willing to swap kids with you so that when you and your husband are out, they are taking care of your kids and then you can do the same for them. The advantage of this is that neither your parents or his need to know that you are leaving behind your kid to go out to play. And your child gets a play date while you are out with each other, which is a win-win.

☐ Take your husband out on a power business lunch. On a special occasion, bring by some roses and cholocates just to reverse the male/female role.

☐ There are some wonderful places that provide reasonably priced messages for two. Getting a foot or body message together is a good way to relax together while chatting.

☐ Parks are wonderful places for a nice walk and enable you to recapture the wonder of looking at the beauty of nature. Somehow a stroll among trees and flowers just refreshes the soul and connects you to your soulmate.

☐ Vacation villages provide activities for those that need to be doing things together, whether it be water sports, bike riding, horseback riding, go cart racing, or fishing.

☐ Your cell phone is a powerful and convenient tool to send little messages to let him know that you are thinking of him, that you love him, and that he is the best thing that ever happened to you.

☐ For those husbands that pack lunches, love notes are a good way to help his digestion as he reads an encouraging note from you before unpacking his lunch.

The possibilities are endless, no matter your budget or time constraint. In the blinking of an eye, your child will be grown and gone, to raise a family of his own. When you are left with just the two of you, my hope and wish for you is that you will still be as madly in love with each other as the day you first met, and that your love will have grown in depth and richness after weathering all the ups and downs of life and raising a family together. I bless you with the lyrics from Wendy Liu's latest love song: may these be the words that your husband will sing to you at whatever stage of your life together:

You are in my thoughts day and night, my only longing, the reward for my hard work;

When time ceases to exist, the seas are dry, and rocks have decayed, you are still the one I love the most.

For Your Growth

1. What is one thing you can do to add more romance into your marriage this week? Make a date and concrete plans to execute this intention.

2.4 SEVEN U-TURNS THAT SAVED MY MARRIAGE

These days, many people look at my marriage and family life with much envy, thinking that we are just naturally nice people who get along well. The reality is far from that fantasy. In fact, we are two quite imperfect people who made a lot of mistakes along the way. At our wedding, our classmates had a running bet on how long our marriage would last, and the longest bet was three years. We married at the very young and immature age of 22, a year after graduating from college. We both came into the marriage with many ideals and personal character flaws, and I in particular carried many bad habits from my family of origin into my marriage. However, as I look back, I found that during critical times of crisis in our marriage, I had some key help and insights that enabled me to make some critical decisions to turn my marriage around. I would like to share with you these 7 U-turns that saved my marriage:

1. No back doors: Before dating my husband David, I had a long relationship with another boyfriend which lasted for most of my college years. He had the qualities of a typical "Prince Charming": tall, smart, good looking, and from a rich family. Our relationship was full of turmoil as his indecisiveness and inability to commit to the relationship made me increasingly insecure and broke my heart several times over, but when I broke up with him, both our mothers were more upset about it than we were, and neither were willing to forgive us until I got back together with him. When I met David, he was quite the opposite, and was serious about our relationship from the start. Whereas my ex-boyfriend was laid back and quite indecisive, David was intense, passionate, and fully committed. It was those qualities that drew me to him, and I later willingly committed to spend a lifetime with him. However, those exact same qualities caused problems for me after we married. I was a young woman of many interests and played many leadership roles in community activities. I constantly developed new interests and new friendships, in addition to maintaining old ones. My problems with over-commitment caused him to raise questions of loyalty and calls for me to re-prioritize. Where does he weigh in on the list of my interests? During those times when he would call me to account, my first desire

is to run away, instead of taking his warnings seriously and shed some of the less important commitments. This running away would take the form of fantasizing about "what might have been" with the ex-boyfriend. Even though the first relationship was turbulent and harmful, with the distance of time, those painful details began to fade and what I began to remember were the qualities that were the opposite of David. Once I opened that door in my mind, I would begin to make unfair comparisons and would become quite unsatisfied with the marriage I ended up with. What began as wisps of thoughts of the other guy would bloom into full blown contempt of my husband as the comparisons went on, and would sometimes come out of my mouth in ways that hurt him greatly. A few years after David and I were married, these fantasies would interfere with reality, making me dissatisfied with my marriage. For the first time after the break-up, I contacted my ex-boyfriend to clarify the reasons for our break-up, because at that time he was still single. He reminded me of our painful history and specific incidents that made being together impossible. After our final exchange, I was finally able to close that back door to my mind and make a deliberate decision to never allow thoughts of him to re-enter my mind. I made a decision to be grateful for my husband, and to appreciate his unique qualities. That U-turn has ensured that we worked together to improve our marriage, instead of having one side with a divided heart and divided loyalties. After I made that decision, I would remind myself to keep that door closed every time I'm feeling bad and tempted to escape in my mind through indulging in harmful self-pity and fantasy.

2. Leaving my home to become one with my husband: Growing up as the oldest daughter in a family of daughters, I played the role of savior and hero. My mother and I were unusually close, and we would confide our deepest secrets and struggles to each other. This became an obstacle after I got married, because every time David and I had a fight, I would go tell my mother to get some sympathy. My mother was not approving of my choice of marriage partner. Because of the differences in our family backgrounds, she always thought that I married beneath me and that we were not equally matched. Every time I would confide in my mother, it would further confirm to her that I had made a mistake, and would further fuel her attempts to

make me divorce him, which would further deepen the distance between me and my husband. I vividly remember one day when we were living in Vancouver, and David and I had a fight. In my typical impulsive fashion, I packed up both my boys and drove off in our van, ready to spend the night at my mother's house. I as drove on the road, my mind turned from rehearsing all the wrong that I perceived that my husband had done to me to what my mother would say. Words like "I told you so, why didn't you listen to me, and still insist on having children with him? When will you leave him?" rang through my mind. I was confronted with two unpleasant choices: face my husband and take responsibility for my own rash actions? Or go home to face my mother? At that moment, I made a decision that I would close that door and finally cut the umbilical cord. I had made a commitment to my marriage: For richer or poorer, for better or for worse, in sickness and in health. The commitment was not to run away whenever things got difficult. I immediately made a U-turn on the road and drove home to apologize to my husband for all the hurt that I had caused him. The expression of shock, relief, and gratitude on his face is still firmly etched on my mind. Every time I am tempted to run home, I remind myself of that face to stop no matter how bad things got. I have since made the deliberate effort to "curate" my comments to my mother about my husband, to praise only his positive qualities and to never say anything negative about him. Today, my mother has developed a lot of respect for my husband as a result of my efforts, and my husband is thankful to me for making that critical U-turn to return and fight for my marriage.

3. Curating my comments in front of others: My parents and relatives are very traditionally Chinese. They never showed any affection in public and are humble people. By that I mean that when others complimented me, my sisters, or my father, my mother would deny that and say something negative about us to demonstrate that we are really in fact very humble. The result is that I have never heard my mother speak kindly or positively about my father in front of others, but usually hear her speaking about his faults and shortcomings. I continued in this pattern like a good and humble daughter, until one day, a friend pulled me aside when we were having dinner to give me a very wise word of advice. She suggested that when I spoke

negatively or criticized my husband in front of others, I was making myself and him look bad, and eventually he will live to fulfill those negative words that I am pronouncing about him. She encouraged me to leave words of criticism for private moments when his heart is open to me and he is asking for my input to improve himself, and I am able to voice those criticisms with love and gentleness. Only then can internally motivated changed occur in him, because they are response to my words of love. If I criticize him in front of others, I am effectively cursing him to become the kind of person I am describing, and he will also criticize me in front of others. This caused me to reflect on my unconscious behavior pattern and see the increasingly negative reactions of my husband to me in public situations. I determined to change this behavior, and asked for help from my friends to catch me when I lapse into this pattern and to make immediate course corrections. As a result, my husband also responded in kind and began to praise me in front of others, starting a positive cycle.

4. The only person you can change is yourself, not him: My husband is an engineer who's not schooled in the art of romance and sweet talk. When I asked him to speak more words of love and encouragement to me rather than criticize what is wrong with me, he responded that he is an engineer and only looks for things that are wrong to fix, and leaves things that are not broken alone. I used to get really frustrated with his inability to praise and appreciate me, and started to complain and nag him about his speech. I would read books on self-improvement and try to make him read them. I would try to get other friends to talk to him to change the way he spoke. These actions only alienated him more from me, and were not effective in changing him one bit. One day, I read the story of a wife who had always wanted her husband to love her but did not begin to see change until she changed herself. I realized that the only person I had control over was myself, and if I depended on him for my happiness, I was playing the role of a helpless victim rather than being someone who is in control of my own destiny. I determined that I would become a more positive and grateful person regardless of how he treated me. To my amazement, once I started praising and appreciating him, he started to return the same kindness and appreciation without me expecting

anything in return. I found that when I worked on being a better wife, I became more attractive to him, and he became a more loving husband.

5. I am not his competitor, but his helper: In the workplace, I was used to the dog eat dog rules of the jungle, where competitiveness and making sure that you received proper credit and recognition for your work was the way to success. In the home, my ways to make sure that we shared 50-50 of the load at home only made my husband more hostile and resentful, causing us to keep records and constantly compare to make sure that the other person acknowledge our part and that we don't do too much for the other person to cultivate the habit of them taking advantage of us. This pattern of behavior only decreased the trust we had for each other because at the core, we were looking out for the interest of ourselves, not the other. We went to a marriage seminar where the speaker mentioned that marriage is a race, and it's a race to out give and out sacrifice for our spouses and to lay down our own interests for him/her. I realized that in my unwillingness to get hurt, I was hurting him. I determined to become his helper to help him look good, succeed, and get more credit than me. He began to trust me more and became more dependent on me, consulting me for opinions on decisions and trusting me to make the best decisions for the family. We became a team, working together toward a common goal of serving others, rather than rivals working against each other to further our own interests.

6. Catching the danger signals: Best-selling author Malcolm Gladwell mentions in his book "Blink" about an interesting research on signs that a marriage is headed for divorce. Surprisingly, the indicator was not the frequency of conflicts within the marriage, but when one spouse begins to treat the other with contempt. Often after conflicts happen, I can close my heart to my spouse and treat him as my enemy, rather than recognizing that we need to attack the issue that needs to be resolved. Once I clarified in my head who my real enemy is, I can stand on my husband's side to tackle the issue needing to reach a compromise or solution rather than on him as a person. Refusing to harden my heart enabled us to stay on the same side

during conflicts so that we can creatively work out win-win solutions rather than having one side win at the expense of the other.

7.   The children and me on one side, or he and I on the same side? When I had my first child, I would get into arguments with my husband about the "right" parenting method. As my son grew older, and disagreements came up, I started to describe the situation to my child in a way as to win him to my side against my husband. However, having read enough parenting books, I knew how important it was for the kids to look up to their fathers, especially for boys. I would literally witness that as I tried to enlist my child to be on my side, his respect for his father would decrease in proportion, to the point where David was unable to discipline him without his heart becoming rebellious. This backfired too when I tried to discipline my child, because he was able to take advantage of our disagreement to pit us against each other. Just as I did with my mother and in front of my friends, I began to stand on my husband's side. When the children would come to me to complain about their father, or how unfairly he was treating them, I would lovingly remind them that they have the best father in the world. Who would spend so much time with them, coach them in all these sports, and discipline them to build good character in them? Who sacrifices so much of his personal recreational time to be with the family? I found that as I led by my own example of genuinely appreciating my husband, the children were directed to respect their father more, and that in turn made my husband want to live up to their high estimation of him. More and more, he became the person I praised him to be, in front of my parents, my friends, and my children. A good father is a result of much praise!

There are many misconceptions about marriage. First, marriage is never the graveyard for love and romance! However, good marriages don't just happen because two people are just naturally good people, either! No one is perfect, and good marriages take a lot of hard work and a lot of hard choices. Feelings come and go, and will go through cycles of ups and downs. However, good feelings come as a result of you making those hard choices for yourself. The benefit of a good marriage is that you will give your child the best gift in the world: a happy and healthy family of origin, a classroom for his own future happy marriage. Are you ready to make those choices?

For Your Growth

1. Are there unhealthy patterns of behavior in your marriage? If so, what do you need to stop doing?

2. What do you need to start doing?

2.5 THE SECRET OF GETTING ALONG

Stephen: "Caleb, you're my hero!"

Caleb: "Stephen, you're my little bro!"

This summer, Jonathan went to the U.S. by himself to attend a summer music camp to improve his drumming skills, leaving his two brothers behind at home to spend more time with each other. These days, every time Caleb gets home from his internship, I always hear this greeting, and can't help but smile at this sweet exchange. Caleb and Stephen are 8 years apart, so it was hard for them to get into fights. Stephen kind of worshipped his big brother. In his eyes, Caleb could do no wrong. In the meantime, Caleb treated Stephen like a little pet, letting him have his way all the time.

Last night, the two brothers had the worst fight ever, and the two of them went around with angry faces, each retreating to his own room to sulk. Used to playing the role of detective and police in my investigative work in helping my children resolve their fights, I went into each boy's bedroom to find out what happened to cause such unhappiness.

Caleb said that he's had a lot of time with Stephen lately and spent a lot of energy to teach him things, play a lot of childish games, talk about many childish topics, and answer a lot of childish questions. Stephen always accepted each word with absolute trust, worshipping this big brother who seemed to know everything. Last night, Daddy returned from a business trip from the U.S. and brought back a spherical Rubick's Cube. Stephen played with it all night, but was unable to solve the puzzle. However, when he passed it on to Caleb, he solved it after 90 minutes. Stephen wanted Caleb to teach him the secret, but Caleb said that there was no secret to teach and no manuals to read. Stephen didn't believe him, absolutely convinced that Caleb was withholding this secret from him because he didn't want to share. Caleb felt that lately Stephen was less willing to trust him, and is respecting him less and less. The only thing he wanted Stephen to understand was that Daddy taught him about how gyroscopes worked when he was little, and it was these principles that helped him to solve the puzzle, not any methods. Caleb wanted to use this opportunity to remind Stephen to take care to listen to what he and Daddy tell him, because although he can't use a lot of those things right away, everything will be useful to him some day.

However, Stephen has his own way of thinking now, and doesn't want to learn from his brother anymore. He felt that Caleb won't let him have his own opinions and thinks that he's always right. Stephen felt that he can solve this puzzle without learning any gyro principles from physics, as long as he learns a method or approach to solving it. Both felt that the other was only willing to talk, but not listen, and this is unbearable. I asked Stephen: "What is Caleb's love language?" He said: "For someone to spend a lot of time to listen to him talk." I asked Caleb: "What is Stephen's love language?" He said: "For someone to spend time listening to him." Hmmm, both need to air their opinions to feel loved, but neither is willing to listen. What do we do?

I called both brothers to the living room, and gave them each a change to describe what happened and how they felt about it. Both felt that the other person was unbearable. I asked them:

"Are there things about Mom that Dad just can't stand?"

Both nodded their heads vigorously. "Of course!"

I asked again: "And are there things about Dad that Mom just can't stand?"

Again both heads bobbed rapidly up and down.

I asked again: "So did these weaknesses change with time?"

Both heads shook. "No."

"So how did we solve this problem? Do you guys think that Mom and Dad will divorce as a result of these weaknesses? Do you think you guys still stop being brothers? No way. So have Mom and Dad been fighting harder?" I followed with these questions.

Both brothers thought about the answers in surprise, and then said: "It seemed like you guys love each other more, not less. How can this be?"

I asked them: "So do you know what's the secret of getting along?"

Both brothers thought for a long time, and couldn't come up with an answer, but were very curious. Finally I told them that it's an extremely simple word. It's easy to say, but extremely difficult to do, but is absolutely the secret of getting along harmoniously in a close relationship. This word is – acceptance. The really weird thing is that when I am willing to accept the other's weakness, the other one, because he knows that he is accepted, is more willing to accept my own weakness, too. Thus a virtuous cycle is begun.

It's as if a light came on in both brothers at the same time, as each felt like he found a priceless treasure. Stephen said: "Caleb, what are you thinking in your head right now? I want to listen!" Caleb smiled: "Actually, I'm thinking about that BP oil leak, and how to solve this problem. . ." Big hand took little hand and walked into Stephen's room. When I walked in to take a peek, Caleb drawing a diagram, explaining to Stephen the different solutions that BP is considering. I reminded them that it's time to go to sleep. Before Caleb left Stephen's room, the brothers gave each other a big "man hug".

"Caleb, you're still my hero! Good night!"

"Stephen, you're still my little bro! Good night!"

Acceptance. Such a simple word, but is the biggest secret in a loving home.

For Your Growth

1. Are there thing about yourself that you find hard to accept? Write down the top three and start each day this week by seeking to accept those things.

2. Next make a similar list for your spouse of the top three things you find difficult to accept about him, and do the same this week as you seek to learn acceptance: of yourself and your spouse.

2.6 WALK ANOTHER MILE

Marriage is a race, a race to out give and out sacrifice for our spouses and to lay down our own interests for him/her. In the workplace, I was used to the dog eat dog rules of the jungle, where competitiveness and making sure that you received proper credit and recognition for your work was the way to success. In the home, however, if we tried to make sure that we shared 50-50 of the load at home, we will only make each other more hostile and resentful, causing each spouse to keep records and constantly compare to make sure that the other person acknowledge our part and that we don't do too much for the other person to cultivate the habit of them taking advantage of us. This pattern of behavior only decreases the trust we have for each other because at the core, we are really looking out for the interest of ourselves, not the other. In our own unwillingness to get hurt, we are shortchanging the person we love.

I remember that before the kids came, it was easier to divide the work or do it together, and there wasn't so much responsibilities that it proved to be crushing to us. However, after the kids came, and I became a full time mother, we discovered that it was much easier to lose balance in either direction. For my husband, it was easy to assume that since he worked to provide the income for me to stay home full time, that it was my responsibility to look after all aspects of running our house and raising our children. From my standpoint, while I did want to be the best wife and mother, having given up my career to stay home, I could not help but feel resentfulness occasionally bubbling to the surface. After all, he didn't have to give up an ego boosting job where he was recognized for his accomplishments to perform an endless series of meaningless tasks. His work ended when he left the office, and my office hours never ended. When my son was first born, I felt shackled to him, and felt guilty for even leaving him to take a shower, especially during the times when my husband often had to travel out of town for work. When we do reach across these feelings to help out, sometime we would overstretch over our capacities, become resentful, and start keeping scores. During those times, each of us would feel unappreciated, tired, and alone while the other mate was also unable to reach out to help him/her get up.

What do you do then? Who is supposed to make the first move? The answer is: both!

I remember the first time I attended a marriage retreat, when I arrived tired and resentful at my husband. I wanted him to hear the messages so that he will change first and apologize to me for saying some insensitive things to me on the way to the hotel. The story that I heard on the first day shook me to the core and challenged me to take a hard look at myself and how far I was willing to go in this race. The speaker told the story of a couple who was set to celebrate their 10 year anniversary one evening. The absent-minded husband was a professor. That morning, as he left for work, he was reminded to arrive home by 6 pm that evening to celebrate. Unfortunately, he got busy writing a paper at the office and totally forgot about the anniversary and the dinner. When he arrived home after 11 pm that night, he saw to his shock a beautiful home cooked steak dinner, complete with candlelight, flowers, and his favorite desert, all uneaten and cold at the beautifully set dinner table. All the candles have burned out, the house was dark, and the children were asleep. Filled with deep remorse and shame, he tiptoed into his bedroom, hoping to find his wife asleep so that he can quietly sneak into bed, but his wife was awake and waiting for him. Just as he opened his mouth to apologize profusely for forgetting, she covered his mouth, put on a new negligee, lit some candles, and made love to him. This act of love did more to increase the husband's gratitude, love, and devotion to his wife than any punishment ever could.

I was touched and challenged by the story. When the story progressed to the part where he found his wife awake, I was imagining what I would do if my husband did that to me. It probably would have involved yelling or throwing things, and maybe a few tears shed in self-pity. I was shocked to hear what the wife chose to do. I know how much work goes into preparing that kind of meal and setting. Not only did she need to deal with her own disappointment and tiredness, but also had to willingly surrender her legitimate right to be angry, put it aside, to attend to the needs of her husband. Did I have what it takes to be that kind of a wife? No. But I desire to become that kind of wife!

This resolve was put to the test many times, starting with the small things. That weekend I made a small start by putting aside my right to demand an apology from my husband, and I initiated the reconciliation process. We had a wonderful weekend of renewing our love for one another.

Sunset Fatigue

Psychologists have coined a term called "Sunset Fatigue" to describe what often happens to people at sunset, when a long workday is winding down and all our energies are depleted from a long hard day of work. For those who work in the office, it could be from having to think so hard to find solutions to so many problems, or emotional exhaustion from handling office politics or employee tensions. For those who stayed at home, it could be a child who is in a cranky mood, growing teeth, or sick and in need to much constant and vigilant care. On top of that, add all the household chores that need to be done and meals to be cooked, the home maker can be both physically and emotionally drained. Experts estimate that most marital conflicts are triggered by Sunset Fatigue, when our defense mechanism against more demands for our mind, physical, or emotional energy are at their lowest. Before seeing each other after the long work day, both spouses should prepare themselves mentally and emotionally. Husbands can do a self-check before opening that front door: How am I doing? Has it been a good day? Am I tired, discouraged, jubilant, angry, relieved, frustrated, or feeling proud? What kind of expression am I putting on for my wife? It's a good idea to take a moment to stop, breathe deeply, and perhaps even send a quick text to let your wife know when you will be arriving home, and what condition you will be in. The old proverb "being forewarned is forearmed" is very true. If I knew how my husband is doing, I will be better prepared to know how to best interact with him when I see him. If I am taken by surprise, I might react out of instinct and end up creating more hurt because my instinctual response was incorrect. There are times when my husband would call me before coming home to let me know that he's had a very tough day, and to ask for some space to de-pressurize. When I receive an appeal like that, my compassion arises and I can immediately put aside my own needs and demands for now to attend to his needs. If he hadn't warned me ahead of time, came home when I was eager to share some happy news with him, and appeared inattentive or impatient with me, I would be hurt and might end up lashing back at him in my hurt, further depleting him of whatever energy he has left. Similarly, I can do the same self-check and appeal to him for help when I need it, as long as I don't abuse his kindness.

My friend and mentor helped me to gain valuable perspective on understanding my spouse when she painted his world as a battlefield, and my role as a nurse whose responsibility was to create an environment that was conducive to speedy healing of battle wounds, whether it's emotional or intellectual. This really helped me to take to heart that one of my primary responsibilities was to be a good nurse to his "battle wounds". I believe the man I married is one who will respond in love and gratitude when I choose to attend to him first, and he has proven that to be true. I believe most men will respond the same way.

The question that naturally arises is: "What happens when both of us has a pretty bad case of sunset fatigue?" Who goes first? That "anniversary wife's" example spurred me to desire to win this race. I can't begin lifting her kind of weight to go to that level of sacrifice, but I can start with small things first.

When he arrived home tired and cranky, I made little choices to put aside my demands for him to make decisions on purchasing that new appliance, fixing that broken faucet, or to have him take the kids so I can take a break, and instead to give him a hug or a backrub to ease his tired muscles and emotions, or to serve him something to drink so that he can relax and take a break. It moved to bigger things such as respecting the decisions that he makes on behalf of the whole family even when I disagreed with him, or refraining from saying "I told you so" when the decision turns out to be wrong.

Just as in weight training, if I set a goal at the start to lift weights that can only be lifted after long periods of training, I would fail and get discouraged, or get injured in the process because my body is not used to handling that kind of weight. The same is true of loving and giving in marriage. You might be thinking, these people are superheroes! How can I get to that point? Well, just as in weight lifting, don't hurt your back lifting the weight that only world champions can bear. Start small. Do one thing consistently for a period of time. Then add something else, a little at a time. You will find that your heart becomes enlarged over time and you can carry more weight than you realize. Just as I fretted over each additional pregnancy, thinking to myself: "How can I possibly handle yet another child when I am already overwhelmed just raising one, or two children?" Yet somehow, I found a way, and in the process, my patience increased, my love increased as well. I find that my capacity to love enlarged with each decision to give and love unconditionally, and that I became a more gracious person over time as a result of my willingness to put aside my "rights" and my notion of equity and fairness. D.L. Moody's words are really true: "We often overestimate what we can accomplish in one year and underestimate what we can accomplish in three".

As you both commit to this process, and as you commit to be the one to initiate, you might be surprised to look back after a few years and realize that the things that used to bother you no longer do. That's because your heart has grown large, and so has your husband's.

For Your Growth

1. This week, look for opportunities to go the extra mile for your spouse, and note to see if at the end of the week, there is any response either way. Do you feel taken for granted or unappreciated? Did your spouse notice the difference in you this week? How did he respond?
2. Share with him your experiment, and ask for his feedback. Make adjustments accordingly, or, if appropriate, invite him to try out the experiment in the future as a surprise to you, to see if you can notice a difference in him.

2.7 WHAT'S YOUR STYLE?

In biology, we learn that animals in physical danger or threat have two coping mechanisms: fight or flight. We humans have similar mechanisms in the face of perceived threat, except that nowadays there is no longer any physical danger of being attacked by wild animals in the forest, but rather, attacked by feelings of hurt or anger in the face of a conflict with another human being. The most frequent of these conflicts naturally occur with our most intimate relationships, which, in a marriage, would be with our spouse. There is abundant research to prove that the divorce rates among couple who fight frequently is no higher than couples who don't fight very frequently. Clearly the key to a happy marriage is not the frequency of conflicts, but how couples choose to resolve these conflicts or leave them unresolved.

In pre-marital counseling class, we had a session to analyze our personalities and the potential conflicts that might arise from those differences. Certain types of personalities will attack when conflict arises while others will withdraw. Couples who both attack will end up having loud and violent confrontations. We've all heard couples like that are always shouting at each other in our neighborhoods because when they have a conflict, the whole neighborhood will hear it. Couples who both withdraw will avoid the problem, but never resolve the issue and can continue in a cold war for long periods of time. There will be apparent peace and calm, but the relationship will actually lack warmth and intimacy. We've also all observed plenty of old couples like this who are in this frozen state of withdrawal. My husband and I have quite the opposite styles. When in conflict, he will first criticize or command, insisting on his way, while I will give in to his demands but carry resentment inside. When the conflict continues without the issue being put on the table to be discussed and resolved, I will eventually blow up when I can no longer hold in my feelings, and in the face of this anger, he will then run away to avoid this negative energy.

In the chapter about single mothers, I discuss about various coping mechanisms for pain. I am rather afraid of pain, and most of the time, choose to either deny it's there, or avoid direct confrontation with the pain. Therefore, my default coping mechanism is always escape, whether it be through reading romance novels, watching TV, work and achievement addiction, or even physically running away. Some of these coping mechanisms seem harmless, and even laudable at times, but are actual ways to redirect my attention away from what I really need to pay attention to. On the other, David's coping mechanism of getting angry right away before obtaining a clear picture of what happened tends to also undermine the sense of safety I felt in the relationship. In time, I learned more about the process of conflict resolution, and even began to teach on this topic to others. It all began with a weekend to remember.

We were living in Los Angeles at the time, and heard friends raving about a marriage retreat weekend, where we get to renew our love for each other. The analogy our friends made was that if even cars need regular tune up to function properly, then what about marriage? We decided to give our marriage a good 100,000 mile tune up, as a wedding anniversary gift to ourselves. It was a Thursday, and we had already arranged for our children to stay with friends, and were all set to leave on Friday evening when our children's school called us to let us know that a few kids at school had lice, and our kids were possibly infected. This means that we had to shampoo their hair thoroughly and wash all their bedding with special detergent. Since our house was thoroughly carpeted, it also meant that I had to have every room shampooed. I asked if David can take some time off work to help me with this physically and emotionally exhausting work, but he told me that he was rushing to finish an important project so that he can leave on time for the retreat. I struggled all day Thursday and Thursday evening while David worked late, and then all day on Friday, and had to pack for our weekend for the kids and myself. By the time I packed up the kids and dropped them off at our friends, and then get us ready to head off to the retreat while David drove home like it was any normal workday to go off with me, I was exhausted, resentful, and fuming. He didn't seem to know how much work I had done, and seemed preoccupied in his own thoughts. At that moment, I didn't care if we had already paid in full for the expensive weekend outing, I just knew that I hated the man sitting next to me, and I didn't want to renew any love for such an insensitive man.

One of the first lessons we learned at the weekend was about feelings. The speaker told us about the cyclical nature of feelings, that sometimes there was just no love left, and the only thing remaining is our commitment to each other. By sheer willpower, we commit to continue actions of love despite the lack of feelings, and eventually, positive feelings will cycle back and not only will love and romance return, but at a deeper level.

At that point, I was so upset that I didn't even have the will to reach out to try, and I didn't have much hope that we would be on good terms, because I was still seething inside. One of the first lectures we heard upon arrival was about conflict resolution, and I was surprised to find that I got stuck at the same spot that everyone else got stuck at. The speaker explained that the cycle begins when your spouse says or does something that hurts you. Whether or not s/he is aware of what's been done, the reaction to a wrong done to you is usually anger. Even though anger is a noble emotion designed to help us take corrective action in the face of a wrong committed against us, we often mishandle this emotion instead of using it as a motivating force to help us communicate it in a loving manner to restore the relationship that was broken as a result of this hurt. Usually, if we were at home, David would be too tired or pre-occupied to notice that I was angry or unhappy, and even if he did, I would deny it by telling him that nothing is wrong. Then I would continue to stew in my anger at his continued insensitivity, until I finally explode in rage at some small thing later. This would then take everyone by surprise and end up hurting everyone even more. Fortunately, I was able to slow down the development of my anger and begin to ask myself some deeper questions. I know that the anger is usually caused by a hurtful action or word, but underneath that hurt is usually an expectation that was not met. I needed to find out what that expectation was, and to dig even deeper to uncover the real legitimate need underneath that expectation. In this case, I had asked for help with handling the lice, but the deeper need was for all that I've done above and beyond what I'm usually doing to be noticed and appreciated. The fact that I was left alone, and then to have my efforts go unnoticed, made me feel hurt and the sacrifices I've made unappreciated. Once I've understood my need beneath the anger, I was able to lay aside that anger for awhile to lovingly confront my husband with my hurt. Once I was able to lay before him my hurt in a loving manner, he quickly responded and apologized for the hurt that was caused, but also communicated how he was struggling with feelings of guilt to have left behind his teammates to finish the project at work while he took off early to come enjoy this weekend with me. He felt bad that he was not a good team player, and was feeling resentful for having to do this for me, even though we had planned it weeks in advance. Once we both had a chance to calmly lay out the facts, we were able to rationally ask ourselves if the other person was the right person to meet our need, and the obvious answer was no. Once we saw that, we were able to think about what other ways we could have found to meet our needs. With the additional information, we were able to apologize to each other, ask for forgiveness, and give forgiveness. Then we were ready to go to the next stage, which is to rebuild the trust that was lost in our relationship. I was able to extend forgiveness and also to ask for his forgiveness at not being more appreciative for making such a huge sacrifice in order to attend this retreat with me, and he was able to apologize for being so engrossed in his problems at work that he didn't notice how much help I needed and how much work I had to do all by myself.

The most important thing to remember in a conflict is that your spouse is not your enemy. The conflict itself is. If you and your spouse can stand on the same side against the problem, seeking to find a win-win solution by finding ways to meet both your needs, then the conflict will actually work to enrich your marriage, not weaken or destroy it.

Miraculously, my feelings had made a 180 degree turn within 24 hours, and love, gratitude, and appreciation flowed quickly back into my heart once again. By the time the weekend ended, it felt like we had just experienced a second honeymoon. It was then that I realized that we can have all the willpower and commitment in the world, but without those feelings of love and romance, the marriage will not have lasting power. We need to learn to renew our feelings of love and romance for each other, so that when the feelings are gone, we have hope that they can and will return again.

It was a weekend to remember. Recovering those necessary feelings of love and romance helped to realize that while feelings are important, they can be deceptive. Sometimes right actions will lead to right feelings, and that takes willpower and commitment. It was the beginning of a process of my learning to subject my feelings under my will and reason, so that I can through my actions lead my feelings back to where I need them to be.

For Your Growth

Action or Speech ➜ Hurt ➜ Anger ➜ Loving Confrontation ➜ Seeking & Giving Forgiveness ➜ Rebuilding Trust

To re-cap: The stages in resolving a conflict begins with an action or speech that hurt. This hurt causes anger, which often derails your love for each other. If you can remember to slow down, dig deeper to understand the underlying unmet expectation and need, and then communicate and confront your spouse in love, seeking to give and receive forgiveness, and then find ways to re-build trust, your relationship will be that much richer.

1. Try to remember the last time you got into an argument with your spouse. How did that get resolved? Try going through the steps of re-building trust to see if you can improve on this process.

2.8 MARCH TOWARDS ONENESS

It was not long after I announced to my mother that I had decided to stop working after my first baby was born to become a full time mother, that my mother brought up the topic of saving up some private savings (Chinese for private savings of wives that husbands aren't aware of). She shared her wisdom with me, that no matter how nice or loving a husband may seem, he will always be selfish and there will always be times that I will want to spend money that he does not approve of. This is when it's a good idea to just spend what I have without having to argue with him or even let him know. It means that there will be more harmony in the marriage because there will be less disagreements and tensions over money. She shared with me that most of her and her friends' arguments with their husbands are over the use of money.

I had always been an obedient girl, and did everything my mother told me. When she brought up this idea to help me start saving up my own private stash of savings without David's knowledge, I was very uncomfortable. I knew she was right. There would inevitably be tensions over money, especially now that we would have to live on half of our income before the baby arrived, and would add a lot more expenses because of having a baby. We would have to make many more financial decisions on a tight budget, and I would want to have my way, not for my own selfish needs, but for my baby's. I was accustomed to not having to check prices before I made a purchase, and did not know how to live on a budget. Yet when David and I got married, we had made a commitment to each other to be one, which meant total transparency and honesty, and sharing 100% of what we had with each other. I knew that if I began to save up my own money, it would undermine that trust and transparency, and while being more expedient, will be more hurtful to the marriage in the long run. When I communicated with my mother about this, she offered to help me save up some money and keep it for me, so that he would never know. I declined. My mother confidently told me that I would change my mind and be back.

The first test of that resolve came when all my neighbors joined Gymboree class. I participated in the first free trial class and fell in love with it. I knew that my baby would so enjoy it! The only problem was that these classes were expensive and not anticipated in our budget. I told David that we could borrow money from my parents to pay for it. In fact, I'm sure that my mother would be more than happy to pay for it as a gift. He refused. He said that we had set a budget based upon our income, and that we needed to be disciplined to live within our means. I wanted to give our baby the best, and didn't want him to miss out on Gymboree classes when everyone else was getting them. We got into a fight, and he would not budge on his principles. So I called him a stingy man and all kinds of bad names that I can think of and then considered my options. The easy way out would be for me to call my mother, admit that I was wrong, and have her pay for weekday classes while David was working, so that he would never have to know. However, this will start me on a slippery downward slope towards deception and the keeping of secrets in our marriage, sealing off certain compartments of our lives from each other. I sought out another trusted friend who also had a baby whose age was close to Caleb, and asked her what she would do. She confessed to wrestling with similar issues, having quit a lucrative job as a real estate agent to stay at home full time with her baby. We decided that there must be other mothers facing the same predicament, and decided to look for them. We found a group of friends in church, and established a new mother's support group, where we could meet weekly in my house to support one another. Our friendship, which would develop over the next two years would endure over many years of separation as we moved away to different places, and helped us through many difficult times when we seemed to be the only mothers in our community that did not go with the flow of popular trends in society at the time. Instead of paying for expensive Gymboree classes, we took our kids to outings to parks and hikes, found many cheap or free places to visit, and got to know the museums and beaches of Los Angeles like our own backyard. Our kids became friends with each other and learned the rules of socialization under our care and guidance. Most of our kids have now graduated from high school and are starting college, some at top tier U.S. colleges. Not one of them seemed to have suffered developmentally from not having Gymboree classes. Of greater importance was that I learned to find ways to swim against the tide of the latest popular child-raising fads and resist the inner feelings of guilt and anxiety, because I knew that the unity in my marriage is worth far greater than any developmental advantage that my child can gain.

My husband is very frugal, and keeps tight track of how we allocate and follow our budget. I used to rebel against this kind of strict discipline, thinking that he was stingy and cheap. However, as I determined to respect him and follow his decisions, I discovered a strange change in him: he became more generous than I was. Whenever we encountered someone in need, and we are considering how much to help, the number that he comes up with keeps being surprisingly more than my number, and I used to think that I was pretty generous! I realized that by being more frugal on ourselves, we are able to be more generous to others, and this generosity brought about much joy into our family, as I began to respect and admire him more and more for his character.

The next challenge to our unity came during the dot com boom days, when David was awarded a lot of stocks working for a prominent Silicon Valley company. On paper, we looked to be like millionaires, and I asked him if we should sell off our stocks to pay off our mortgage. He told me that I didn't understand economics, and that it was smarter to keep our stocks for the value to rise than to pay off our mortgage, which was very low in interest. I didn't believe in debt, and didn't feel comfortable owing stocks when we are in debt to the bank, and could easily have paid off our entire mortgage. He disagreed. I decided to respect his opinion and decision instead of fighting to convince him that I was right. Not long after that, the dot com bubble busted, and our stock papers suddenly became virtually worthless. While it was a very expensive lesson, every dollar was worthwhile, because after that, my husband consulted me on every single financial decision and took my words very seriously. The preserved and deepened marital unity was worth every dollar of this tuition.

There are many things, big and small, that sought to divide us or pit us against each other, whether it's our children looking for us to disagree when they requested something from us, in-laws seeking to divide us against each other when they make a request of us, or financial decisions, especially when it came to spending on the children. These are the three biggest reasons for divorce in the U.S.: money, child-raising, and in-laws. Through each challenge, we sought to preserve our unity, and kept no secrets from each other, despite many temptations to do so. As we kept this a priority, we now enjoy a deep friendship and admiration for each other, and the sacrifices we each make towards our unity. Today, we are best friends, soul mates, and co-workers in serving others who share everything with each other: no secrets, nothing to hide. We often experience the strange phenomenon of being able to finish the sentence that the other person begins.

Unity in marriage is hard to achieve and preserve, but it ultimately enables us to last longer and be more effective, together. A house divided against itself cannot stand, but in marriage, 1+1 does not equal 2, but 1 x 100 times the impact of us separately. In the words of Mother Teresa, "Together, we can do something beautiful".

For Your Growth

1. Are there ongoing issues in your marriage that is dividing you? Disagreements that are keeping you apart? Are you willing to be the person to submit to him and let him have his way? If not, what will it take for you to let this issue go?
2. Are there secrets that you are keeping from your husband? How do you plan on sharing them with him in a way that will build up your marital unity?

2.9 THE MOST INTIMATE OF BATTLE BUDDIES

My husband and I took two classes together in college. The first one was a music class where we had no interaction or any feelings for each other. I took the class for an "easy A" because of my heavy course load full of lab classes and many activities outside the classroom. He did not have a favorable impression of me because he felt that I was wasting my opportunity by skipping many classes, coming in just to put up party or school event posters and still doing well in the class because I had a lot of previous music background, while he worked hard because he really wanted to learn more about music. In his mind, he had no interest in me and nothing in common with me.

In our last year at college, he got sick with pneumonia and landed in the school infirmary, where I worked as a dietician to put myself through school. He was sent home during the long Thanksgiving holidays, and knowing his condition, I visited his dorm room to bring by some food for him out of pity, knowing that the dorms will be empty and he will likely be sick and lonely. This act started a friendship that evolved into a dating relationship. Through the process, I discovered that we were as opposite as night and day, and had virtually nothing in common. I was used to a more lavish lifestyle, having grown up in a family that did not have limitations on spending. He was from an immigrant family, where his parents sacrificed a lucrative banking career in Taiwan to immigrate to America for his education, and they lived a very frugal lifestyle. He was hard working and a straight forward engineer, while I was a social butterfly, always coordinating events on campus and knowing all kinds of people through my large networks of friendships. He thought dancing was frivolous, I loved parties and dancing and couldn't imagine life without it. He thought quickly, spoke quickly, and acted quickly. I liked to amble and linger, took my time in considering an idea, and acted slowly. He loved classical music. I loved rock and popular music, and took part in musicals and attended Broadway shows. He planned everything. I wanted to do things spontaneously, preferring to go by the feeling of the moment. He attended a Chinese church, I attended an all white church, where Asian faces are rarely seen. Except for our common faith, we didn't have anything in common.

The second class we took together changed our lives forever. It was a world history class. Before the class, we were just like two dating college kids, doing fun things, having long chats, and checking out each other's strengths and weaknesses to see if we are compatible together. When David convinced me to take this "Perspectives" class with him, I signed up to establish a point of common interest with him. History always bored me, because it was just an endless list of dates and places to memorize and pass a test, and never had any relevance to my life. However, this class examined the progression of history, the rise and fall of empires, and asked students pointed questions about our role in history and its progression. It was the first time I had been asked to look at the meaning of my life that way, and it shook me to the core. Both David and I felt that we had experienced a call, a sense of mission for our lives.

That winter, we both attended a conference with a desire to use our summers to do something meaningful in history. I wanted to go to China, because it would be easy for me, already knowing the language and the culture. David felt that we as Chinese always want to help our own people, and wanted to resist what he felt was "ethno-centric" behavior. He wanted to cross cultures and language barriers, and go where Chinese were less inclined to go. He signed up to go to the Palestinian refugee camps of Jordan. I signed up to go tour Xinjiang, but because the project was not confirmed, signed up to go to Istanbul. At that time, we were not sure if this summer experience would take us in different directions and we would have to part ways, or if it would end up confirming our desire to be together, but we were both willing to take that risk to see where our paths would take us. My Xinjiang project ended up getting cancelled, and I ended up spending a summer in Istanbul living among Iranian refugees and falling in love with the Iranian culture (mainly because Iranians loved food and dancing!). I came back to the U.S. with a new love for the Middle Eastern culture and a sense of mission for my life. I wanted to expend my life to make this world a better place, and serving society and the poor will be a part of my lifestyle. Much to my surprise and delight, David came back with that same sense of mission and love for the Middle Eastern culture, and after much thought and discussion, we decided that we wanted to get married to run in the same direction, living a life that is free of greed and pursuit of wealth, fame, or vanity, but is rich in faith, meaning, adventure, and purpose. We wanted to play a part in the advance of history as people of Chinese descent, and were willing to expend our lives to live out that ideal.

Our decision to marry encountered parental opposition, because both of us decided not to pursue advanced degrees. That was the first test to our resolve. The second test came from our classmates at MIT, because they have seen how different we were, how lacking we were in common ground or compatibility. We were too headstrong – did we want to wait a few more years? Our decision was a resounding no. That was the beginning to our difficult journey towards becoming one, even though we had no idea what lay ahead of us. Our outlook was not good.

Because we started out in marriage with such great odds against us, we knew we had a lot of hard work to do to make it work. We started by trying to establish some common ground. All we had in common was our sense of mission and destiny about our lives, but it was enough to establish common core values, and then to build common interests together. Since serving society and the poor in particular, and living a lifestyle of sacrificial giving was not an option, but a core part of who we wanted to become, we began our marriage by becoming volunteers in the community, serving underprivileged youth together. After we moved to Los Angeles, we became volunteer counselors to college kids and high school youth. At one point, we said yes to a friend who had asked us to befriend a fringe group who were sentenced by the court for various crimes and were assigned to our church to perform community service. Other families and youth at our church shunned them, and we befriended them and became their big brother and sister. We got involved with prisoners and their children, the homeless and orphans. Through it all, we experienced being taken advantage of, misunderstood, having our things stolen, and even losing our life savings at one point. However, because of our common sense of mission and values in life, we were able to put aside our differences and work through them.

When we built our lives together based upon this sense of mission, we developed common interests together: music, hiking outdoors, exploring, camping, and all kinds of sports and new hobbies. We learned together and learned to accept each other's differences through the conflicts developed when trying to work together as a team to help others. We learned communication and conflict resolution skills through these almost daily conflicts. This "iron sharpening iron" process helped us to value our differences, because when we accepted those differences, they became our protection and completed us, so that we can balance discipline and fun, reason and emotion, and planning and spontaneity. He learned to dance because of me, and I learned to live within a planned budget for him. The more of our own ideas and habits we were willing to lay down for each other, the more we were able to respect and appreciate the other.

Years later, shortly after Caleb celebrated his first birthday, an MIT classmate came to visit us. He had witnessed our tumultuous courtship and our dramatic fights at school, and was a bit tentative when entering our house as to what he would find. When he saw David patiently crawling on the ground playing with Caleb and helping out with the housework, and me, who didn't know how to fry an egg when I got married, now serving a delicious home cooked meal to our dear friend, he kept shaking his head, saying: "I can't believe this is the David and Rossana I know! God's grace is so amazing!"

I believe that husbands and wives are together for a greater purpose than to procreate and extend the family line. A family is society's most basic unit, so changing the world starts with the family, one family at a time. When there is a sense of mission to your building a family unit together, you can overcome all kinds of odds against you, including lack of common interest or differences in personality, interests, family, culture, language, and race. We started out with much against us, but having a common faith and a common sense of purpose and mission about our marriage defeated the odds against us. Now we are instilling that same sense of mission and purpose in our children. We are on a collision course with destiny. There are urgent problems to solve in our world and at this crucial time in human history. Will we, as Chinese people, decide to choose petty personal comfort and "security" or go all out, living a radical lifestyle to serve humanity, achieve greatness together in the process of trying?

For Your Growth

1. Have you and your spouse every sat and dreamed about what you
    want your family to contribute to the world? Make a date to dream
    and discuss together.

2.10 SKATING INSIDE THE RINK

I played ice hockey when I was in college. It was exhilarating to feed that need for speed inside the ice skating rink. In addition to going fast, I could make all kinds of crazy moves gliding on that ice on top speed that I could never do on flat ground. Suited up in my pads, I zipped around on the ice with perfect freedom. The walls of the rink protected me from falling outside, and when I fell or got wacked by an opponent's stick, my pads protected me from injury. Yet as soon as I got out of the rink, the same movements only produced frustration. I knew in my head that the same laws of physics inside the ice rink did not apply outside, and trying to move fast on my skates only produced sore muscles because the carpet on the ground impeded my every move. I once heard someone make the analogy that marriage is like that skating rink. When you are within the boundaries of the marriage, or the borders of that rink, you can do anything you like, and enjoy yourself in whatever creative and fun ways your mind can imagine. However, once you go outside the protective borders of that rink, or what's covered inside that marriage vow, you will find that the same rules that applied inside the rink no longer apply, and that the protection is gone as well.

A good friend who married multiple times told me that when she was single, she kept thinking that only if she could get married, she will finally be happy, but then discovered that marriage couldn't make her happy. Then she thought that if she could get finally a divorce, she could finally be really happy, and then when she did, she discovered that the problem was with herself not being able to be happy. Through each successive marriage, the desire and will to stick to the commitment became tougher and tougher as it was easier and easier to undo the promises made at the marriage ceremony. Elizabeth Taylor even went as far as to marry nine times, twice to the same man. My friend discovered that when she left a marriage because of certain issues, and did not remain to resolve them, the same issues would come up to haunt her in the next marriage, and she discovered that the baggage was actually her own to deal with, and did not go away by switching mates. Only two people who are willing to work on being better skaters inside the boundaries of a lifelong committed relationship have enough safety to truly discover the joys of union of two souls. The borders of that rink are actually for protection, not to lock people in. Marriage is a garden – you must till, weed, water daily in order to make it beautiful. Neglect it, it will become unruly and hard to manage. The home is a place where love, not reason, is the primary language. Marriage is not a bamboo, it's a cedar tree. Patiently cultivate it, it will provide rest, covering, protection, and blessing for those around it. Neglect or abuse it, it becomes a curse and source of hurt for those around it.

When this garden is unattended because of neglect or busyness, third parties can easily crash the party to steal the heart of you or your mate. It doesn't need to be a person, but can be work, pursuit of money, fame, or power, computer gaming, KTV, golf, shopping, or spa with your friends, and even good and right things such as filial piety or parenting your children! Long before the appearance of a third party, there is usually already a functional divorce, or an emotional distancing between the couple, that opens the doors for that third party.

Growing up in a family that socialized in wealthy circles, in a time when male chauvinism was in fashion, I saw the consequences of what happens when couples try to skate outside the borders of marriage, from insecure forty year old aunties getting chest enlargement operations and facelifts in a desperate attempt to stay young and attractive to their husband's wandering eyes, to fifty year old uncles going through belated midlife crises divorcing the wives of their youth who endured hardships with them to build up a large financial empire, in favor of young twenty somethings with vacuous expressions and shimmering red painted nails who gush and fawn all over this "older uncle" and claim undying love and admiration for his looks and talent when everyone else knows that without his money, he is nothing. I saw the little girls who grow up to be women who are unable to trust men, boys who go through serial affairs or relationships, but are unable to commit to marriage, for fear of not being able to live up to their commitments. I see children who grow up thinking that their parents' broken marriage was their fault, as they spend their lives trying to perform or be good enough in order to make amends.

Some Asian men regard extramarital affairs as normal, even a badge of honor of a real man, as trophy mistresses are a demonstration of his wealth. In their eyes, women are private property and something to be shown off, not someone to complement oneself or a soul mate and companion. At the same time, with the release of women to the workplace, it is now also fashionable for women to have extramarital affairs as a sign of their independence and freedom. Marriage has become a tool for self-actualization or promotion instead of a promise of a lifetime where "neither sickness nor health, neither riches nor poverty can split us apart." In this kind of relationship, one side is treated as a tool for satisfying the self-centered needs of the other, not as a companion to be loved and treasured. The biggest losers in a marriage based upon exchange are the children, who grow up lacking love and feeling of security. Because of the confusion growing up in a home that lacked healthy role models for a healthy marriage, they grow up to further perpetuate and extend this confusion of roles.

In the shadow of traditional Chinese culture, wives close one eye to their husband's infidelity. This is why before relocating to China, all our friends and relatives around me warned me of the temptations that my husband will be exposed to. We made a decision to protect our marriage, and to set clearly defined boundaries around our marriage and family life, so that our marriage will continue to thrive and trust can be preserved. This is just like cultivating a garden, which requires frequent cultivation in order to thrive. Without this kind of awareness, a person will just fall when unwittingly faced with temptations. Even if ultimately nothing happened, certain appearance or hint of impropriety will already rob a person of his integrity.

These are the boundaries that my husband David and I drew around our marriage to preserve trust:

- When talking with a coworker of the opposite gender alone, to always leave the door open. Otherwise, we will arrange to meet in a public space.

- Unless there is a third coworker, to avoid riding in a car with a person of the opposite gender.

- When in an enclosed space with a coworker of the opposite gender, to be sure a third person is present.

- When a coworker or friend of the opposite gender asks for our help, we will try to get his/her permission to invite our spouse(s) into this situation or introduce him/her to our spouse, and explain that this kind of teamwork is more effective in helping him/her.

- When traveling on business, notify a friend to check up on us: on the one hand, a phone call will dispel the sense of loneliness that might overcome us; on the other hand, a friend who calls to check on us would motivate us to keep away from temptation, keep us accountable on what we promised to stay away from.

- When traveling on business, bring some things of interest to alleviate the sense of loneliness. For example, once when I was traveling, I brought some drum sticks to practice drumming on the hotel cushions. I will also bring books and magazines, edit some family photos, call family members back home, and share what I've been seeing or experiencing on the road. My husband is a storytelling expert, so when he is traveling on business, he will always make up a new series of stories to tell our kids.

Safeguarding our marriage against third parties is the best way to manage our marriage. A wise friend once told me that no man would willingly go out looking for another women unless his needs weren't being met at home. If husband and wife have an agreement on work-life balance and arrange their schedules and lives accordingly, and maintain those boundaries, they will have won half the battle. Even though children occupy a lot of time, they will all eventually leave this home. Therefore, besides paying attention to the children, parents should also invest time to cultivate common interests, hobbies, and goals. In actuality, it's tougher to excel at managing your family relationships than your work, and is more important. This is because we take off our masks at home and show our family members who we really are. Love reigns supreme, not logic. If a person has no healthy family life, work loses balance and meaning, and can become a form of escape.

The boundaries around our marriage also pertain to those relationships within the extended family, whether it's with our parents or with our children. We will discuss this in the next chapter.

For Your Growth

1. Sit down with your spouse to do a health check on your marriage. How often do you have sex? Is that enough for both partners in terms of satisfaction, emotional connection, or frequency? I ask these embarrassingly intimate questions because sex is usually a good indicator of how well your marriage is really doing. Do you have time to be alone together? Do you intentionally make positive deposits in each other's emotional banks on a regular basis?

2. Take an inventory of your life's priorities in terms of mind share: how much of each day do you think about your spouse vs. work, child, school, or other things? How can your spouse's mindshare increase? Do you need to allocate time for each other, and if you do, what will you do other than talk about your child, or the "business" of running your household? Some ideas include taking dance, photography, cooking, painting, or some other classes related to something you'd both be interested in.

3. What kinds of boundaries and mechanisms would you like to implement around your marriage to safeguard it?

2.11 A FATHER IS
INDISPENSIBLE IN HIS CHILD'S LIFE

David Lin was my classmate in college. Ever since he started teaching me guitar, we became music buddies and best friends. Impulsively, we married a year after graduating from college, and went through many hard times because of our immaturity and friction. However, because of our common faith and values, we have already journeyed through over half our lives together. Now I can say with certainty that I have no better friend in this world who knows me better. In this month before Father's Day, I want to introduce to everyone my family's greatest secret weapon: my husband David Lin. In our family, he is the captain of our ship, the head of our household. He is a man of few words, but in the area of parenting, I tend to say more, but he does more. The best gift that he gave to our children is insisting on loving me more than them, and this insistence has given the children a healthy model of a happy marriage, laying the foundations for them to build their own homes in the future as we use our own marriage as their primary classroom. In order to be the primary source of influence in their lives, he learned soccer and basement, and have been their soccer, baseball, and tennis coach throughout their childhood, using sports and coaching to teach them character and train good habits, showing them how to play by the rules of the game of life. He is an expert at child discipline, drawing firm boundaries and administering consequences consistently without letting emotions cloud the picture, and is always available to instruct and communicate. Even though he is very busy with work, but he devotes massive amounts of time and energy to his children, always learning and growing, turning down many opportunities for career promotion because of too much travel. He is the most curious learner in the whole family, constantly seeking out new things to learn, new challenges to conquer, and new adventures to live out. It's tough to win a thumbs-up of approval because he's always challenging our kids to take risks and break their own barriers, but when the kids fall down, he is their most loyal cheerleader and patient coach. He's not afraid to let other's see him fail, and often lets us witness how he fails, laughs at himself, never taking himself too seriously. As a result, we also lose our own fears of failure, and become willing followers to try new experiences, reach new breakthroughs. He is brave to own up to his responsibilities, and fights to be the first to apologize, as a result, has won our respect.

David Lin, you will always be the biggest hero in our family!

Fathers: Are they relevant in the upbringing of a child?

A common sight these days is to see a mother who takes care of everything related to the raising and care of a child, but there seems to be no trace of the father's hand in the child's life. It seems that most fathers feel that a child's education is the sole domain of the mother, not the father, because his primary responsibility to the family is to provide financially. This simple belief can be fatal to a child's healthy growth.

A general survey of American prison inmates and their relationships with their parents uncovered that while some have loving relationships with their mothers, over 95% of the inmates were abandoned or rejected by their fathers. The majority of them, especially men, also struggle with issues of anger from the feelings of abandonment and rejection. Many additional studies demonstrate that there is a direct correlation between crime and the absence of fathers in the home.

This impact is powerfully illustrated with the research done by sociologist Richard Dugdale on the descendants of two men. First, Max Dukes (born 1700) was a man who lived in New York City over two hundred years ago. He had a reputation as a hard man, and married a "free-lovin' woman". Of his 1,200+ descendents, 130 spent time in prison (7 for murder, with the average prison term of 13 years), 310 were nomads, 190 were prostitutes, 60 were habitual thieves, and 680 were admitted alcoholics. His family cost the state of New York, where they lived, over millions of dollars just to incarcerate them and put them in rehab programs, and they made no contribution to society whatsoever that was viewable. The family raised by Max Dukes became a tremendous burden to society.

At the same time, another man named Jonathan Edwards (born 1703), who was a Puritan preacher, also lived in New York. His eloquent and powerful speeches and writing are still widely quoted today. Of his 929 known descendents, 430 became preachers, ministers, or theologians, 100 were attorneys, 60 were judges, 60 were doctors, 60 were authors of fine classics, 100 were university professors, 14 served as university presidents, 3 were mayors of large cities, 3 were state governors, one was controller of the U.S. Treasury, 7 of them were elected to the US Congress, 2 were elected to the US Senate, 1 of them was vice president of the United States, and to date his family has never cost the state or the nation one cent, but they have enriched and contributed immeasurably to the life of plenty in America.

A Father's Impact on His Daughter
Linda's Story
When Linda was born, her mother got very sick. The fortune tellers told her mother that Linda is her hex: if Linda is well, her mother will not be well, and if her mother is well, then Linda will not be well. Ever since then, Linda's mother never had anything nice to say to Linda or about her. Each time the mother is in a bad mood, she vented her negative emotions on Linda, on several occasions breaking the sticks with which she spanked her. What hurt Linda the most was not that she was frequently unjustly punished, but that her father always sat idly by, never saying a word to defend her. Linda concluded that men are never to be trusted or depended upon. She grew up determined to show her family that she is capable and worthy to be loved, went to a top university, and became the CEO of a large company. However, she went through 3 marriages and after the 3rd divorce, finally decided that she's better off alone, without the burden of a man. It seemed to her each time before she married, the man was very successful, but not long after the marriage, he would stop doing his part in the marriage and would become dependent upon her for even the smallest details of living. Her second husband was an executive of a big IT company but shortly after they got married, lost his job and fell into depression. During the years they were married, he was drunk most of the time. After her third divorce, Linda decided to see a therapist to see what part she's contributing to these divorces, as they all have the same element in common: that the men in her life all became useless after marrying her. She eventually traced the root back to her relationship with her emotionally absent father.

Cindy's Story

Cindy's father was a successful businessman, but was rarely home. Even when he was at home, he was usually busy with work and rarely had time for her. She grew up longing for her father to love and cherish her, and hoping that some day he would notice her enough to appreciate her. After Cindy grew up, she discovered that she kept getting involved with married men who would promise to leave their wives for her but never did. The last affair with her married boss ended in disaster because he promoted her several times within 2 years to placate her unhappiness at his not leaving his wife for her. As a result, she found herself ostracized by coworkers who were disgusted at her quick promotion despite being unqualified for her job. When her boss's boss audited the department and discovered that the funds were being misused and company performance suffered as a result, both she and her boss were fired. She never saw her boss again. Heartbroken, she went to see a therapist, who helped her to see her pattern of falling in love with successful but emotionally unavailable men, who promised her the world but never came through for her, just exactly like her father.

Psychologists will tell you that a father is the most important man in a daughter's life and his relationship with her will directly impact what kind of woman she becomes and the kind of marriage she will end up with. Most daughters of alcoholics end up marrying alcoholics. Conversely, if a daughter grows up with a father who spends time with her and cherishes her, she will be less likely to be involved in pre-marital sex and to settle for a man who does not appreciate her. She will also be a lot quicker to walk away from a destructive relationship while another less secure woman will continue in a negative cycle. A father's impact on his daughter cannot be measured, but his absence will be felt forever.

A Father's Impact on His Son

A 1999 episode of a famous TV new show "60 Minutes", documented the process of population control gone awry in an African animal sanctuary. Scientist proposed that the baby elephants be moved to another area to protect them from extinction. In the beginning, everything was fine. However, after about a decade, some of these baby elephants became young adult male elephants, but they began to exhibit violent behavior, attacking and killing the rhinos that lives in the same area as them. After some close analysis, scientists figured out that these young male elephants lacked adult role models growing up. Despite fear that it's too late to correct this, scientists sent these young male elephants to areas with larger number of adult male elephants. Under the leadership and discipline of the older male elephants, these young elephants learned to follow the rules of the crowd, and quickly stopped all aggressive behavior.

If adult males played such an important and critical role in the lives and development of baby elephants, how much more so human males?

You may ask why mothers can't replace fathers in the process of parenting. John Eldridge in his book "Wild At Heart" talks about the three major needs of a man as: a beauty to rescue, an adventure to live, and a battle to fight. A mother's natural instinct is to nurture and comfort her son, providing a warm, safe, and comfortable environment for him, while a father will challenge his son to take risks, compete, to courageously confront his fears to overcome them, and rise up to be a man. He can affirm the manhood in his son in a way that no mother can. He does this by modeling for his son what a man is and can be a hero to his son in a way that a women can't be. He can see the big picture and think in long range rather than situationally & personally. Also, he can make decisions based upon rational thinking rather than be too easily swayed by emotions, as mothers have a greater tendency to do.

What we commonly see before us are overly anxious mothers and

emotionally or physically absent fathers. Some fathers check out emotionally either because they lack the skills and knowhow, or because of their desire to avoid their overly anxious wives. As a result, more and more boys are growing up with gender confusion, are more effeminate, or have become very timid and risk averse. We need to redouble our efforts to bring fathers back to the forefront of home life, to prevent emotional disaster happening to another entire generation of children.

How Can Fathers Be More Involved?

When my eldest son Caleb was born, my husband told me that I was the gatekeeper. Because Caleb was totally dependent upon me for sustenance, but not on my husband, I had an important responsibility as a mother not to let my anxiety to be a perfect mother make me become too possessive or perfectionistic about raising my child. I need to invite my husband in to participate in the parenting process, as well as to be willing to take a back seat sometimes to let my husband care for my child his way, even if I don't think he is doing a good enough job. I needed to create opportunities for him to be involved rather than take care of everything myself, thinking that I am making life easier for him. In my house, I respect my husband's leadership and expect him to take the lead in parenting decisions, even if I think they are wrong or some of them cause me anxiety. My decision to respect him helps him to take his leadership and responsibility seriously and want to improve himself as a father.

Parenting is the ultimate in teamwork. Just ask any single parent how tough it is to raise a child alone, and you will want to begin right by making sure that both parents are involved in this most sacred of missions in life. May fathers and mothers work together to make sure that fathers make the most significant and positive impact during the most formative short years of a child's life! Fathers, being actively involved in parenting your child will be the best investment you can make in your life.

For Your Growth

1. In what ways have you contributed to excluding your husband from the parenting process? How has your anxiety and perfectionism affected the way you parent? The way you evaluated your husband's help in parenting? How can you weaken yourself to give him more freedom to parent in his own unique way?

2. How can you invite him in more with more acceptance and affirmation rather than dissatisfaction and criticism? As a first step, think of three things that you appreciate about the way he is fathering your child and tell him.

3. If you have a chance, read "Love and Respect" together. In what ways have you disrespected him and made him feel inadequate for the job of fatherhood? In what way can you encourage him more as a father?

4. One of the most important aspects of parenting is time, and time is what fathers are most lacking in because of work and other obligations. How can you help your husband to free up more time for the family? Sit down with him to discuss creative ways to do this.

2.12 WHAT ABOUT SINGLE MOMS?

We were freshly married at age 22, barely adults ourselves, when Alex, our groomsman at our wedding, approached us with a strange request. Would we be open to be the legal guardians to a teenage girl who needed legal guardians in order to keep her scholarship at a well-known girl's boarding school nearby? Lillian's mother had passed away when she was young, leaving her doctor Dad grieving and clueless as to how to raise her. She was smart and talented and won a scholarship to this boarding school, but her father lived in a different city, and will not be nearby to help her when things came up. Lillian needed guardians in the same city who can be on call in case of emergencies. Alex was her youth counselor at church, but he was not qualified because he was a single man. The only couple he knew would be us. Would we consider being Lillian's legal guardians? That was a daunting question for a newly married young couple who were barely out of college themselves, and how would we know how to parent a 15 year old girl who was raised by a single Dad? After some thought, we decided to do it. That was our first of many encounters with children of single parents. We took on a teenage girl with boy problems, issues with curfews and schoolwork, as well as struggles with a father who was dating and getting re-married. That year, we had our hands full learning about the issues and heartaches facing a child of a single parent, and developed a firm conviction that we wanted to work hard on our marriage to make sure that our children are raised by two parents who loved each other, together. Lillian is now happily married to a successful executive who adores her, and mother to three boys of her own. The journey of healing she went through is a testament that children of single parents are totally capable of having happy marriages and being successful parents.

One of the most prominent features of single parenthood is the grieving process associated with the loss of a spouse, whether it's through death, divorce, or other means of permanent separation such as institutionalization or illness. I remember when I was back in California, a respected physician friend recommended a book to me which had impacted her deeply. When I read the book "A Grace Disguised" by Dr. Jerry Sittser for the first time, I cried and cried because it touched me so deeply. He had lost three generations of his family all at once in a car accident: his mother, his wife, and his daughter, and was faced with raising the 3 remaining hurting children all alone. Reading through his own account and analysis of the process of grieving, I realized that all of us have grieving issues to resolve, whether it's the loss of some treasured friendship or the loss of childhood and innocence. This would be a book that I would read again and again and recommend to many friends who had to confront loss and go through grieving. Many of the beneficiaries include single parent friends, all of whom found the book helpful from both a mind and a heart level. Because this book is not translated and published in China, I will take the liberty of summarizing some main points on the milestones of grief. I say that they are milestones because they don't necessarily progress sequentially in a linear fashion in stages, but rather are components of the whole process of grieving:

- Experience loss & pain: Dr. Sittser talks about the analogy of darkness and pain. He describes a vision of trying in vain to chase after the vanishing sun and its accompanying warmth, but losing sight rapidly, and of feeling the accompanying despair that came with the sight of the vanishing sun. His sister told him about the connection between east and west, and although they seem at opposite ends, they are actually around the earth. Therefore the quickest way to find the sun again is not by trying to run after it, but by running backwards into the darkness and through it. Pain has to be faced, and grace must be found so that we are transformed by our suffering, and our hearts enlarged because of our sorrow. I find this to be true of my own life, which has consisted of long series of attempts to run away from my own pain. Yet reading this book gave me courage to stare my pain in the face, confront it, and grow from it. In the words of Dr. Sittser:

> *"Choice is therefore the key. We can run from the darkness, or we can enter into the darkness and face the pain of loss. We can indulge ourselves in self-pity, or we can empathize with others and embrace their pain as our own. We can run away from sorrow and drown it in addictions, or we can learn to live with sorrow. We can nurse wounds of having been cheated in life, or we can be grateful and joyful, even though there seems to be little reason for it. We can return evil for evil, or we can overcome evil with good. It is this power to choose that adds dignity to our humanity and gives us the ability to transcend our circumstances, thus releasing us from living as mere victims. These choices are*

141

never easy. Though we can and must make them, we will make them more often than not only after much agony and struggle."[1]

How does your soul and heart get enlarged?

"The soul is elastic, like a balloon. It can grow larger through suffering. Loss can enlarge its capacity for anger, depression, despair, and anguish, all natural and legitimate emotions whenever we experience loss. Once enlarged, the soul is also capable of experiencing greater joy, strength, peace, and love. What we consider opposites—east and west, night and light, sorrow and joy, weakness and strength, anger and love, despair and hope, death and life—are no more mutually exclusive than winter and sunlight. The soul has the capacity to experience these opposites, even at the same time."[2]

Do you ever get over the darkness? How can there possibly be any benefit to the darkness?

"Even if we really do overcome our own pain (which is doubtful in my mind), we nevertheless find ourselves more sensitive to the pain of others and more aware of the darkness that envelops the world. The choice to enter the darkness does not ensure we ever completely come out the other side."[3]

- Denial, shock, and numbness: The pain of loss is so great that there is a tendency to want to run away from it or deny its existence or impact. People use escape and develop addictions as a coping mechanism to push away the presence of this pain. They pretend it doesn't exist and put on a brave face, staunchly believe that a miracle will happen to make everything restored to pre-loss conditions despite all circumstances indicating otherwise, become workaholics, watch TV incessantly to numb the pain, or conversely rage and go on a mission to seek revenge, try to find substitutes in new relationships or become

---

[1] Sittser, Jerry (2009-05-11). A Grace Disguised: How the Soul Grows through Loss (Kindle Locations 463-469). Zondervan. Kindle Edition."

[2] Sittser, Jerry (2009-05-11). A Grace Disguised: How the Soul Grows through Loss (Kindle Locations 490-494). Zondervan. Kindle Edition.

[3] Sittser, Jerry (2009-05-11). A Grace Disguised: How the Soul Grows through Loss (Kindle Locations 514-516). Zondervan. Kindle Edition.

addicted to food, alcohol, sex, shopping, or any other way to produce short term pleasures to replace the feeling of pain. However, pain exists for a reason, to alert us to the need to heal a hurt. Numbness or denial will insulate us from pain for awhile, but will also deny us the ability to heal and feel joy and pleasure again.

> *"Denial puts off what should be faced. People in denial refuse to see loss for what it is, something terrible that cannot be reversed. They dodge pain rather than confront it. But their unwillingness to face pain comes at a price. Ultimately it diminishes the capacity of their souls to grow bigger in response to pain. They make the same mistake as patients who, following major surgery, refuse to get out of bed and put damaged muscles back to work. They pretend nothing is wrong and tell everyone that they are feeling wonderful. But denial of their problem causes muscles to atrophy until they cannot get out of bed at all. In the end denial leads to a greater loss."*[4]

- Other emotions that result from this intense pain include: anger/hatred at self, the person who caused the pain, others, and God, fear, confusion, loneliness, guilt, and depression. This is all a natural reaction to intense pain, and should be confronted and accepted.
- The person experiencing this loss might cope with these feelings through **withdrawal and isolation** from others, because no one can understand or identify with the pain, and because there is no energy to interact with others. It's important that this remains a temporary state, and that we remain in community with other friends and relatives who can walk with us through this darkness.
- Acceptance: When reality sinks in, pain is faced, and life continues with the heart enlarged to accommodate the pain as a part of this new reality, acceptance comes slowly but surely, along with a new ability to experience joy and pleasure more deeply and poignantly, as the simple things in life take on deeper meaning.
- Being comfortable alone: Solitude is no longer feared, but welcomed, as we learn to enjoy being alone, not lonely. We are

---

[4] Sittser, Jerry (2009-05-11). A Grace Disguised: How the Soul Grows through Loss (Kindle Locations 578-583). Zondervan. Kindle Edition.

comfortable with our own presence and develop quiet pleasures that refresh and rejuvenate us.

- New relationships: We begin to treasure old relationships, especially those who have walked with us through the grief, and to develop new ones who are able to accept, know, and understand us in our new reality.

- Renewal of strength: As our souls and hearts are enlarged to encompass the pain, we also find our capacities to experience joy and pleasure, as well as our compassion for others, also enlarged. With this enlarged capacity comes renewed strength for living more fully, deeply, and authentically. We gain a new humility and grace towards ourselves and others. Hope and self-confidence are also renewed as we emerge from our loss stronger, after seeing how we have survived and continue to grow through our experience. We gain a new way of thinking and relating to others that is different from the easy triumphalism and optimism of our pre-loss days. We grow in wisdom as we allow ourselves to become tempered by pain.

- Ability to help others: Because our hearts are enlarged, we are able to understand the pain of others more deeply, extend compassion, and be able to come alongside to help others with the help and comfort that we have received. We are less prone to offer easy and tidy answers that we know in theory, less prone to judge, and able to cry and offer our presence to others.

Why did I not characterize the above components as "stages"? Because stages imply that people go through this process once, until all the pain is finally all gone. This is not true, but the later components do get larger while the earlier components tend to reduce and become a part of our beings. In the words of Dr. Sittser:

> *"I did not find it helpful, therefore, nor did I find it true in my experience, to identify these various responses as "stages" through which I had to pass on my way to "recovery." For one thing, I have still not moved beyond these stages, and I am not sure I ever will. I still feel anger, I still want to bargain with God, I still face the temptation of indulging my appetites, and I still want to that the tragedy is true. Not that I feel the urge to escape as intensely as I used to, but that is because my internal capacity to live with loss has grown. I have more perspective now; I have more confidence in my ability to endure. The*

problem with viewing these avenues of escape as stages is that it raises the false expectation that we go through them only once. Again, that has not been true for me. I have revisited them again and again. If anything, I have not moved beyond these stages but below them." [5]

The reason that I found Dr. Sittser's book so compelling is that he writes in the first person, as someone who has wrestled with the pain, not just having studied and analyzed the problem from a distance as an expert. I believe that part of the healing we receive comes from hearing the stories of others who have traveled on the same road of healing as we will embark on, and finding hope at what we hope to find when we do the hard work of healing. I have invited two of my friends to share about their own personal journeys of being single mothers.

ᘓ

Story 1: Changing for Love

I am ZL, 35 years old, work in the media industry. I've been raising my son as a single mother for 6 years now.

My father had been having an affair with another woman since I was very young, finally divorcing my mother when I was 18. Since then, he disappeared from my life forever. This even cast a big shadow of hurt in my life. Although my mother remarried, and my stepfather was nice to me and my little sister, deep within me I lacked a father's love. This shadow would ultimately impact my own marriage.

In my thirst for fatherly love, I entered marriage at the young age of 22, marrying my ex-husband, who was 6 years older than me. However,

---

[5] Sittser, Jerry (2009-05-11). *A Grace Disguised: How the Soul Grows through Loss* (Kindle Locations 627-634). Zondervan. Kindle Edition.

married life was totally different from what I had imagined it would be. I still did not get the fatherly care I craved because my ex-husband was the youngest in the family who was spoiled since birth. He had no idea how to care for another human being. I gave birth to our son when I was 25. At the time, I had to work as well as care for my husband and my baby son. I felt my heart breaking and my strength running out. As a result, marital conflict escalated in intensity and frequency.

When my son was 2 years 9 months old, I was hospitalized because of a pregnancy where the fetus was implanted outside the uterus, leading to an operation that led to my being bedridden for over a month. During a time when my body was the weakest, my husband left me completely alone in the hospital in order to care for my son. As I lay there alone in the darkness of the night, suffering from pain and sleeplessness, I gained sudden clarity. As I reflected my process of growing up, I discovered that I actually missed my own birth father very much, and desperately hoped that he could come to my aid in this time of most desperate need to bring me some warmth. It was only after this realization that I also realized that my husband could never give me the fatherly love and care that I needed and expected. This illness drew my marriage to a close. A year later I took my son and left my home town to raise my son alone in Beijing while I worked. I became a single mother.

When I first arrived in Beijing, pressure from work was huge, and I traveled frequently for business, leaving almost no time for my son. My son, who was not yet 5, could only stay with a nanny all day. After losing his father and then having a mother who could never be with him brought him great hurt. He became easily angry and emotionally unstable. Sometimes his eruptions of negative emotions were difficult to bear, even for me! As I watched my son live through similar pain that I went through childhood, my body and spirit went to the edge of breakdown.

At this time, friends suggested that I go through inner healing and rebuilding. During the rebuilding process, I received systematic processing of the contribution of family of origin issues to the breakdown of my marriage, and from a psychological standpoint learned to forgive myself and my family. I improved a little, and matured a lot. However, I was still deeply lonely, even feeling that the world had abandoned me and my son.

Through my American neighbor who helped to drop off and pick up my son from school, I was introduced to Rossana.

Rossana and her family have very harmonious relations. The help they gave us was such a precious gift from heaven to me and my son. When I first met Rossana, my son was asleep and I was crying alone on the couch. My cell phone rang. It was a text message from Rossana. Someone is thinking of you. You are not alone. In addition to Rossana's family, I also got to know other families in the community, and joined the Mommy Princess group.

Together, we learned about parenting and studies different books together, sharing our problems and thoughts. The help and care of friends brought me out of isolation and loneliness. The parenting skills learned from these classes effectively improved my relationship with my son. Regular therapy sessions and inner healing classes helped me to walk out of the shadows of my past, allowing me to interact with those around me in a happy and healthy way. My son finally got a mother who was healthy and whole on the inside!

What was ever better was that my son has his own companion and role model: Rossana's youngest son Stephen. Under Stephen's acceptance and modeling, he learned to treat others with respect. Now when we are walking together, he will automatically help me carry things, and his burst of anger disappeared. Laughter can often be seen on his little face, and the light of happiness is there!

I no longer worry that my son will grow up with a single mother. When we receive love and care from many people around you, your heart will be filled with gratitude and happiness, and will have the desire to pass on this love to warm even more people around you. At the same time, your own life will become even more healthy and abundant.

છ

Story 2: Single Mother Can Also be Happy and Fulfilled

I've already been a single mother for 13 years. Besides supporting a son who is studying overseas, I am also caring for two aging parents. My mother has been bedridden for 8 years before passing away last year. My father is 86 today. Bearing these responsibilities is only a tiny part of my life. Besides my work, I am also a student, working towards dual master degrees of marriage and family therapist and psychological health. When I'm with my friends, I'm always happy. They say that I am a woman who is full of life and confidence. Therefore even my good friend Rossana did not find out that I was a single mother until recently. When she did, she invited me to share my personal experience.

Since my marriage failed until today, I did not become a woman full of complaint who is full of pain and bitterness. The first reason is that I was lucky to have learned the right way to let myself become healthy in my soul and my spirit.

Right after my divorce, I came to Beijing as a graduate student, **wanting to forget my past and have a fresh start.** This thinking I think many can affirm and understand, and can even be admired by many, because I am a strong woman who can take up and put down. I thought the same way all along. However, in reality, it was never that simple. The wounds from marriage cut to the bone (I left a marriage full of domestic violence). Fear of the future constantly invaded my heart, causing my emotions to go up and down. I often felt loss and sadness, and then rage. I hated my ex-husband, and hated myself, to the point of gnashing of teeth!

With the help of friends, I tried learning to "forgive", forgiving those I hated and myself. After the hatred decreased, my emotions stabilized. My sleep and my studies all improved. My own transformation made me want to help even more people, so I sought formal certification through the fields of marriage and family counseling and psychological counseling.

The process of learning is also one of constantly seeking personal growth and breakthrough. For example, I needed to confront and grieve my own loss, to experience the changes in emotions, body, and mind when I grieve, to experience to hurts in my heart, every area of my body, and my soul. Why do I need to do such painful things? Because if I don't process these losses but bury them deep in some corner in my heart, then when pressure comes, these negative emotions will all rise to the surface and

overwhelm me. When I am unable to bear them, they can turn into depression, anxiety, and all kinds of emotional blockages, even cause physical ailments.

After experiencing this kind of process of healing, I was able to face a lot of people and things that others want to run away from. I can face the future no longer with fear, but with boldness. My whole person experienced a renewal. So I encourage every single mother to bravely face your pain and embrace the tomorrow that belongs to yourself.

When my spirit received healing and growth, the beneficiary, besides myself, are my son and my parents. When I can express my emotions in a healthy way, I no longer feel so tired and nervous, and won't get angry because of big and small things. After mother learns to relax, the son who is beside her can also relax. In an atmosphere of safely and relaxation, mother and son are then able to discuss many sensitive topics such as the girl he likes and all kinds of issues and quandaries in the process of maturing. We can talk about all these. I can also accept and respect my son more as a result.

I remember last year he mentioned in an email to me that he hopes he can continue to grow, and hopes that I can point out his shortcomings. After reading the email, I was very comforted, because I seldom blamed or criticized him at home, but encouraged and supported him more often. Although I am a single mother, but a healthy and mature mother is enough to help a child grow up healthily.

As someone who's gone through the process, I would like to share my own insights and experiences with more people. Three years ago I formed a single mother's support group. These mothers each have their own unique difficulties, and also have plenty of common problems. Some mothers have serious emotional blockage, depression and anxiety. Some mothers lack knowledge, having warped views of self and others which seriously impacted their judgment. Some mothers cannot get along with their child and family members. Mother's problems negatively impacted their children's development, to the point where some children can't attend normal school.

In the past three years, we met every week to encourage and support each other. Together, we learned how to listen and to accept one another, as well as to not judge others. In the single mother's group, everyone found safety and belonging, became happy to help others, and found the courage to share their own experiences of healing. Every single person experienced growth and change. Mothers who were once in depression were able to be free of dependence on medication and return to regular work and study. Overly self-obsessed mothers became willing to help others who were more needy. Mother-child relationships are improving little by little every day.

My experience and the experience of every single mother in my group proves one point: stop complaining, continue growing. Single mothers can also be happy and fulfilled!

CB

From these single mothers' stories, here are some suggestions for single mothers:

- Make a choice to develop a positive attitude, thoughts, outlooks, and beliefs about life. As we have learned from Dr. Sittser, we cannot do anything to control our circumstances. However, we definitely have a choice over our attitudes and way of responding to our circumstances. Make your choices helpful for your growth, not a hindrance.
- Believe that you will heal and not always feel bad. Even though the pain will always be there to a degree, believe that you will be able to also feel joy again, if you are willing to do the hard work of confronting and working through your loss.
- Take some time to be alone to face your feelings of guilt, shame, anger, sadness, grief, and rejection. Learn to overcome the feelings of guilt and self-condemnation.
- Learn to forgive, beginning with yourself, your spouse, and others.
- When you feel anger, self-pity, or sadness, choose to forgive and let go. I find it helpful to visualize an image of myself holding balloons filled with hate and anger, and releasing them one by one as I name

my hurts and disappointments. Forgiveness is not about letting the other person off scot-free, but about letting ourselves out of our inner prisons of bitterness that is poisoning our souls and disabling us from moving on to emotional health. When we let go, we free ourselves from those feelings, give up our rights to take revenge into our own hands, and choose to move on to enjoy the other positive parts of our lives.

- Take the time to learn about the grieving process and to go through it, not allowing yourself to run away or shortcut the process. Take time to confront your pain and heal.

- Accept your own imperfections and limitations, and believe that what resources you have is enough for you to prosper.

- Affirm yourself as worthy of love. Remember that just because your spouse left, does not mean that there is no one else who loves you, or that you are unlovable. At the very least, you should try to remind yourself of your strengths and positive aspects, and affirm yourself that you are lovable.

- Remember that failure in marriage does not mean failure in life. As long as you continue to have a positive outlook in life, you too can raise a healthy and happy child.

- Do not become isolated. Develop friendships and be in community. Learn to depend on others and help others in a healthy way. YET

- Do not become desperately dependent or clingy to others because you fear being alone or fear facing your pain.

- Learn to be alone and enjoy being alone. Find hobbies that will re-charge your batteries and renew your energy. Take time to think and reflect on life and what you want out of it.

- Develop concrete short term and long term goals

- Find ways to help others with the comfort and healing that you have received. This will help you to find purpose and meaning in your pain as you use your own growth to help and enrich others.

- Learn and live the Serenity Prayer

"God grant me the serenity
to accept the things I cannot change;
courage to change the things I can;
and wisdom to know the difference. "

--Reinhold Niebuhr

Throughout our marriage, we have had many close friends who are single Dads and single Moms. It is through being in the same community with them that we know their struggles and learn how to come alongside as friends to help and journey together, so that they are not alone. Parenting is tough enough with two parents, but it is particularly difficult for a single Mom or Dad who has to do it all alone without any help or relief. This is why having a supportive community is key to thriving as a single parent. Even though I can't offer advice to single parents because I have not lived or struggled through what they have to face each day, I can find ways to be part of a community of healing for such single parents. Here are some concrete suggestions on what has worked for our family as we seek to be part of that larger family for single parent families:

1. Give them hope: Whether or not they get remarried, help them to enjoy life in the present, being thankful for every provision and relationship that is already in their lives to live a full and meaningful life. Encourage them through your words and actions that you care about them, and that their presence in your life matters to you and enriches you.

2. Seek to understand them; walk with them: companionship: Instead of trying to offer advice or judge them, offer your friendship, presence, and help on a practical level. Have their children come over to play with your children. Offer to babysit their children so that this single mother can have a night off to rest. Cook a meal and bring it over, or invite them over for dinner.

3. Seek to understand and help with practical challenges and issues facing single parents. Try to read up on books related to the challenges that single parents face, and find ways to deepen your understanding of them.

4. Help children of single parents to develop friendships and learn to interact socially with other children, as well as provide models of healthy marriages and two parent families. The best thing you can

do for single mothers, especially those with boys, is to allow them to see and experience healthy marriages and families, so that they can model their future families after the ones they've seen and experienced. It's not about saying anything, but including them in your daily living and letting them observe the dynamics between two parents and how they interact with their child. It's letting them experience normal healthy family life with a male model. If there are older children in your community, they can be big brothers or sisters to them, to teach and instruct them on socialization amongst peers, and to give them healthy peer role models so that they learn how to relate to other peers in a healthy way.

5. Help them to feel a sense of belonging in a larger family identity. Instead single mothers isolating themselves out of a sense of shame and inadequacy because they are "different" from other families, we should enfold them into our midst so that they can feel a sense of belonging to a larger family, so that the next generation can grow up healthily in the a loving community of relationships. This will prepare them for success as they build families of their own in the future.

As you have read in the lives of these three women, being part of a single parent household does not mean the end of hope for a full and fulfilling life. It all begins with a new heart which believes and new eyes with which to see the world. Let it begin now.

I would like to share a poem that my son Caleb wrote last year when he was facing some loss related to a friendship. We had not previously discuss this analogy with the sun, but when I share with him this chapter that I was writing, he shared this poem with me. I thought it would be an appropriate ending to this chapter.

Westward Sunrise (December 2010)

I watch the ephemeral sun
setting over glistening silver and gray,
and I can't help but think
that I rather miss it all.

I feel as if I have been cheated,
that in a fleeting second

the God-given gold has faded away--
We had to replace them with our very own eyes

and the sunset--
Oh, what a fleeting bittersweet
lux aeterna, *(Note: Latin for "eternal flame")*
red and yellow symphony.

We've got a good view from the blue
but I daresay it'll get cold when it sets in,
that we've chased away the sun
into its rocky abode beneath the concrete.

Why are you hiding,
afraid of the night of our making?
We fashioned it from words and tears,
something of an Atlas for our fears

My dear,
its shoulders will not grow weak,
that is, if we can survive the dark
and face the coldness of our hearts.

For surely if we run westward,
we'll catch up with the sun,
reaching up,
as if we might take back yesterday.

But no, we have learnt from Icarus,
And so our wings are fashioned from steel--
Towards the eastern horizon I will fly
in search of tomorrow's sunrise

For Your Growth

1. If you are a single mother, what is the one thing from the above list
    of suggestions that you will carry out this week?
2. If you are not a single mother, but have a friend or relative who is a
    single mother, how will you try to better support her? Make a plan
    to communicate this intention and plan with her.

SECTION III

GROWING UP WITH OUR CHILDREN:

WHOLEHEARTED MOM LOVES RIGHTLY

3.1 WHY AM I A MOTHER?

It was the early spring of 2000, and Caleb and Jonathan were 5 and 7. I was feeling restless. My boys were rambunctious and seemed to be constantly getting into trouble. They just couldn't seem to sit still, and were constantly squabbling about this and that. I felt that I was contributing little to my home in tangible ways, and that my talent was unacknowledged and unused. Just to test the waters, I went for job interviews and received several job offers. I went to see a trusted mentor to talk about my desire to return to the workplace. Perhaps it would be better for my boys if they were in a good school, where professional educators can reform their ways. I certainly have tried all I can and nothing seemed to be working. I missed being able to dress up, act professional, talk adult talk, and be admired and rewarded for my performance. Is this enough time to pay my dues as a full time mother? My friend gave me a piece of valuable advice that I've kept as a constant reminder to check my motives for being a mother. Similar to a word of advice I received earlier about leaving a job, he told me that I should always leave a place to go somewhere greater, not because I couldn't stand my current circumstances that I had to leave it behind. It's better to run TO something than away FROM something. The same is true for motherhood. I should never use my children's performance to validate my worth as a person or evaluate my performance as a mother. Otherwise they will go through life wounded by my conditional love, weighed down by my expectations. Another pearl of wisdom was this mentor shared was that when God created humans, He did not intend to give himself a problem to solve, but a gift to open. Did I look upon my children as problems to be fixed, or gifts to be discovered and opened each day? I took a hard look at myself, at why I chose to stay home with them. I asked myself how I would react if someday my children turn out to be mediocre people, if I would be able to live with myself, or with them. I thought of the hurt they would feel if I can't accept them when they fail to measure up to my expectations, and after long talks with myself, made a decision to stay put at home until I've sorted out my heart's desires. Once I settled the question of performance and separated it from my children, I determined to accept them unconditionally and to just enjoy them as they are.

Then, just two weeks after I packed up all their baby furniture and related items and gave them away, I found out that I was pregnant with baby #3. It must be God giving me a chance to start with fresh motives. I am not a mother because I want them to turn out to be superstars to affirm my worth as a person. I am given the privilege of opening three gifts every day, the gift of relationship, of knowing and loving three people who will love me unconditionally in return. When people look at me with a look of pity, saying: "What a waste of your education!", and then say that my kids must become very smart or accomplished because of my efforts and my investment, and then wishing me that my investment will eventually pay off, I would smile and say with honesty: I am grateful to know and bring up three precious little souls, to influence them for eternity. No matter how they turn out, they will always be a delightful gift to me. Even if they never amount to much in life, I am grateful for the privilege of knowing them and growing up alongside them. I neither need nor desire any other validation. The greatest gift of motherhood is the gift of relationship.

For Your Growth

1. Reflect upon your reasons for becoming a mother. How do you view your child, as a problem or as a gift? There is always a mixture, but which view occupies the larger proportion of your thoughts each day as you think of your child?

2. When other people criticize your mothering or your child, what is your first response? Are you able to objectively evaluate others' criticism of how you go about parenting, or do comments from others affect you more on the emotional level? What kinds of comments trigger irrational reactions within you? What kinds of preventive measures can you take to react in a more healthy and rational manner?

3. Seek out a friend, or tell your husband of your resolve to enjoy the relational aspect of motherhood without the need to validate with external performance on your child's part.

3.2 LOVE MEANS
ACCEPTANCE AND GIVING GRACE

This morning, a mother called me on the phone to tell me that her son finally admitted to borrowing a friend's internet gaming card to play when she wasn't home. Even though she already knew about this a long time ago, she was waiting for her son to take the initiative to tell her. When she finally forced it out of him, she was extremely angry and gave him a heavy punishment. Her son cried for a long time, refusing to be comforted or to draw close to her. She deeply regretted her actions, and felt that her actions were a bit extreme. Racked with feelings of guilt, she was unable to sleep all night. I shared with her this story to help her gain some insight on how she can repair the broken relationship between them and rebuild trust.

Last October 1st Holidays, I had a dream in which I saw Caleb emerging from an underground sewer tunnel. His face was lined with fatigue, as if he had been walking for a long time, as he emerged wet, dirty, and stinky. However, it looked as if he was at the end of his journey, because there was a patch of blue sky at the end of that tunnel, and outside it looked as if the sun was about to rise. The dream switched over to another scene of Caleb sitting cross legged on a pristine white sand beach in front of a clear, placid, and blue expanse of water, as if he was facing a giant mirror. Caleb's eyes were shut, an expression of peace and rest on his face. At the same time, he was floating on a cushion of air, quiet and still. I felt from my heart that the name of this cushion of air was "grace".

The next day was the first day of the week long holiday period. I shared this dream with my husband. We felt that we needed to ask if Caleb has been under more pressure lately, and to offer to pray for him. I speculated that it might have to do with this impending college applications, and wanted to go with my husband to offer him some encouragement. When we asked if he would like for us to pray for him, he agreed right away. Halfway through, I described the two picture to him, and told him that I felt that he was struggling on his own in using his own ways, but that I felt that he can be like the second picture, floating on a cushion of grace. Caleb's response gave us a huge surprise.

He let out a loud cry, made a beeline for his room, shut the door, and started weeping on his bed. After he was finished, he finally came out to share with us what happened: Yes, I've been trudging along in the sewer for a long time now, and I'm so tired. These past two years, his friends would go out to the bars in Sanlitun to relax and hang out every Friday night. Because Caleb sings for two rock bands at school, he is quite popular and is invited each time. Finally, he went without letting us know. He knew that we would not support him to go to a bar, so just decided to not even ask us about it. Instead, he waited until we were all asleep to climb out of his window on the second floor and jump off the roof to go. After he's had a drink with his friends, he would head home. While we were still asleep, he would climb in through his window to go back to sleep. In the past two years, he went out in this way several times. Each time he got back, he would be racked with guilt and would stop for awhile, until he got invited again and again and couldn't refuse anymore, and would do it again. In the meantime, we thought that he was just tired from all the studying during the week, and would let him catch up on his sleep on Saturday morning, never even suspecting that something was amiss. We've always had a pretty close relationship with Caleb, and never suspected that he would hide anything from us. After the summer was over, he asked us if he could occasionally go with his friends to Sanlitun to hang out, just to socialize with them. We totally trusted him because he had always proven his responsibility. Also, because we've had previous conversations before about him being the butt of his friends' jokes when he refused to drink beer, we felt that he was able to withstand the peer pressure to refuse alcohol.

After hearing this news, I was very discouraged, feeling that I had failed as a mother. Before summer vacation, I had just finished writing a blog about his refusing to drink beer, and was so proud of him for doing that. Now I felt like a hypocrite. Should I disqualify myself from giving parenting advice now? How I have failed as a mother! All these thoughts floated through my head, but at the same time, I began to feel enormously grateful. If it hadn't been for this dream, would there be any possibility of my finding out about this? Isn't this dream pure grace from God? Having benefitted from this grace, do I have a right to judge my son and withhold this grace from him?

My husband and I almost went up to give Caleb a hug at the same time, letting him have a good cry in our embrace. I asked him: "now that the truth is finally out, do you feel better?" He nodded his head in rapid succession, a smile beginning to appear on his face. We sighed. "The people to be most pitied are those who know they are sinning and are unable to enjoy their sin with abandon! When you know right from wrong, that conscience inside is always warning us as we struggle alone in that sewer. When you face the fight in you own strength, there's just no way to win." Caleb told us that he didn't lie about beer, because he really dislikes the taste of beer, and will always refuse beer. However, what he didn't tell us what that he preferred whiskey! My eyeballs just about fell out of their sockets! He continued: "But rest assured, Mom and Dad, because I have self-control! I go every time just so I can hang out with my friends. Also, because I have to use my hard earned money to buy the very expensive liquor, I am only willing to buy half to one glass each time. I continued to ask: "So is that everything you want to tell us? Anything else that we don't know?" He nodded and went into his room, emerging with two bottles of hard liquor that he pulled out of the back of his closet, both birthday presents from his friends. I asked Caleb what he wanted to do with them. He said that even though they are really expensive and it hurt to see such waste, he is happy to say goodbye to them. Very quickly, the contents of both bottles were emptied down the bathroom sink. Just like that, all the secrets came to light, and were gone down the drain, along with the alcohol.

My husband and I have typically placed our expectations of our kids in the area of character. In their studies, our attitude has typically been: "Do your best with what you've been given." We keep emphasizing the principle that: "All things are lawful for me, but not all things are profitable. All things are lawful for me, but I will not be mastered by anything. " It's not that we forbid our children from drinking alcohol, but that we have no confidence that they are able to drink responsibly. In the past, we have drank red and white wine at the dining table, but have not given them any to drink. However, if they were curious about the taste, I don't think we would have refused, either. This incident made us realize that it's time to teach them about drinking responsibly in social situations. We told Caleb that the greatest disappointment was that he didn't trust us and discuss this with us and get our buy-in on this. As a result, the trust between us has been damaged. He will need to spend some time to rebuild this trust between us. He expressed willingness to bear the consequence and work on rebuilding this trust. He was just relieved that this secret that has been hidden for the past two years has finally come to the light, bringing him the peace that he longed for. He gave some suggestions on how he can repair that trust, and we agreed to set those measures in place. Now he has emerged from struggling alone in the dark sewer to face the rising sunlight, and the blue sky is within view. Caleb can finally float on that cushion of grace!

The root of a person lying is fear, because he knows that he's done something wrong, and his conscience has brought forth feelings of guilt and shame. He felt that instead of exposing the mistake to learn from this mistake and start over again, he felt a need to hide and cover over this wrong. Only when this person knows that he is totally accepted and loved as he is, is be able to emerge from this perfect love to chase away the fear within. Under the high expectations for personal integrity, we all need constant grace, to experience grace, and even more to extend grace.

Only in this kind of acceptance and love can a person who has done the wrong thing get up the courage to face and admit the thing that he felt ashamed about, to accept the responsibility and consequence for such an action, and to begin again. This is not the same as indulging a sin, because in this context, a child know right from wrong, because what parents have communicated their standards, and that "right will always be right, even when no one else is doing it, and wrong will always be wrong, even when everyone else is doing it." We don't compromise on our standards, but our kids know that they can always find grace in our love, and kindness can lead them to repentance, washing their past transgressions white as snow, giving them a change to begin anew.

One of the songs we love lead sing together is one that was popular during SARS. The lyrics are very appropriate to this lesson that we are learning. I share them here with you. May love never fail in your family, chasing away all fears, so that your kindness can lead your child to repentance.

Love Never Fails

Sea of humanity, deep expectations

Let life be filled with the peace of true love

Blessing you, listening to you

Walking with you through the valley of tears

Love never fails, chase away the fear in the heart

True love in my heart, peace just descends

Love never fails, let life become a miracle

Blessing you deeply, the dark night will soon pass.

For Your Growth

1. Reflect on your own process of growing up. What kinds of things have you hidden from your parents? If your child were to hide these same things from you, how would you feel today?
2. Find a time to sit down with your child to ask him/her if he did something really bad, if he thinks you will still love him. Then ask him why he thinks that.
3. What kinds of "bad" behavior do you find difficult to accept in your child? Which areas can you work on in terms of increasing your acceptance of your child?

3.3 HOW DO YOU GET PASSION?

These days, the phrase I most often hear is "interest is the best teacher". I am also seeing more and more parents who want to cultivate their kids to pursue their interests. As a result, all kinds of "interest" classes have sprung up to meet this need. Ironically, these "interest" classes is exhausting our kids, making them lose all interest. How do you spark interest in a child, and help him to preserve his passion? If you read the biographies of many masters, you will discover that they all encountered a teacher, mentor, or parent who was passionate in a certain area. This is to say that passion is not taught, but caught. It's like a positive virus, and no one who has not come into contact with it can get infected. Just as William Butler Yeates said, "Education is not the filling of a pail, but the lighting of a fire."

In my book "The Competitive Edge of the Next Generation", I talked about my experience of learning to play the piano. I was on a trajectory to be like many kids today where I would pass qualification for the highest level in a musical instrument and finally earn the right to never touch this thing that I have develop such hatred for. However, I met a teacher during high school who helped me to use my piano skills to play my favorite top 40 pop songs. As a result my relationship with the piano went through a radical transformation, and my passion for music was ignited. If I hadn't met this teacher, I would probably not have touched my piano to this day.

Now, my eldest and second sons' passion for music is being ignited. Caleb very much regrets the fact that I never forced him to practice the piano when he was growing up, because it is such a critically needed skill to him. He loves composing music, and is writing a symphony for his graduation ceremony. Because he was never forced by me to learn music theory, he saw the huge gap between him and the master composers in the process of studying their works. He determined to spend the entire summer after he graduates from high school to teach himself piano. I firmly believe that with this kind of motivation and passion, he will learn better and faster than if I was forcing him to learn against his will.

Jonathan fell in love with the first violin chair in his school orchestra, and began dating her under both sets of parental supervision. We gave them very clear boundaries, encouraging them to serve the community together and to cultivate common interests. Before knowing her, Jonathan was a pure rock drummer, with a propensity towards heavy metal music (not necessarily for the song itself, but because heavy metal music has the greatest complexity in drum beats). After getting to know his girlfriend, he began to play jazz drums, and even began to learn the double bass in order to accompany his girlfriend in performances. This summer, he went with her to a Jazz music school for summer camp and returned a completely different person. Now, our house is filled with jazz and classical music all the time. In two short months, as a result of playing daily with his girlfriend, practicing songs being played by the school orchestra, he is already able to play more difficult pieces, and plays for three classical music ensembles. Every day after school, he would practice 1-2 hours on his drums and then another hour on his double bass without any reminder. Last week, I discovered that without us noticing it, Jonathan had already become a very technically advanced musician. Where did his passion for music come from? He was infected by his girlfriend.

There are two more reasons that Caleb and Jonathan love music. The first one is his family. Because we have a Lin Family Band, music is our common love and bond. They naturally grew up immersed in an environment filled with all different kinds of music and love of music. This exposure enabled them to like and play all different genres of music. The second reason is that they go to a school with a teacher who is passionate about music. His students all got infected by him. As a result, the school culture is such that people everyone wants to form their own band to play for different occasions in different venues. All the most popular kids are members of a band. This is the contribution that this teacher made to their school, and has helped this school to gain a reputation as a school that is excellent in music.

So the question we should be asking is not "whether or not to enroll in an interest class", but "where are the passionate teachers?" If a school or classroom has a passionate teacher who can ignite a child's interest in a certain subject, then we should try our best to get our kids in contact with this teacher to "get infected". This world is filled with teachers that have the knowledge and degrees, but rare is the teacher that is passionate and willing to pay the price to help their students on their own time to fall in love with what they love. If we can't find such teachers, then we need to be that kind of a mentor to infect our kids with our passion. This is how schools and homes complement one another. Of course, if our area of interest is not what we are good at, then we can only take them so far before helping them to find a teachers who is skilled enough to bring them further along. Our Lin Family Band ignited in them a passion for music, but our knowledge of musical instruments is not as professional as their teachers in school. When Jonathan's drumming got to a certain point, the teachers at his school are no longer able to help him. As a result, he needed to find a teacher from outside to help him to progress further in order to keep breaking new ground.

When the fires of passion have been ignited, our kids no longer need our supervision to learn. Instead, they are infecting us in return. Now, I am furiously reviewing the classical music that I learn so long ago, because I no longer want to be left behind in the dust.

For Your Growth

1. Reflect on your life thus far. What have you been passionate about? Why? How could this passion infect your child and allow it to become a positive motivating force in his life?
2. Ask the same question of your spouse. How can he infect you and your child with his passion so that it can become a positive motivating force in your lives, and also to draw you all closer to one another in this common interest?
3. If there is no common interest among family members right now, sit down together to discuss what new interest you would like to pursue and learn together, and make concrete plans to develop this new interest together.

3.4 INFECTIOUS TEACHER, INSPIRING STUDENT

One day I brought Stephen to his ceramics class. Ms. Yao, Stephen's ceramics teacher, came over to talk to me alone. A bit embarrassed, I thought that it was to discuss the Winter Break class schedule, because Stephen kept bugging me to call Ms. Yao repeatedly to schedule sessions in hopes of starting as soon as possible. It turned out that she wrote a letter to share with me. After reading it, I was so touched that I asked for her permission to share this letter with everyone. She agreed.

Ms. Yao said that Stephen really touched her. However, throughout the process of Stephen learning ceramics, he and our whole family has been the really beneficiaries. Making ceramics is Stephen's spiritual food and a tool that he uses as an outlet for his emotions. I thought about what would be left in our spirits if a "hobby class" is unable to help us relieve stress or heal our damaged emotions / spirits, but is only able to help us win awards or get on the stage, and then those awards rot and the limelight disappear.

Passion is more important than talent, because not only can passion motivate, but it can also heal the spirit. In the process of going to all kinds of extracurricular classes, if your child has the fortune to encounter a teacher that is able to infect your child with his passion, you must seize this opportunity to let your child be in contact with this person to get "exposed" and "infected". As parents, what we are after is not the applause or acknowledgement from others, but that our child's spirit can be enriched as a result of his interest, and his becomes more persevering. These are the greatest rewards in the world. Here is Ms. Yao's letter

Persistent Stephen – My Student
Chinese New Year just passed, and Stephen's Mom already called twice to ask when he can start ceramics classes. I know that Stephen's hands are getting "itchy", and he misses his clay. Because of curriculum still needing to be completed, Stephen needs to wait another week before he began. As a teacher facing such an eager student who loves ceramics so much, I have a lot of thoughts – it's time to write something for my student Stephen.

Initially, my letter was entitled: "My Student – Persistent Stephen", but as I reflected on all that happened in Stephen's ceramics classes, I changed the order. He is Stephen, a persistent Stephen.

When I first met Stephen, he was in second grade when he came in to attend my ceramics class. He was a quiet yet articulate little boy. Using his not very fluent Chinese to tell me that He is Stephen Lin from America.

I noticed him not because of his works, but because of his tenacity, patience, and orderliness. He joined the class in the middle, when other classmates already have significant foundation, so his works were not outstanding. At the time, my request to the students was: good product that is affirmed by others can remain and get stained; product that was not satisfactory should be kneaded back into the original clay pile. Many students couldn't accept having to destroy their own works. Looking back, I really didn't know how to evaluate my actions. Actually, I knew that every child worked hard to create something, and all original expressions are all good, but I don't know why, I just wanted them to be better, and know that they CAN be better, and I wanted them to experience the joy of breaking through their own limitations. When I saw those breakthroughs, I was more excited them they were. Some students were willing to receive the criticisms from their classmates and began over again without any complaining. Some students gritted their teeth to bear it while others couldn't accept it and backed out of the class. Stephen welcome it, and even thanked his classmates for every single critique. Once, twice, three times… he gladly destroyed his works.

That semester, we all knew that Stephen did not have one piece of work that remained. Later I would often talk about this with my students, and they would admire his refusal to give up, but Stephen didn't think anything of it. He felt that he should work hard and harder. Now, every time I think back, my heart would ache for this 7 year old boy who comes to each class full of enthusiasm, plunging fully into the process of creation, and then to destroy his work without any regret. This process repeated for a semester. I often regret my own stubbornness – why so stingy towards the students? Wouldn't encouragement be better for them to accelerate their development? I just couldn't turn that corner, but I met a student who is even more stubborn than me – Stephen Lin.

I especially remember that last day of school. While everyone was getting ready for vacation, Stephen ran to my classroom to tell me: "Ms. Yao, see you next semester. I will still be taking ceramics class."

I began to look at this clean cut little boy in a different way.

Next, Stephen's works went through a fundamental change: from project design to style of expression, all began to show his unique way of thinking and expressing himself, and began to win the affirmation of teachers and students alike. Every time someone made a positive remark on his work, he would say in all seriousness: "Ms. Yao said…. This classmate said this, and I improved upon it…" What astounded us the most was that he remembered just about every word that teacher said in class, remembered every strength in a classmate's work, and kept incorporating everything into his own works, while experimenting, improving, and re-creating them into his own unique creations….

When a teacher sees her own words, thoughts, and theories affecting her student deeply, and how he applied each concept rigorously, occupational satisfaction rises immediately, bringing satisfaction and inspiration.

Stephen's improvement was evident for all to see. His freedom of expression, attention to little creative twists in his work, beautifying methods and intentional application of these methods, bring much inspiration and surprises to the spirits of his classmates and me. At the same time, his steady confidence in creation and his attitude enables him to enjoy being with his clay, as he also experiences the joy of evaluating and enjoying a work of art with his teachers and classmates. And this steady confidence is at the same time accelerating his improvement in other subjects and areas of study. I often hear him say with pride: "Ms. Yao, my whole person is improving!"

Stephen is almost 11 years old. In these four years of growing alongside him in ceramics class, Stephen has used his insistence to prod me and his classmates to also grow and improve. Stephen's persistence encourages me constantly, and gives me passion to encounter the spirits of my students in the classroom with my own.

Every time I observe Stephen's intimate dialog with his clay, to the exclusion of all else, I am always reminded of Raphael's words:

"In art education, art is just a means to achieve the goal, not the end in itself. The goal of art education is to enrich a person's creativity through the process of creation. Regardless of where this creativity is applied, when the child is grown, and he is able to increase his creativity through his experience with beauty, applying this creativity to his life and work, then the objective of art education has been achieved."

Persistent Stephen has used the paths of his own growth to prove these words, and let everyone see and feel the real power and attraction of art education.

Stephen, bless you!

For Your Growth

1. Reflect on your life thus far. What have you been passionate about? Why? How could this passion infect your child and allow it to become a positive motivating force in his life?
2. Ask the same question of your spouse. How can he infect you and your child with his passion so that it can become a positive motivating force in your lives, and also to draw you all closer to one another in this common interest?
3. If there is no common interest among family members right now, sit down together to discuss what new interest you would like to pursue and learn together, and make concrete plans to develop this new interest together.

3.5 GRADES COME FIRST?

Have you ever tried to pick green fruit that is unripe and had a very difficult time with it? The function of examinations is in actuality like the color of that fruit. Tests reveal to us the ripeness of a fruit, whether it is ready to be eaten or used for its purpose. However, today, tests have become a symbol of what we base our self-concepts on, and is bearing a burden it is not designed to bear. Tests, like the color of the fruit, is merely one of the many signs of the condition of the fruit, and cannot be altered to suit the preferences of the gardener. In North America, farmers had developed a chemical to spray on green tomatoes to make them turn red overnight. The tomatoes look ripe and attractive when displayed on the shelves in the market, but when brought home, are hard and tasteless.

Today, parents and teachers, as gardeners of the souls of our children, have succumbed to the lie that we can hurry along and change the color of the fruit, and that by changing the outside color, just like those chemically altered tomatoes, they can cross the narrow plank of Gaokao (Chinese College Entrance Examination, China's SAT Equivalent) and be ready for life. What most parents who focus on test scores or the outward color of the fruit will discover is that the inside of the fruit is often quite green, very difficult to pick off the branch, and not ready at all to be put to its real intended use. The timing of the ripeness of the fruit cannot be controlled or speeded up by the gardener, and any means to manipulate the outcome can only end in fooling others, leaving the inside unchanged and ultimately ruined and of no use to anyone. There are seasons of growth in a living thing. As gardeners, we are to observe the stage of growth, cooperate with that stage by providing the best conditions for growth during that stage, and allow time to do its work to mature that living thing. As people who are infinitely more complex than plants or animals, we are even more difficult to manipulate.

Today tests in china function like a filter for the limited amount of seats in the limited number of universities available to help society and industry provide a qualified work force. Unfortunately, the qualities that are needed for the best jobs will not be cultivated with a test centered system. Like frogs in that proverbial well, we parents can only see the filter as the obstacles to our children obtaining that job, but cannot see beyond that filter to see what keeping that prize really requires.

So what should we do as parents of young children, whose peers are being pushed earlier and earlier to achieve impressive skills and obtain an amazing body of knowledge? Should we really not worry about test scores at all? Would that be irresponsible? Grades are an indication of proper growth. What are the main responsibilities of the gardener for a young person's soul? Here are a few of the key areas of focus that we should cultivate. Once these foundations are properly laid, the grades will fall in their proper place at the right time later on in a child's life:

Living Habits: children should expect to take care of their own responsibilities such as making their beds, keeping their desks and rooms clean, and helping with household chores. These good habits help him to learn self-mastery as well as responsibility, skills that will be foundational to him when he begins his working life. Recently I interviewed a student whose father contacted me to schedule for an interview on his son's behalf as well as send me all of his background information so that his son can focus all of his time and energy competing in a science Olympiad. I was rather disappointed to learn that this person has not had any opportunity to learn to manage his own time, his activities, his college applications, or even his own future work. While his academic achievements were definitely impressive and outstanding, I am concerned that once he arrives in college and his faced with all the dizzying array of choices he is to make, he will be lost because he has never learned to be responsible for his life or own his decisions.

Attitude towards studying: When my son Caleb was growing up, he had no interest in learning the piano and refused my offers of lessons. Now that he has his own band and has begun to write his own music, he requested that I teach him piano so that he has the needed skills to compose music. He is now motivated to practice on his own without me ever reminding him because he wants and needs to use those skills. Even though he is learning the piano much later than his peers, many of whom started very early in life but have now lost interest, he is catching up quickly, putting his new knowledge to good use, and enjoying the process of learning. Practicing the piano at age 16 is now motivated by his passion for music rather than an obligation to his parents to make the piano lessons count. As parents, we can help our children to have the right motivation for learning by fueling their interests and providing opportunities for them to learn.

Habits of Studying: One of the great things about the Chinese educational system is that our children receive a very solid foundation in their basic education. Certain knowledge that are critical to future learning, such as basic math, reading and writing, are skills that are required for higher learning. The best thing we can do for our children during the elementary years to cultivate healthy study habits, which means that they get used to doing their homework before playing, watching TV, or getting on the computer. After that habit has been established in our children, then we can work on their motivation for learning and help them to discover various interests. One college applicant who was an exceptional biologist credits his passion in biology to trips taken every weekend with his father to catch cicadas when he was a child in elementary school. Another worldwide astronomy champion credits his fascination for astronomy to gazing at the stars every night with his grandfather while he told stories of the mysteries that are yet to be explored in the heavenly bodies. He says that when he remembers those days, he is still filled with a sense of childlike wonder. Once an interest is discovered, than it is also up to the parents to cheer their children on and encourage them to persevere in exploring their interest and developing the skills to be excellent in a particular area. There is a saying that "genius is 99% inspiration and 1% perspiration", which I find to be very true in every master that I know.

Relationship with Family Members: A home filled with the presence, love, and attention of both parents who love each other, firm discipline and guidance, elderly who are respected, and opportunities to socialize with other children will teach our children to have the right view of authority, have strong EQ, know how to know and master himself in consideration of others, gain ability to follow instructions and gain a sense of responsibility for himself and others, and be able to trust and depend on others in a healthy way. These are the most foundational skills needed for success in life in general, as a child needs to grow up to be an adult who not only knows how to hold down a job but also to be an upright citizen of the country as well as a good son/daughter, husband/wife, and father/mother.

This semester, right before finals, because of expiring flight mileage, we had to take our youngest son Stephen out of school for a week to take him to the U.S., where he had a great time going to Disneyland and all the theme parks nearby. However, because he also got sick coming back to Beijing, he ended up missing a total of 10 days of school, and those 10 days were the most critical and intense days of pressure and review for finals. Instead of being able to score at the top of his class for various subjects, now we were told to be happy to expect him to pass. To our surprise, he did rather well for someone who did not cram during those last days, even though he was not at the top of the class. This showed us that what test score he got was what actually was absorbed into his brain during the normal course of classes that semester, and we were quite happy with his progress. In fact, he was able to write something from his actual experiences of traveling in the composition portion of his test rather than having to make something up. What we were most happy with was his progress this term mastering the character of being able to go to his desk to complete his homework on his own without complaining or playing first. He is still very, very slow in completing his homework, at times working until well past his bedtime to get it all done. However, he has stopped complaining or trying to get out of doing all his work. This is a critical self-mastery skill that he must have in order to be able to learn on his own. We are proud of what his teacher wrote in his Report Card :

I am very happy, because you have improved once again this semester. You can complete your homework on time, and in class, you are able to pay attention and proactively raise your hands most of the time. That's amazing! Can you turn the "often" into "every day?" Try it! I think you can do it! And when you do, you will be the pride of your Dad, Mom and teacher!

For Your Growth

1. Out of the four areas mentioned above, which one do you need to work on more with your child? How will you set concrete and measurable goals to monitor your progress and improvement in helping your child grow in this area?

2. How can you enlist the support of your spouse, parents, and other caretakers of your child to lay a solid foundation in this area of weakness?

3.6 HIGH IQ = SUCCESS?

This morning, a friend came and told me that the whole year, her child's teacher from school has been pressuring her and her husband to take her child to the hospital for an IQ test. The reason is that the teacher was unwilling to take responsibility for the child's grades (this child got a 90% on the most recent math test, which made the teacher very unhappy and caused her to pressure my friend once again to go register for an IQ test). I already stopped her several times, but she had reached her limit, and was caving in to the pressure. I am always saddened when I see a sunny and happy child become a lying and angry child as a result of a teacher's misunderstanding about test scores. These parents are willing to do anything to get their child into a "better" school, but his teacher, who is willing to destroy the spirit of his pupils in order to achieve higher test scores, send daily text messages like a madman to complain about their child and call them to leave work early to go to the school office for more lectures. The child's self-respect is trampled on the ground, and the parents don't have enough courage to go face the teacher. Now this child has grown rebellious, and would erupt in fits of anger as his emotions spin out of control. I am worried that when he enters the teenage years, he will become extremely rebellious. I appealed to her to hurry up to save the situation now instead of waiting until the parent-child relationship has broken down. I cry for so many of these kids and their parents. I hope that you will spend more time with your children to give them a happy childhood. This weekend, please lay down your homework, your IQ tests, and take your children out to play in order to build a good relationship with them. Don't let them think of scolding, guilt, tiredness, and criticism every time they think of you, leading them to give up on themselves. While there's still time, please rescue the friendship and goodwill you have with your children!

Not long ago, two news headlines caught my attention:

"Child Prodigy Class" Strange Test Questions Designed to Select Strange and Unusual Talent
According to the article, these two extremes of questions can isolate the kind of strange talent that can adjust to the prodigy class, and those trained

by trainers who rely on memorization will not do well.

198 kids were selected from 1239 of the 10 and 11 year-old kids in the city. Then 60 are selected to "trial study". Finally, 30 people are then formally admitted. These 30 students will finish all 8 years of public education in 4 years and participate in Gaokao at age 14.

While "Prodigy Class" Process in Session, Hospital "IQ Test" Sessions Are Oversubscribed

These days, it's increasingly popular amongst parents to administer IQ tests to their children. Dr. Zhang of Beijing No. 3 Hospital IQ Testing department tells reporters that many parents bring their children here for IQ testing at the urging of their children's teachers who want others to verify their pupils' low IQ so that they can escape from taking responsibility for these children's low test scores. Of course, there are also significant numbers of parents who are there to prove that their children are "unusually bright". Right now, these testing sessions are oversubscribed with a minimum waiting list of one month.

When I read news like this, I want to cry: "Parents, wake up!" When can we regard children as children, as precious and unique gifts to be treasured instead of machines and tools to be used? We have fallen into misconception about IQ Testing!

The Truth Behind IQ Testing

Modern IQ testing originated in 1916 from Prof. Lewis Terman of Stanford, when it debuted as the Stanford-Binet Scale. This test was used after WWII to test for which kinds of people are suitable for spy work. The original IQ test, called the Binet-Simon Scale, was put together in France to identify which kids are lower in intelligence and thus need additional help. As one can see, both tests have different purposes, but should never be used as a tool to measure and predict a child's future success.

I wanted to quote bestselling author Malcolm Gladwell in chapter 3 of his book "Outliers" related to genius to explain and reveal the truth behind IQ testing and its limitations. I don't want so many parents to worship an incomplete concept and use it as a one-size-fits all tool to judge and determine a child's fate, to forever pin a label of "genius" or "dumb" on a child.

"In 1921, Terman decided to make the study of the gifted his life work. By the time Terman was finished, he had sorted through the records of some 250,000 elementary and high school students, and identified 1,470 children whose IQs averaged over 140 and ranged as high as 200 (author's note: 120 is normal, and only those whose IQ is above 130 is considered "genius"). That group of young geniuses came to be known as the "Termites," and they were the subjects of what would become one of the most famous psychological studies in history. For the rest of his life, Terman watched over his charges like a mother hen. They were tracked and tested, measured and analyzed. Their educational attainments were noted, marriages followed, illnesses tabulated, psychological health charted, and every promotion and job change dutifully recorded. . . all the time recording his findings in thick red volumes entitled Genetic Studies of Genius. . . But, as we shall see, Terman made an error. He was wrong about his Termites. Terman didn't understand what a real outlier was, and that's a mistake we continue to make to this day.

Change It is amply proved that someone with an IQ of 170 is more likely to think well than someone whose IQ is 70," the British psychologist Liam Hudson has written, "and this holds true where the comparison is much closer – between IQs of, say, 100 and 130. But the relation seems to break down when one is making comparisons between two people both of whom have IQs which are relatively high . . . A mature scientist with an adult IQ of 130 is as likely to win a Nobel Prize as is one whose IQ is 180." . . .

But given what we are learning about intelligence, the idea that schools can be ranked, like runners in a race, makes no sense. . .

This was Terman's error. He fell in love with the fact that his Termites were at the absolute pinnacle of the intellectual scale—at the ninety-ninth percentile of the ninety-ninth percentile—without realizing how little that seemingly extraordinary fact meant.

By the time the Termites reached adulthood, Terman's error was plain to see. . . Few of his geniuses were nationally known figures. They tended to earn good incomes—but not that good. The majority had careers that could only be considered ordinary, and a surprising number ended up with careers that even Terman considered failures. Nor were there any Nobel Prize winners in his exhaustively selected group of geniuses. His fieldworkers actually tested two elementary students who went on to be Nobel laureates—William Shockley and Luis Alvarez—and rejected them both. Their IQs weren't high enough. . . By the time Terman came out with his fourth volume of Genetic Studies of Genius, the word "genius" had all but vanished. "We have seen," Terman concluded, with more than a touch of disappointment, "that intellect and achievement are far from perfectly correlated.""

Other Factors Affecting Success

Does a misconception that took a professor and his team from a top university an entire life's worth of work to prove require our nation to prove it all over again through our children? Do we want to pay this heavy price with our families' only precious children?

Everyone is looking for the genius, strange talent, and prodigy, but who is going to raise a happy and healthy ordinary child? What kind of results will an elitist society produce? Don't kids with low IQ have the right to pursue education, success, and happiness? Is the purpose of education to select the elite at the cost of eliminating the majority of the "remainder" , or to satisfy every child's desire for learning? Every chicken has in its nature a love of eating rice, just as every human being has in his nature curiosity and a desire to learn. Why is it that in our schools, we will only feed those chickens that eat the most and the fastest, but neglect the majority of those chickens that still have the same need to eat rice? How will these elites find high quality plumbers? Painters? How scary will it be for an entire nation to be composed of elites! Will geniuses or strange talents have high integrity or character? In my eyes, an illiterate yet considerate migrant worker who is willing to sacrifice for others will always far surpass a selfish, arrogant graduate from an elite university. Why does every parent and school want to fashion every child into an elite? Or desperately try to "rescue" those children who have lower grades? Our society has already made our children into slaves of scores and grades! I think that the fundamental responsibility lies with parents.

In the 4th chapter of the book "Outliers" , we discover that the biggest factor in a child's success is family background. The same two people with equally high IQ, one did not even graduate from college, the other because of his family's concerted cultivation and creation of opportunities, giving of confidence and affirmation, became recognized in history as a "genius".

The difference you see is because certain families teach their children to show their best side to the world, while other families neglect this. The example mentioned above of the high IQ genius who never even graduated from college lacks an environment, and this environment can help them cultivate the correct attitude to face the world.

As parents, we need to help our children become adults with high character, to let him produce a sense of pride and value in his work, no matter what profession he chooses, because his life has value and dignity. There is no higher or lower worth in any job or profession. The way that we evaluate a person should not be based upon what kind of car he drives, the house he lives in, or the diploma hanging on his wall. We need not complain about the unfairness of life or the injustice of society, but need to examine our own hearts and actions. We need to help our kids cultivate the correct attitude to face the world. Besides words, nothing can be more powerful than our own example.

For Your Growth

1. Growing up, what has been your reaction to the way you were educated? How has that affected your attitude towards how your child is being educated?
2. Are there attitudes within you that are not healthy or helpful to your child's progress in his current education system? What do you need to stop doing? What do you need to start doing?

3.7 DISCIPLINE PRODUCES CHARACTER

Many parents grew up in an environment that is high in pressure and low in affirmation. When they see the word "authority" (composed of the characters "authority" and "power"), they see "power", which produces in them an extreme sense of repulsion and resistance. In reality, they have already entered into a misunderstanding of the true meaning of authority. Nowadays, some parents have swung to the other extreme, which is to completely let their children do whatever they want in total freedom, allowing them to decide everything. When they discover their children doing something wrong, they refuse to correct them. This philosophy produces children that are selfish, prideful, and stubborn. When they are grown and enter society, they have a tough time getting along with others, and are unable to maintain healthy relationships with friends or family, not to mention being able to bear the responsibility for family members or become loving and responsible citizens who are able to contribute positively to society. The "Happy Education" that is so trendy these days places children's happiness and right to decide in the highest priority, sacrificing the need for parents to train and discipline their children to cultivate good habits. Because some parents were wounded by discipline when they were growing up, they now try their utmost to protect their children from all the pain they had suffered when they themselves were children, not willing for their children to suffer any setback or difficulty. However, because their own patience has limits, they will occasionally lose it and explode, unwittingly taking out their repressed emotions on their kids. Then they end up feeling guilty afterwards for their loss of control. This guilt pushes them to apologize to the kids, which in turn negates any legitimacy of the parent's attempt to correct or discipline. This vicious cycle will ultimately produce an insecure child who will act according to what he observes the parent is feeling at the time and adjust his behavior accordingly. When these children enter school, many parents out of their protective instinct will oppose teachers who are trying to correct their children, placing all the blame on the teacher or the school. Although sometimes the teachers do have problems, many times the parents are unable to see the responsibility of their children for breaking rules or hurting others. According to many of my principal or teacher friends, most kids who excel in school have parents who seek to maintain positive and mutually respectful relationship with the school, collaborating and growing together with teachers. In other words, in the process of a child's growth and learning, parents will rarely see a child who never suffers setbacks or difficulties.

In reality, if parents fail to train and discipline their kids in the process of raising them, they are spoiling them, even tacitly expressing their approval of bad behavior by doing nothing about it. However, households that overly emphasize discipline often lack adequate expression of love and acceptance, causing children to grow up lacking in self-confidence or pushing them to rebel. At the ends of either spectrum, these children grow up unable to maintain healthy and respectful relationships with authority figures, whether it's their teachers, bosses, or the police. The process of parenting must be built on the foundation of acceptance, affirmation, love, and time spent together, before training and discipline is effective. Only when a child has been trained and disciplined can he mature into an adult who seeks to serve those around him – someone high in CQ, EQ and AQ.

In my last Sina Weibo (Chinese Twitter) online Q&A on the topic of "How to Discipline Your Children" (http://talk.t.sina.com.cn/ft/20110218283) , I shared some concepts related to discipline. Because it was very difficult to break up entire concepts into 140 character chunks, I will give a fuller explanation here:

"Train up a child in the way he should go: and when he is old, he will not depart from it." -- An old Jewish proverb

Discipline and punishment are entirely different! The Chinese word for discipline is composed of the character "correction" as well as "teaching". Correction means to bring correction in reaction to a wrong attitude or action, while teaching means to proactively encourage the correct heart attitudes and teach/train the right behaviors. Discipline needs to begin when children are small, not later when they are older. As children grow older, the freedom given them can increase in proportion to the responsibility that they are able to handle.

Discipline needs to be built on the foundation of a loving and close parent child relationship. Therefore, in order for such a relationship to grow, the child must feel the unconditional love and acceptance of his parents.

Discipline without love will produce rebellion, because the child cannot experience the protection from rules and regulations, but only the pain from not following the rules. The goal of discipline is to train our children to have good character and habits, ultimately to hand over to him the freedom to manage himself, going on to fully mature adulthood. The goal of punishment is to add pain to a wrong that already happened, and makes a child unable to emerge from the experience without shame and low self-esteem.

Discipline is proactive. It's training the appropriate response and behavior before something happens. Punishment is reactive. It's trying to determine how the mistake was made and what caused it to happen. Parents who discipline their children based upon principles are building on a foundation of a love relationship, calmly executing consequences, concluding with loving reassurances that helps a child understand that his parents will always love him, but desire to help their child overcome poor habits, attitudes, and behavior that will be harmful to him in the future. On the other hand, parents who punish their children after something went wrong are hostile, angry, and frustrated, executing consequences with negative emotions and anger. Sometimes, those negative emotions are caused by feelings of awkwardness or shame on the parents' part.

Discipline will produce further feelings of security in the heart of a child, because he knows that the world has order, with clearly defined boundaries. This kind of children will be able to see that they are protected by rules in life, and will trust and affirm the need for rules. When they are grown, they will respect the law, and will have a heart for justice. The hearts of kids who are punished will be full of shame and guilt. This kind of children will grow up learning to behave according to how they observe others are feeling, and will learn to manipulate their parents using their emotions. When they are grown, they will tend to follow rules less. In society, we often will observe people who talk about "humane understanding" at the cost of justice, often asking those who are hurt by breaking of laws to exercise tolerance towards those who hurt them.

Discipline uses logical consequences, not threats (if you don't turn off the TV now, I won't let you play!), compromise (OK, I'll let you watch 5 more minutes. After that, you will stop, right?), repression (I'm counting to 3, you'd better turn it off! 1-2-3!), or wearing down (Please turn off the TV, OK? Turn it off, please! Please, please, please turn off the TV now! Nag, nag, nag…) Discipline is following previously agreed upon rules and executing the previously agreed upon consequences for violating those rules. The consequence must be painful to be effective. The final outcome of discipline is the reward of good personal character itself, because good character will naturally bring about the affirmation and admiration of the parents and others around.

Discipline and consequences must be set according to each child's personality and uniqueness. For example, Jonathan can't stand being lonely and hates being isolated, but Caleb loves his own personal space. Therefore, a time out will work effectively for Jonathan but not for Caleb. The best times for disciplining a child is before age 6. As a child matures, the parents' role will evolve from a being a good teacher to a trusted friend. As a child's heart attitudes and habits become more set with age and maturity, discipline change from external consequences to internal motivation, letting the conscience become the dominant voice.

Discipline is a very long process, and is a great endeavor that is worth devoting all of a parent's heart and strength to do well.

Cultivating Good Habits

"Sow a thought, reap an action. Sow an action, reap a habit. Sow a habit, reap a character. Sow a character, reap a destiny." - Seneca

Cultivating good life habits is a necessary process in childhood. Without good habits, it is difficult for children to increase self-control or learn to delay gratification. When children are small, cultivating habits uses two external factors to help children develop internal motivation. There's an expression in English called "carrots and stick" (In Chinese, it's "toasting wine vs. punishment wine"). Carrots refer to some time of external reward or affirmation leading to positive motivation. In our work life, an employee who does excellent work is rewarded with some "carrot system" such as bonuses, awards, promotions, "performer's" travel club, etc. An organization that is not concerned with internal motivation will more often use the "stick system" such as ducking of pay, warnings, surveillance, elimination of the bottom 10% of performers, etc. In the home, "correction" often uses negative reinforcement while "teaching" uses positive reinforcement. Below are some of the "carrots" and "sticks" that we used in our home when our children were young. They are more suitable for preschool children. After elementary school, these kinds of measures need to gradually decrease, allowing habits and motivation to internalize because at that stage, our child can tell the difference between right and wrong and will begin to formulate his own values based upon what we are transmitting to him.

Boundaries

My good friend Caroline Huang, who has a master's degree in education from Harvard, in this January's Root Education Magazine, talks about "How to Formulate Family Rules to Cultivate the Character of Self-Control" mentioned three factors: 1. Family Rules are larger principles for the purpose of building character, teaching them how to be mature people, and is different from other rules that are aimed at cultivating daily living habits. 2. Family Rules must be built on the foundation of agreement between husband and wife.3. Family Rules must be written down into words. Those parents interested in formulating Family Rules for their children can consult "Lin Family Rules" (attached in appendix).

After putting in place Family Rules, you can set some short term goals for immediate living habits such as get up without being awakened by adults by 9am, finish homework before TV, or no snacks 60 minutes before a meal, etc. These "habit goals" can be built and reinforced with rewards.

Rewards

We will never buy a toy for our child because he just passed by, saw it, and wanted it, because every desire can be an opportunity to help our child learn delayed gratification. In "Rossana Teaches Children Etiquette", I suggested building a new habit every week, and gave a chart of age appropriate suggestions at the end of each chapter to help parents build concrete goals.

Charts are very useful tools. Every child likes stickers, and loves to use tangible behavior to obtain beautiful stickers that they choose, and to accumulate X number of stickers to exchange for a larger reward. This is very visual for them. This larger reward can begin with something tangible such as a small toy, book, stationary, sticker, etc. It can also be a privilege, such as inviting a friend for a sleepover, or a trip to the museum with parents. Slowly, the reward becomes verbal affirmation from parents, until a positive character is itself the reward, because it begins to benefit the child himself and others around him.

Our house had a cup, which is empty when we begin building a habit. When our children see something they want, we will put our heads together to think of a new habit or goal that we want to set up to challenge ourselves. For example, to get up and brush teeth and make bed every morning without being reminded by Mom. Every time he succeeds, we will put a marble in the cup. When our child watches the cup becoming full day by day because of what he did to fill it, there is a very visual reminder: I am reaching my goals! When the cup is finally full (we consider 30 marbles to be full), our child can then open his designated gift. Every time our children open their gifts, it is always such a happy moment, because this gift was earned by his own effort and perseverance, and is something he paid a personal price for. They will usually value these items way more than if they were just given them freely.

Timers are also great tools. Agree with your child that if he can complete a task after X minutes, you he can then do or get something. When your child is watching the timer wind down, he is given a fun and visual reminder of how much time is left to complete the task. In our home, timers have helped us to avoid many unnecessary arguments and anxiety. Children naturally like to please their parents. Timers are their helpers.

Logical Consequences

Logical consequences result from an action. For example, if your child won't eat his lunch, he will need to go hungry until the next meal. If we cave in because our child cries for a snack before the next meal because of his hungry, we have deprived him of an opportunity to experience a logical consequence, and are therefore helping him to build a bad habit. In addition, he has learned to use tears to manipulate his parents.

Logical consequences needs to have a price and needs to be painful. Usually after a child experiences a logical consequence, there will be negative emotions or even tears, but parents must remember, this is a consequence that the child has chosen with eyes wide open. As a result, he must understand that this pain is his own choice and must be his to bear, not because parents for no reason want to torture their child. He needs to understand that if he wants to avoid future pain or experience certain joys or rewards, the right to exercise that choice rests in his own hands, not his parents.

Every child has a different point of pain. We need to understand our child's love language and pain points. For example, one of Caleb's love languages is physical touch, so corporal punishment is very painful for him. On the other hand, it is not one of Jonathan's love languages, so spanking produces no effect. His pain point is in his hatred of boredom, so a time out would be a much more effective pain point than spanking.

Spanking

We have a wooden spoon in our home that is designated for the purpose of spanking. We don't' use hands because parts of our body are used to express love, not inflict pain. Our children all know the purpose for the wooden spoon and what specific actions or words will invite it out. Rules are set ahead of time, so when the wooden spoon comes out, they are not surprised. Please remember that spanking can never be administered in the heat of anger, and parents must be fully in control of their emotions to administer it. If parents are unable to control their emotions, I am completely against spanking, because parents lack self-control. Please also remember that the basis for spanking is love and must also end with a hug or a kiss to reassure our children of our love for them. As we process with our children, we help them to understand that the wooden spoon is to chase away bad behavior, but we love them. We ask them which particular action brought the wooden spoon out, and ask them how we can avoid bringing out the wooden spoon next time. After that, we comfort them and tell them that we are on their side in the fight against the common enemy of that bad behavior, tell them that we love them, and end with a hug.

Famous Taiwan economist Charles Kao said: "Without people you won't accomplish things, without talent you won't accomplish great things, without character big or small things will be bad things." No one in this world will automatically become a responsible adult with good character, but the training parents provide for their next generation in the home, can help every child to become a hero. Let us begin one family, one child at a time. Guide his thoughts to produce right action, build good habits, cultivate good character, and change his destiny!

If you are interested in more specifics on discipline, you can consult the books "The New Dare to Discipline" and "Boundaries for Kids".

For Your Growth

1. Which area do you need to improve when training your child to have more positive attitudes, speech, or habits? Do you need to be more accepting, loving, or more strict or consistent in setting and enforcing boundaries?
2. What kinds of rules or boundaries do you have in place in your home? How can it be adjusted to better reflect your child's current maturity level and needs?

3.8 MANIPULATION OR REAL LOVE?

A story that my mother used to tell me when I was small made a deep impression on me, and is still impacting me today. On that day, Mom fried up a wok of super delicious rice vermicelli. I could not control myself, and wolfed down bowl after bowl. When mother told me to stop, I kept begging her to just give me one more bowl. In order to tell me to stop, she told me that just the week before, there was a news story about a girl in the next village whose parents rushed her to the hospital because her stomach hurt really badly from eating too much rice vermicelli. Soon after she arrived in the hospital, she died before the doctors had a chance to save her. When the doctors cut her open to see what happened, they discovered that her stomach was full of thin strands of vermicelli because her stomach had exploded from too much of it. As soon as I heard the story, I immediately stopped, but this fear that gripped me continued to linger. Even now, every time I eat too much, I would remember this vermicelli story, and this inexplicable fear would arise within me. By now I know that there is no scientific basis for this "old wife's tale", but how powerful childhood lies can be!

After I gave birth and was spending the month long recovery period (called "doing a moon", a Chinese tradition), mother would not allow me to climb the stairs to fetch things. She told me yet another story. There was an old woman in a particular village in Taiwan who had to carry around her uterus everywhere she went as she was farming because she didn't recover well and because she didn't listen to others and instead of resting was climbing stairs. This is why her uterus kept descending until it fell out and she had to carry it around. I had to laugh out loud then. I didn't want to argue with mother, who insisted up and down that this is a true story, and if I won't heed her caution I proceed at my own risk. Obviously, by this time in my life, my medical knowledge had surpassed hers (even though mother was very smart, she could not go to college because of the war), I also saw that she was using this "method" for my own good, and she was also used to using these "kind lies" to make me listen to her. However, she did not realize that I still cannot shake the shadows cast by these "kind lies" even well into adulthood.

During mother's time, she was a well acknowledged "master" of parenting, because all three of her daughters were super obedient. She was always calmly reasoning with us and talking sense into us. These days, mother is using these same "methods" to teach my kids. Last time my son went back to visit her, he wanted to message her by pounding on her back. She told him some stories about how a boy shattered all the bones in his hand from messaging his parents too much. After Stephen came home, he was full of fear. Mother also called us to reprimand us for making our kids give us message, because this will impeded their bones from growing. I understand that she doesn't want the kids to work too hard, and thanked her for her reminder. However, after I encouraged Stephen to go online to investigate the reliability of such a thing happening, he realized that correct posture will not hurt the growth of his bones, and there was no possibility of a healthy boy shattering all his bones from messaging others.

This morning a friend called me to ask for advice on her child, for fear that the situation would worsen. The whole summer, he was cared for by his grandparents. They have a lot of worries and fears, warning him not to do this and touch that. Her son seems to be more obedient now. The grandparents didn't need to get upset to get him to listen, but rather reasoned with him. Not long ago, to train the child to be more independent, the whole family decided to enroll him in a summer camp that involved 10 days of overnight stay. They also discussed with their son and gained his agreement, but from the first day he arrived, he called home daily to cry loudly, complain, threaten, and beg to come home because he wasn't used to it. When the parents asked him to persevere, he would be shamelessly angry, demanding, and disobedient. Towards the end, in order to complete the last few days of training, they had no choice but to send the grandparents to go to camp to stay with him, where they were with him every moment of the day. Ever since their son returned from camp, he became a totally different person, becoming distrustful, suicidal, and unable to be cheerful. It was supposed to be a happy experience, how did it turn out like that? Why is it that other kids had no trouble adjusting, but her son would be hurt so badly? I know this family. The parents invest a lot of energy into educating their son, and always treat him lovingly. When I heard about this incident, I remembered my mother's "kind lies", and her various "tricks". I also remembered my own turning point in this area.

Once, when my son wanted me to buy him something, I refused. He began to get mad and used words that made me feel guilty to manipulate me to make me want to give in out of guilt. He told me that I've been spending too much time taking care of his little brother and didn't give him enough time. Therefore he couldn't feel my love. I clearly felt that these words were said to manipulate me, so I told him: "1. We had not budgeted for this item because it is a want, not a need. 2. I am not responsible for his feelings. He needs to take responsibility to manage his own feelings. 3. I apologize for not spending enough time with him the past week. I will definitely adjust my schedule next week to make sure that I make enough time just to be with him." The answer I gave him woke me up. I made the decision that I will refuse to use these types of emotional manipulation to get my children to listen to me: "Mom, sometimes when you want me to obey you, you also tell me certain things to make me feel bad. So I am saying these things to you to get what I want, too!"

So these tricks that we learn from the previous generation are actually a form of manipulation using negative emotions, not using logical thinking to allow children to experience the consequences of their own choices, training them to think for themselves and internalize their own values. Therefore, although near miraculous results are immediately apparent, proving that we are "parenting masters" what we transmit to our children are not proactive internal motivations, but rather hearts that are worried and fearful of everything. Kids are robbed of the courage to face new challenges or to get up again after they fall. All the more worrisome is that as they grow up, they begin to use the same "tricks" on us to make us "obedient". This kid who went to summer school successfully use his "trick" to make his grandparents listen to him, to stay with him in summer camp.

If we use fear, worry, negative emotions or guilt to teach and manipulate our kids, always under the cover of "safety", our kids will also use the same "tricks" to train us. If we use emotions to force our kids to do things we want them to do, they will also use emotions to force us to do things they want us to do in the future. In this way, both sides will learn to observe how the other is feeling at particular points in time to use more and more dramatic and charged emotions to force the other. This phenomenon is called "enmeshment" in English, ultimately leading to co-dependence between the two generations where the next generation is unable to grow independently or bond with peers and future mate in a healthy way. When he begins building his own family, he will be unable to understand, build, or maintain clear and healthy boundaries. From a psychological standpoint, the me in an enmeshed relationship makes you responsible for my happiness because you want to control me and make me obey you. Therefore, I do not need to take responsibility for my own happiness and give the right and responsibility for my happiness to you, making you to blame when I am unhappy. From the outside, it looks perfect and loving, but people co-existing in an enmeshed relationship live with more and more pain, because they are in bondage to "love". I will mention two examples here.

1. Several parents came to me in despair asking for help with all kinds of problems of their middle school children. Because school admission pressure was too great, parents gave their children too much pressure to study during elementary school. They usually use their negative emotions (such as anxiety, anger, or tears) to make the children feel that their lack of performance was the cause of such emotions. By the time these kids are in middle school, because they neither got any sense of accomplishment from their mediocre studies nor received any affirmation of any abilities to give them confidence, they despised studying, lost any internal motivation, and therefore gave up on themselves, refused to go to school, staying at home all day. If parents asked their kids to go to school, they would blow up in a rage and threaten suicide. As a result, the parents dare not bring up any more requests of their children. These children will have stayed home fore several years, reading comics, watching TV, playing computer games, and refusing to do any housework or contribute to the family in any way. These parents have become enslaved to their children's threats of suicide.

2. A college grad, because of his inability to find an ideal job, has stayed home for several years, waiting for his parents to find him a job and a spouse. When friends and family around him ask why he doesn't go make plans for his own future, his response is: "Whatever jobs I get they will feel that it's too hard for me, whatever friend I get introduced to they feel is not good enough. I

can't decide, so I'll just let them decide. Whatever they feel is good enough for me I will follow and my life will be OK. In the end they always call the shots anyways. It makes no difference what I say or do." I have also seen friends of family in North America like this who are single, jobless, in their 40s and still living with their parents. Every time the parents want to force these children to go out to find a job or friends, they will use emotional language to place all the blame on their parents for being overly controlling and forceful before, making the parents feel guilty and helpless. Both parents and children live in increasing despair, not knowing when this entanglement and mutual torture and guilt will end.

On the other hand, working hard to build reasonable boundaries feels very cold at first, even cruel, but every person is then able to take up responsibility for his or her own life, happiness, feelings, and wrong decisions, bearing their own consequences. Through learning from their own mistakes and falls, they are able to grow and improve. Only then will they regain the right to proactively extend unconditional love and grace to others, allowing both sides to finally be free. The West is a society that is ruled by law, which can feel at times cold and inhuman. For example, when parents would tell their children that after they are 18, they will leave the home and live independently because they will be adults responsible for their own livelihood. Parents will no longer be obligated to provide for their needs after this. This kind of talk is a real turn off for Chinese parents, feeling so cold and unloving. However, this is a manifestation of the Western family system which is based upon rules and related consequences, which is a kind of a mini-society that is ruled by law. Even though it feels uncompassionate, it is very objective and bypasses future enmeshment. I also believe that in a loving Western family, if the adult children need help from their parents, they will get it, but parents will set the right expectation to build healthy boundaries so that it does not create a lifetime of dependence and enmeshment. Eastern society emphasizes rule of man (such as owing a debt of gratitude), feels more "humane", but easily falls into an entanglement without personal boundaries, where children have no way to mature and leave their parents, no permission to build personal boundaries, and no ability to bear responsibility for himself and others. These kinds of enmeshment often begin with "kind lies" in childhood. May parents be careful to monitor the way in which they teach and reason with their children, not letting their own love to descend into mutual bondage, and try their best to be constrained by honest and objective pre-set rules and consequences to set one another free, to allow all three generations to have freedom to grow and mature.

To promote the rule of law in the home instead of the rule of emotions, you can consult Lin Family Rules as an example.

For Your Growth

1. Growing up, do you obey your parents because of their moods or because of well established rules within the home? How are you continuing the pattern set in your home?
2. Reflect on your interaction with your child this past week. How much of his poor behavior has been corrected by you through your display of anger, sadness, or displeasure? How much is by administering consequences related to previously agreed upon rules?
3. How can you remind yourself to stick more closely to rules?
4. How can you get help to keep you accountable to manage your emotions before you discipline your child for bad behavior?

3.9 THE TRUE MEANING OF HAPPINESS

Every time I teach parenting with my husband, we would always ask the parents present what kind of a child they want to raise? Most parents will say they just want a happy and healthy child. One Weibo fan said this: "We want him to achieve this realm where his happiness is not dependent on things, he is not sad because of himself, but he can maintain a happy heart, healthy and happy!"

Happiness is something that the whole world is pursuing, yet is the hardest thing to get a hold of. The U.S. even wrote the pursuit of happiness into their constitution! Having lived all over the world, my personal experience and observation is, the more you make the pursuit of happiness your motivation for living, the more difficult is it to capture true happiness. However, it is actually much easier for those that don't deliberately pursue happiness to capture or attain happiness. You can say that happiness is a byproduct in life, and not the main thing.

No parent in the world does not want his child to be happy. The question is, if a child does not pay a price himself to earn his happiness, but obtains it easily and freely, his happiness is only shallow and short lived. Only when he expends sweat and effort in exchange, will he treasure his happiness.

Ever since our kids were 7-8 years old, we have taught them to manage their money. They have many years of experience in work, saving, and giving. One Christmas, Caleb finally reached a big goal.

My husband David spent a big part of his first paycheck after graduation purchasing a leather bomber jacket which was in vogue when the movie "Top Gun" was all the rage. The leading character was a pilot, and my husband had dreamed for years to be a pilot but never had a chance to realize his dream, so he bought a bomber jacket instead to remind himself. When Caleb was in high school, David gave this jacket to him because it was still in good shape. A year later, as the zipper was starting to break, Caleb had an idea: to earn his own money to buy his own leather jacket that was good enough in quality for him to pass down to his own son some day. After he looked through several stores, he realized that he needed to spend a lot of time and energy to earn and save up for this. The high price didn't discourage him, but gave him inspiration to increase his income. He posted flyers all over our neighborhood to advertise that he can tutor both Chinese and English, and can teach any tough subject. Because he loves kids and is a good teacher, his tutoring business kept getting more customers, to the point where he needed to recruit friends to help handle the requests. However, his friends weren't interested – if they weren't concerned that it would interfere with their studies, they weren't interested in earning money because their families were already wealthy enough to provide everything they wanted. During Christmas, Chinese New Year, and birthdays, when the grandparents and aunties would ask them what they wanted, Caleb would always suggest some lower priced items so as not to be a financial burden, but he never mentioned the leather jacket.

Caleb saved up for two years, until this Christmas. After he finished buying all our gifts, he discovered that he was still 1-200 yuan away from being able to buy his jacket. David and I asked to pitch in this last little bit, and he finally went to the store to pay for the jacket. After bringing it home, he had us wrap it up and put it under the tree until he can open it up two weeks later. When he finally put on his leather jacket, he told us that no words can describe his happiness and sense of satisfaction inside. He told us that he will treasure this jacket for life, because he spent so much time, effort, and sweat in exchange for it. He will take good care of it, until he can give it to his high school son some day.

In my book "The Competitive Edge of the Next Generation", I discussed the close relationship between the cultivation of self-control and leadership. Self-control begins with delayed gratification. When a child can say NO to something he sees in front of him for a greater YES farther in the future, he is increasing his AQ little by little. When he finally obtains that distant goal, his happiness will far surpass the small temporary happiness that he sacrificed to get there. This happiness will be enjoyed longer and deeper. However, this goal needs to be chosen and set by our child himself. As parents, we can only help him to find opportunities to delay his gratification to help him to cultivate the delaying of gratification as a habit. This way, no matter if it's his studies or waiting for his life partner, he will be able to resist the easy temptation right in front of him in order to wait for the best, insisting on refusing to use short term substitutes to bring some temporary happiness and losing long term satisfaction as a result.

Caleb is 17 now, and is still waiting to give his first kiss to his future wife at the wedding altar.

For Your Growth

1. How good is your child's capacity to delay gratification? Does he generally feel grateful for his life, or a sense of lack?
2. In what ways can you help him to feel a greater sense of gratitude about life? Do you need to give in more to his desires or find new ways to help him delay gratifying his current desires? How will you go about doing that this week?

3.10 THE JOY OF CHORES

It was the first summer back in North America after we moved to China. We were spending some time visiting my parents and sister in Vancouver. Our kids were used to spending time with their grandparents in their big house on the summers and during vacations, and took no time at all to settle in. Not long after we arrived, my sister came to talk to me, and was quite upset. "The boys used to help their grandma clean up, and always put away their dishes after they finished eating or drinking something, but now, they leave cups all over the house, some half drunk, some totally empty, and don't seem to be aware of anyone else's needs anymore. One year in China has turned them into self-centered spoiled boys! They are going to become people that are not welcomed by others, and how will they be able to attract nice girls when they start looking for a wife?"

This was a wake-up call for me. Living in the U.S., we were used to doing all the household chores ourselves because the cost of hiring a maid was prohibitive. However, after arriving in China, we were able to hire a helper to help us take care of the household chores. However, we had unwittingly robbed our children of an opportunity to develop their characters of responsibility and faithfulness!

One of the ten core values of our family is responsibility. My husband and I have grown up working to earn our spending money and contribute to our own education expenses. We believe in the value of hard work and being responsible to ourselves, our families, and our society.

Household chores is a critical tool for teaching responsibility in the home. No one is born naturally responsible, but every person, no matter his level of intelligence or ability, can learn to be responsible, but this requires training. In the workplace, only a responsible worker can be trusted with more responsibility, and only the worker with proven track record of being trustworthy with a task or project entrusted to him has any hope of advancing further in his career. No matter how intelligent or capable someone is, if this person cannot be counted on to carry the weight that is placed upon him and complete his work by the required time, he will not be valued as a contributing member of a team. The twin virtue of responsibility is faithfulness, another one of our family core values. Without the character to remain faithful to commitments that we make, we will never be able to complete our responsibilities. There is no area as helpful to training as assigned chores, because the successful completion of chores do not require high IQ or abilities, but on the trained characters of faithfulness and responsibility. Everyone in our family has chores that we are responsible for, no exceptions. This way, we parents can lead by example. We negotiated for an arrangement with our ayi to leave some chores for us to do.

In our home, our ayi leaves before dinner. We do all the cleaning up together afterwards, putting away the leftover food, packing lunch for the next day, and washing the dishes. The kids took turns washing the dishes until we got our pet dog. Then they negotiated among themselves so that one child does the dishes, one walks the dog, and one feeds the dog. Each is responsible for cleaning his own room and organizing his own belongings. On weekends, our ayi does not work, so we do our own cooking and cleaning. Saturday morning breakfast cooking sessions, led by my husband, has become a much anticipated family tradition, where I sit back and relax while the boys in the house cook a hearty breakfast. We often host marriage study groups in our house or guests visiting for dinner. After our guests and their children leave, we enjoy cleaning the house together, washing up, and mopping the floor. Housework not only transmits to the children our family values but has really knit our hearts together as we serve one another and other visiting guests together. Day after day, year after year, the faithful completion of chores successfully cultivates the valuable character of faithfulness that only time can carve. That's something that no maid or PhD tutor can help with, and no money can buy.

The movie that most illustrates this point is the movie "The Karate Kid". In the movie, Danny, who goes to Mr. Miage to learn Karate to defend himself against school bullies, is asked by this ordinary looking person to take the whole weekend to paint his fence using the "Up and Down" motion, and then sent home. Then the following week he is asked to put the wax on the car using the "Wax on, Wax off" motion. When we begin to think that Mr. Miage is only using Danny as free labor, Danny begins to get mad at spending all this time not learning Karate, but in chores. However, in a few short strokes, Mr. Miage demonstrates that Danny has already mastered the basics of the Karate movement through painting and waxing. This reminds me of the stories of the old days when Shaolin apprentices have to fetch water for 10 years before they are allowed to learn Kung Fu. What was the point? First, those who don't trust the instructions of the master, or won't obey his instructions, will get tired, discouraged, or will quit. They won't be able to see the point up front, and demand complete understanding before complying. However, some knowledge can only be internalized after being experienced, not memorized or read from a book. Those who learn to be faithful will earn the right to be entrusted with "trade secrets" of the master with less likelihood of betraying their master. Second, even though the mindless repetitions seem pointless and a waste of time, it is actually cultivating in the apprentice the virtues of faithfulness, patience, and endurance. Those motions that are repeated over and over again enable the apprentice to master the real motions behind real Kung Fu by developing muscle memory, so that when it's time for Danny to react, his movements are automatic and unconscious. This kind of muscle memory comes with practicing piano, figure skating, basketball, or any other physical activity.

In the second chapter of the best-selling book "Outliers", author Malcolm Gladwell talks about the "Rule of 10,000":

"The idea that excellence at performing a complex task requires a critical minimum level of practice surfaces again and again in studies of expertise. In fact, researchers have settled on what they believe is the magic number for true expertise: ten thousand hours. "The emerging picture from such studies is that ten thousand hours of practice is required to achieve the level of mastery associated with being a world-class expert—in anything," writes the neurologist Daniel Levitin. "In study after study, of composers, basketball players, fiction writers, ice skaters, concert pianists, chess players, master criminals, and what have you, this number comes up again and again. Of course, this doesn't address why some people get more out of their practice sessions than others do. But no one has yet found a case in which true world-class expertise was accomplished in less time. It seems that it takes the brain this long to assimilate all that it needs to know to achieve true mastery.""

Lately there is an increasing tendency among young parents to encourage their children with lavish and indiscriminate praise. A lot of this is in reaction to their own upbringing of seldom being praised or affirmed of their talents. However, this kind of indiscriminate praise, or praise for the wrong characteristics, will cultivate either a sense of entitlement (whatever I do, you have to admire, to praise, and to reward, because I'm different from everyone else!), or of false sense of superiority (I'm just naturally very smart, so I don't have to work hard to earn awards or be first because I was already born with the superior genes of being smart, having good music sense, being athletic, etc. etc. etc.) It's true that we are all born with all these innate talents and potential. It's also true that without hard work, or the accumulation of those 10000 hours, even Mozart, as mentioned in the book "Outliers", will just be a mediocre kid with a good music sense.

Caleb is taking his gap year at home right now and tutoring many neighborhood kids to save up money for the future. He teaches a number of kids in math. To his surprise, he discovered that most of his students are very smart, and know that they are smart, but just have not learned good study habits. We had some interesting talks about the importance of rote learning and repetition that Western schools don't like to talk about, but is absolutely critical to master a subject. I speculated to him that of all the subjects, math probably ranks the lowest in terms of need for rote learning, and he told me that what he's doing in tutoring is mostly teaching good homework and test taking habits such as previewing material, doing the homework with the proper formats, and reviewing material. Often the mistakes such as incorrect units (i.e. km instead of m or cm) or forgetting to answer a word problem properly are mistakes of carelessness that can be eliminated by cultivating good question answering habits. Skipping steps and not showing teacher the work, not memorizing certain critical formulas, or lining up numbers improperly also belong to this category. I asked him how he gained those skills, since he also went to international school, and he said that all of his valuable skills related to math were from local Chinese school. Even though he hated the teachers at the time, it was drilled into him repeatedly through tests and points deducted to go through the necessary steps, write his answers a certain way, and to check on units. Those habits became unconscious, and when he got to international school, he pulled ahead of everyone else because he learned and did his math problems with the proper habits while others were still struggling with careless mistakes. As a result, he was able to learn and master even tougher problems and get to a higher level of mastery on the subject of math. Even in math, repetitions and developing a discipline in approaching and solving problems plays an important role. Just raw intelligence is not enough. Even though the understanding of what makes a master includes key ingredients such as desire, passion, and natural talent, just as key are the ingredients of persistence, faithfulness, repetition, mastery of the subject matter, and the Rule of 10000.

This is the reason that in our home, our children receive no reward for their talent, ability, or intelligence, but are praised for their diligence, hard work, persistence, faithfulness, and responsibility. It's only when children have these characters trained in them that they are able to fully utilize their innate talents.

While we may not set out to cultivate our children to become future master, preserving some household chores for them gives them a valuable edge in character training. A faithful and responsible adult will be trusted with important projects or company secrets any day over a smart and cunning man who is not able to honor his commitments or complete his assignment on time.

The following summer, we returned to my parents' house in Vancouver, and my mother had nothing but praises for her diligent little helpers, who helped her to walk her dog, weed the large backyard, plant a yard full of tulips, trim away rotting leaves from her indoor plants, polish the crystal glasses, load the dishwasher, and learn to cook Taiwanese snacks.

For Your Growth

1. Is your child taking care of his own responsibilities such as washing, cleaning, dressing, and changing himself, cleaning his own room, organizing his own things, time, and completing his own home work?
2. What kinds of chores are your children performing in your home? How can you adjust the allocation of your time so that you can use the chores more fully to teach your children responsibility and faithfulness?

3.11 BECOME A PIPE OR A BUCKET?

We are living in a time of incredible abundance of resources in knowledge, as parents are willing to pay astronomical amounts of money for their children's education. However, does that mean that this generation of kids will be more accomplished? Not necessarily.

I've heard from a safety expert that if someone did not use the safety knowledge that he learned within 30 days of learning it, it will be forgotten. Learning a language is similar. Even though you get 100% on your grammar test, if you don't use the language, you are likely to forget it after a year or two.

Grand master Zhu Xizeng used this simple two line poem to express what he gets from reading: "Fresh water comes from a living source". Knowledge is like living water. Only when it is constantly being used will it continue to flow. Smart learners will often use what they learn to help and nourish others. Not only that, the more living water flows, the greater the volume and the fresher the water. In the same way, in the process of helping others, the learner is continually improving himself. If knowledge is only used to adorn oneself or pad one's resume or college application form, it becomes a pool of dead water. No matter how great the pool, there is no flow or movement or sharing. In time, it begins to stink. This kind of a person criticizes others easily, but is of no use to others.

Several years ago, our whole family went to teach English in Gansu. One day, both David and I were sick and unable to get out of bed. Caleb stepped forward to help us teach. In the process, he discovered that he liked teaching and was quite good at it. We began to teach him how to teach and speak. After we returned to Beijing, he began to tutor others for spending money, and also earned the praise and admiration of other parents and kids around him.

Lin Family Band needed a drummer in order to lead worship at church. Jonathan got on YouTube to learn to play to fill in a need. For the introverted Jonathan, this was a huge challenge because he had to overcome his shyness and stage fright week after week even after he played badly. Now he is one of the best drummers in the city amongst high schoolers. When we or other friends have a need, he always gladly offers his help or teach others to play.

I deeply believe that these skills will stay with Caleb and Jonathan for life, not just because they are interested in them, but also because they are using them to help others. In my view, the best starting point to motivate our kids to learn something proactively is to serve others together. In the process of serving, they themselves will grow the most.

No parents want to cultivate their kids to be beautiful vases that are empty on the outside but are of no practical use on display on the shelf. If we hope that our kids will serve others in the future, let's put their knowledge and skills to use as "living water", and go serve the world together.

For Your Growth
1. How do you cultivate the ability to serve others in yourself and your kids?
2. How do you serve others together as a family? Begin today.

3.12 SERVING AND EMPOWERING TO SERVE

The famous philanthropist Bill Gates grew up watching his parents serve in the community, especially his mother, Mary Gates, serving on the board for the United Way, a community charitable organization. It was therefore not surprising when he announced that he was setting up the Bill & Melinda Gates foundation as an extension of that lifestyle of serving and giving back to the community. Instead of serving being a once a year or occasional activity that is engaged in to ease the conscience, to fulfill an obligation, or to list on one's resume or college application, it should be a way of living, and a mother plays a major role in cultivating that lifestyle in the family.

It was that lifestyle of giving and serving that attracted my husband and I to each other and provided a common interest in our marriage. After we started having children, it was a matter of figuring out a way to extend that lifestyle to include our children. When our children were just born, and we were not as mobile as we used to be, we would host a constant stream of visitors in our home, or I would host a group of first time mothers in my home where we could support one another in our decisions take a break from our careers to stay at home with out children. As soon as our children were old enough (when they were 2 and 4 years old), we began to take them down to Mexico over long 3 or 4 day weekends to stay in orphanages. We lived among the children, read to them, played with them, and my husband would repair their broken bikes and toys while I cooked with my children for the other orphans so that the orphanage staff can take a break from their work to rest. Since I loved to clean and organize, it was always a joy to give the kitchens a much needed cleaning alongside my children. In the process of organizing the kitchen, I would also come up with an inventory of things they needed to run the kitchen more efficiently, and this gave me an opportunity to extend our family's involvement after we returned home. I would share this list of needed items with my friends and their children and we would set about gathering these items to send down as a care package for the orphanage. It was in Mexico that our whole family fell in love with Mexican food, a love which has continued to this day. Where we lived, we made regular visits to serve food at Soup kitchens for the homeless and volunteered to help others in the community who needed food or clothing. My husband learned to coach soccer and baseball to serve the community needs for coaches. We tried to model a lifestyle of serving where we were constantly asking ourselves the question: "Where and how can I contribute?" No one was exempt because of his age or lack of "qualification". All that was needed was a teachable attitude and a willingness to humbly identify with those we served instead of being patronizing or acting superior.

A teachable attitude is a critical component of a lifestyle of serving. I remember that we once ran into someone begging for money for food in the street as we were rushing to attend a sporting event. We don't like to give money, because many of the poor people in the streets who beg for money end up buying drugs or alcohol with that money rather than food. However, we didn't have the time to take this man to a MacDonalds to buy him lunch, so we had to refuse the request. Our children felt really bad about it afterwards because we had told them that sometimes these people needing help might be angels in disguise, waiting to shower us with blessings of joy. We returned to our house later and determined to learn from that lesson. The following Saturday, we made a basket full of sandwiches and went looking for people who were begging for money to buy food, and found some. Our basket was soon empty and our hearts full. From then on, we made sure that we had a ready supply of MacDonald's gift certificates to give to people who were hungry. Being teachable to learn from our mistakes, experiences, and even missed opportunities, enable us to find new and creative ways to serve together as a family. As a result, we were constantly finding new ways to serve together. After we arrived in Beijing, we were excited at the many opportunities we had at our doorsteps to serve others together, and made it a regular part of our lifestyle here.

Serving others can take many forms, but the starting point is usually with a lifestyle of hospitality. By hosting a constant stream of guests and visitors, we are always getting to know new people from an interesting array of backgrounds, nationalities, economic and educational classes. We could always find some common interest to identify with, and all of us have become adept at laying aside our personal prejudices and assumptions about people who are different from us to find ways to meet on common ground. A posture of learning and humility helps us to ask questions with the assumption that there is always something valuable each person can teach us, from a seasoned career diplomat to a farmer well acquainted with reading the weather conditions. This skill helps us when we are serving others who are less fortunate than we are because we also need to lay aside our personal prejudices and assumptions about who and where they are and adopt a posture of learning something valuable from each person as we serve him/her.

I would like to end with a tribute to my own mother, who lived a life of serving others without fanfare or expectation of return, always downplaying her role and seeking to upkeep the dignity of those she served. Her example has inspired me to live up to her legacy. The example I will always remember started when I was a small girl living at home in Taiwan. One day a new nanny came to live with us in our new house in Taiwan. She was much older than the other nannies we had, and brought some of her children to live with her. She was an unusual nanny in that she was well educated and knowledgeable about many things. Not only was she a great cook and housekeeper, but she was very good at telling us good stories and answering our many questions about the world. Her children were also hard workers and good students, and treated us like their little sisters. When I asked her about her husband, she told me that her husband was in jail and that they were saving up money so that when her husband came out of jail they can be together again. One day, a lady came banging on our door, demanding to see my nanny. Not only was she mean and angry, but her mouth spouted obscenities and nonsense aimed to degrade and hurt. My mother told her that my nanny not available and told her to go away. This lady was very loud and persistent, and started scolding my mother, too. She said that my nanny owed her a lot of money, and was angry at my mother for protecting her. In her anger, she accused my mother of plotting with my nanny to swindle her of her money, and threatened to bring in the police. My mother stood her ground and would not open the door to allow her to talk to my nanny, who was huddled upstairs with her frightened kids, a worried frown covering her usually kindly face. I was really upset by the whole thing, and demanded that my mother go out to explain to the woman that someone as nice as my nanny would never borrow anyone's money without paying it back. And there must be some mistake, because my family is rich enough that we would not need to cheat anyone of their money, especially when we lived in a big house where we can easily be found. Mother told me and my sisters to stay quiet, and she stayed outside of our front door talking to this angry lady the whole morning in a calm yet firm manner until she finally left. By this time, my nanny was packed with her belongings and told my mother that she felt so bad for bringing trouble upon our whole family, especially when we've been so kind to her and her family. The right thing to do was for her to leave and not bring further trouble to our family, especially now that people know where she was hiding. My mother insisted on her staying on, and patiently explained to her how we couldn't live without the excellent service she was providing to our household. We kids, not knowing what exactly was going on, begged her to stay, because we have all grown really attached to her and her two daughters, who are like elder sisters to us. Afterwards, for a period of time mother would face down a few more angry visitors, some of whom threatened physical harm to our nanny, her kids, or us. Mother alerted our driver to keep a close watch on our home and property to be sure that no one maliciously set out to do damage. At the time, I didn't think much of it, and only thought that bad people were after our nanny. I was puzzled at why there would be such stupid people who wanted to harass us. It wasn't until one time after a particularly nasty man left our house that I demanded my mother to give me a more detailed explanation in order to try to understand the motivations of these people. It was then that I found out that my nanny's husband had actually been a business partner of my father, and had borrowed large amounts of money from many personal friends, including my father, to open a chemical factory that went out of business. He made some deals, signed some contracts, and made some promises that he was not able to honor. As a result, he was sued and sentenced to 7 years in jail. My mother told me that he was a good man who got in too deep over his head, and invested too quickly and ambitiously in trying to make a quick fortune. A really smart and calculating man would have set aside some reserves for his own family, but he put in everything he owned into his business. My Dad also invested a large sum of money that was completely lost when the business failed. However, because he had other investments, we were able to continue with our lives. My nanny and her children were not so lucky. Not only did they lose everything, but they were hounded and verbally abused by many bitter and angry investors, some of whom were former friends, who were convinced that she was hiding away money somewhere. It was even more difficult for her to prove her innocence because they had lived very lavishly before their bankruptcy. She and her kids had nowhere to live and no means to survive. My nanny had not worked since marrying, and had no skills to earn money to support her 4 children, all of whom needed tuition money. Her eldest was in the middle of medical school, which required a large amount of tuition, and she had no way of paying even a small part of it. That was when my mother stepped in and decided that this lady would become our nanny in exchange for tuition and expenses for the kids. She considered it a fair trade because her two daughters were excellent students and would be excellent role models for us girls. There was no talk of debts owed to us, because she and the children were not the ones who incurred the debt, and should not be punished for foolish decisions made by the husband. I don't recall how many more years the nanny and her daughters continued to live with us, but I recalled that both of her daughters graduated high school and went on to college, moving out of our home one by one. Our nanny and her husband reunited after he finished serving his jail sentence, and they travel to various parts of the world, visiting their children and their families. All of her children are now very successful in their careers and families, and have continued to remain close family friends.

Mother Teresa said: "Preach the Good News at all times. Use words only when necessary." My own mother never sat down to teach us about serving others, and said very little about the need to serve others. She merely lived out this message in front of us. Her life is more powerful than any lecture or teaching on the subject. May we teach our own children what it's like to serve others by boldly and transparently living our lives before them.

For Your Growth

1. Sit down with your spouse to ask each other about your parenting styles. What is one thing that you can change to make your behavior more consistent with your talk?

3.13 AWKWARD SILENCE

During our walk on the icy streets of Beijing, my son says his friend XXX asked when we are inviting him to our home for dinner again. I curiously asked him if this is because he ate something yummy last time he came over and wanted me to cook it again? As I was mulling how to get more of these yummy dishes into his lunchbox for his friends at school to try and share, he told me that anything is OK. The main thing is that his friend likes the way we were when we were all eating together. He said that it's better than watching TV. I didn't understand. He explained, saying that among his friends, most families don't joke around, chat, or have lively debates around the dinner table. Most parents would at most ask about how their studies are going, then followed by an awkward silence as the kids rushing all they can to finish eating so that they can escape this awkward silence. His friend told my son that after coming to dinner at our house, he realized that family life can be so fun, parents can like their kids, admire their viewpoints, and eating together can be such a bright spot in cementing family relationships. I told him, maybe this family is an exception, but he told me that maybe our family is the exception, because all his friends tell him that his family is different from others. This is also why when the friends are planning to socialize in the evenings or weekends and we don't allow them to go because they can't miss family dinner, my son gets looks of envy rather than disdain. His friends would tell him that if they were him, they wouldn't want to miss family dinner either.

After we got home, I began to think about what my son shared. Actually, we never plan what we will say at dinner. Sometimes we would laugh so hard that we are crying, unable to straighten up to finish our food. Some other times we are debating an issue so passionately that our faces would be red, but the one thing that is consistent about our dinner table is that if you have something to say, you'd better insert yourself quickly, otherwise someone else will beat you to it and occupy the available space with his opinion. I could never imagine any awkward silences, but lots of collisions in our efforts to say our two cents. I also thought about this news that I just read the other day, an article about a survey that "Zhixin Sister" (translates to Big sister "Know Your Heart") conducted for "Listen To Your Child Day":

October 22, 2010, during the "Listen To Your Child's Heart" activity organized by Zhixin Sister Service Organization, the results of a survey conducted among elementary and middle school children was announced. Over 200 students from schools in Beijing, Shanghai, Tianjin, Hebei, and other cities in over 10 provinces were surveyed. The results showed that only 26.72% of the children surveyed expressed that the first people they would want to confide in would be their parents. Of those, middle schools who chose their parents as confidantes take up 17.79% while elementary kids take up 34.21%, demonstrating that this ratio decreases as the age of the children increase. Also, 13.84% of the children chose to bury their confidence inside, while 5.61% of the children chose confiding in friends over the internet.

The survey shows that 38.92% of the children prefer face to face conversation as their preferred way of communicating a confidence, with diary writing (including online blogs) running second at 19.94%.

In questions regarding which areas you most want to talk with your parents about, 19.31% wanted to express opinions or suggestions to their parents, 13.48% wanted to talk about questions related to friendships, including those with the opposite sex, 11.58% wanted to discuss questions regarding their future, while 3.76% have questions regarding their health or bodies.

In surveys conducted with 107 parents, over 90% chose to listen to their children's reflections and questions regarding studies.

I was saddened when I read that most parents only want to talk to their children about their studies instead of their heart. Children are definitely not the only losers because parents will lose many opportunities to learn from their children and thus miss out on opportunities for growth in themselves. Nowadays, I feel that my children know and come into contact with many more things than me, surpassing me in many areas. In the earlier days I can barely get by in math and science, but nowadays I am relegated to sitting there with them to listen and learn, not daring to air too many opinions out of my own ignorance.

Each of my children have benefitted greatly from our dinner table. We would regularly invite guests of various backgrounds to our house for dinner. We have entertained people from CEOs and diplomats to humble teachers and farmers in rural villages of China. Each guest is fascinating, and has lots to teach us. Learning to be comfortable in interfacing with all kinds of people has given our children a natural confidence when they enter social situations that they themselves are not aware of. Here is how each of our children have benefitted:

Caleb

Being the eldest and the talker of our family, Caleb has interacted with the widest range of people at our dinner table, and is the most composed when in social situations. He benefited greatly last summer when he was working as an intern in an energy policy research company. The first week on the job, he was asked to sign in the guests to a business seminar. These guests included CEOs from national energy utilities as well as multi-national corporations and various government officials. He welcomed them with friendly confidence and was able to serve them refreshments and interact with them during the breaks. The attending guests were impressed with his ability to converse with them in both languages with comfort and ease that they thought that he was one of the full time associates working at the company. When the founder of this company heard the feedback, she increased his job scope. Instead of helping to enter data or file paper as a high school student, he was given an entire research project that other associates with graduate degreed worked on, and in the process, gained valuable work experience that changed the direction of his life.

Jonathan

At my husband's company dinner banquet one year, where employees were invited to bring their families, we sat at the same table as a few senior technology researchers with PhDs. While a kid at the next table was amusing and amazing the dinner guests at the next table with his phenomenal store of knowledge of geography, Jonathan was engaged in conversation with two of these senior researchers and asking questions about their research with deep interest. When my husband walked over to the table with two desserts and suggested that we get some, because they were so delicious, the two researchers looked over at the buffet line, and made comments about the line being too long. At that moment, Jonathan immediately got up and offered to get these desserts for everyone. These two men looked over at us and asked us: "What did you do to teach your children? We see a lot of very smart kids, but most of them are showing off about how much they know and how smart they are. We've never anyone his age who shows interest in other people, is able to ask intelligent and thoughtful questions, and then is able to be considerate enough to serve people without being asked. How do you guys teach them?" My husband and I looked at each other in puzzlement. We couldn't remember specifically instructing Jonathan what to do in specific situations. However, I do know that we have invited a number of accomplished guests over for dinner, and our kids being comfortable in engaging these friends in conversation without being intimated by their titles or accomplishments. Because the conversations took place in the comfort and safety of our own home, they were able to learn about appropriate ways to indulge their curiosity by asking questions respectfully and listening reflectively. Because Jonathan is the shy one in our home, he would ask me what he should do when he runs out of things to talk about. I suggested that since shy people talked less, they are naturally more observant, and that he should look for ways to serve people to fill in the time spent with people. Therefore while others are talking, Jonathan is usually looking for ways to serve to fill in what he feels are his "gaps of silence". When he interacted with adults outside of the home, he just continued doing what they were used to doing with guests who visit our house. What felt natural to him, when observed by strangers, seem so outstanding in contrast to what other kids were doing that evening, including talking about themselves, and burying their heads in a hand held game or a book without engaging anyone else present.

Stephen

Last week, Stephen went to play at a neighbor's house. My friend remarked that he was so friendly and outgoing, and greeted her husband when he came home from work without being prompted. Stephen introduced himself, asked this husband questions, and thanked him when he gave him some snacks. My friend's husband remarked that it was so unusual for a child his age to be comfortable to take the initiative to engage adults in friendly conversation. Again, it was the dinner table conversations that unwittingly trained our children, including 10 year old Stephen.

Family dinner is not a place where you just fill the stomach to get physical nutrition. Neither is it a place to train table manners or teach knowledge. It is a place of nourishment for the soul, body, and spirit, a place to transmit important values, and place to give life, a place to learn respect and sharing, a place to learn to resolve conflicts, and a place to express love. At the family dinner table, the entire family's hearts and spirits can be nourished and grow. It is an irreplaceable place. If your family dining table is not a place that people can't wait to get to, you will have lost a precious treasure, a secret weapon in building, deepening, and consolidating family relationships. My dream is, very quickly, that Chinese families will no longer have a need to experience or escape the awkward silence at their dinner tables.

If you are just starting out with dinner table conversation, here are some ideas of what you can talk about to get your brain moving in the right direction:

- Something interesting that happened at work or school today.
- Read some jokes together. Better still, make some of your own.
- Discuss and debate some item in the news.
- Share about a book or article one of the family members is reading.
- Discuss a movie.
- Play a word game.
- Dream about and plan your next long weekend or vacation.
- Dream about and plan a family service project.
- Invite a dinner guest overly on a regular basis to get to know him and "pick his brain". Some questions we've asked our guests include his favorite childhood games, memories, or something related to his work, hobby, or family.

For Your Growth

1. During dinner, what is the main focus of everyone's time besides eating? Besides studies or homework, what are your favorite topics of discussion at your dinner table?
2. If you feel that your family is spending too much time talking about studies, what kinds of topics do you plan to talk about instead? Some possibilities include stories of your childhood, your favorite moments in life, favorite movies, books, or stories of people at work.
3. This week, challenge yourself and your spouse to not mention school work at the dinner table.

3.14 A MOTHER'S MISSION

Traditions

"Tradition simply means that we need to end what began well and continue what is worth continuing"
-- Jose Bergamin, Spanish Writer

One of my fondest memories growing up is making zongzi (Bamboo leaf wrapped sticky rice) with my Mom and two younger sisters for Mid-Autumn Festival, and making Taiwanese sausages before Chinese New Year. We never made those items other than those special days, and these two items remain one of my favorite foods because they remind me of those special times when we would go through the familiar ritual of preparing the stuffing, making sure to use the best ingredients and spices, and then carefully helping mother stuff the zongzi or Taiwanese sausages, tying them up in bundles or sections, and hang them neatly with the right distance apart. There is something comforting about rituals that gives one a sense of security and predictability. When I first went away to college, I was so homesick that I asked my Mom to make some zongzi to send to me, all the way from Vancouver to Boston. Having those zongzi to eat helped ease my homesickness and comforted me in my initial loneliness. Family traditions serve to punctuate the regular flow of daily life with a sense of rhythm and predictable anticipation and are the building blocks of happy memories in one's childhood. To quote Susan Lieberman: "Family traditions counter alienation and confusion. They help us define who we are; they provide something steady, reliable and safe in a confusing world. "

I believe that one of the roles for mothers is to help create traditions for her home, whether it's inheriting old ones passed down from her home or creating new ones of her own. When I ask my children about their fondest memories of childhood, or what holiday they love the most, it would inevitably involve some family tradition. These traditions often begin with something we all loved doing the first time and decide to make a regular thing, and take on a life of their own, or could be as old and familiar as what all the other families do around a particular holiday. I would like to share some ideas for what has worked in our family, particularly after arriving in Beijing. Hopefully this will stimulate some creative thinking and inspiration for you to start your own family traditions. Creating your own traditions will help you to sprinkle your child's childhood with many memorable events with which to weave together memories of a happy childhood, and gives a sense of continuity to the different stages of growth in your child. When they are grown, they will long for those events and these traditions will serve as a powerful tool to draw them home when they are grown and out of your nest.

Traditions are built slowly, one event at a time. Some work wonderfully the first time and become fast favorites that are repeated regularly with glee. Others don't work so well and fade into distant memories.

One of the earliest traditions that began daily in our home is "cuddle time" each evening before bed. Now that my older two boys have become boys and become more reserved, we still have a time of conversation and prayer together before they head to bed. The content is different every day, but two elements remain a constant: thanksgiving and blessing. We always go over the day to look for at least 1 or 2 things to be thankful for, and to look for the positive side of things that might be perceived as bad. This habit, done day after day since they can understand speech, has helped them in their worldview and the way they process their circumstances, and has given them an attitude of gratitude and optimism that is rare among their peers. The second element that they cannot do without is a blessing from me or my husband. We usually bless them verbally in some way, either verbalizing our gratitude for being a part of our family, being a gift to us, or blessing them with good dreams, healings for an cold or headache, courage to sleep in the darkness, or wisdom to make a certain decision. Even when we have guests over late from dinner and cannot sit with them for prolonged periods of time to talk, they will be sure to pull us aside to get that blessing from us before going to sleep. Even when my husband is away on business trips, he will make sure to call home before bedtime to give them their blessings. Having raised three boys of very different temperaments and health conditions, none of them have ever had problems with their sleep. I believe that the act of verbalizing a blessing gives them a shield or covering over their time of sleep, and is a powerful tool in cultivating a feeling of security and contentment.

Holidays

Certain occasions lend themselves to creating family traditions, because others are celebrating those occasions in their own ways, too. It's always fun to find our own unique ways to celebrate, year after year.

While others celebrated Thanksgiving in the U.S. with eating Turkey and getting together with family, we found other ways to capture the meaning of the holiday. This is because we don't like to eat turkey and our extended family is usually far away. We usually like to have a nice dinner at home and spend an extended time counting our blessings in the past year. We would take turns around the dinner table to focus our attention on each person, starting from the youngest to the oldest. Everyone would go around and give thanks or appreciate one or more things about the person being spotlighted. After coming to China, we have forgone the elaborately cooked meals for special meals out sometimes, but the tradition of sharing our blessings remain constant.

Traditionally, the day after Thanksgiving is typically the day that the Christmas Tree can be up and decorated and the malls start advertising their Christmas sales. The tree decoration day is a special day for us. All evening we would have festive or soft Christmas music playing in the background, depending upon our mood at the time. Each year we would try to put up a new decoration to commemorate that year. For example, on the year Stephen was born, we bought a glass milk bottle ornament. Every time we hung up that ornament on the tree, we would remember Stephen's first Christmas and the joy he brought to our home that year. Another year we put up a Chinese knot that Jonathan made in his handicraft class at school to commemorate the many kinds of beautiful Chinese knot that he learned to make that year. With each new Christmas tree decoration year, we would have more and more memories to remember as we add more ornaments to the tree. From the day after Thanksgiving until we take the tree down after New Year's Day, we would often pass by the tree to look over the ornaments and reminisce.

One of the traditions that we continued from the U.S. is taking a Christmas photo and sending out an annual newsletter to our family and friends as our

Season's Greetings instead of a Christmas card. Since we had a wide circle of friends from our college friends to coworkers, neighbors, kids' friends at their school, and friends from the many circles of relationships we've developed, the Christmas newsletter and photo was a great way for us to write a general update of what everyone in our family did the past year as a way to keep in touch with our friends, many of whom we are no longer keeping in touch with on a regular basis. Often we will get a letter or card back in return, updating us on what our friends have been up to in the past year. In that way we continue to renew friendships that would otherwise have been lost.

When we first arrived in Beijing, Christmas was not a commonly celebrated holiday, and people didn't get the day off. However, since it was one of the biggest holidays of the year for our family, we were determined to create our own traditions to celebrate, Beijing style. On Christmas Day, my husband would take the day off from work and we would head out to town to explore it, acting like tourists as we look for a new place to explore. The first time we did this, we discovered a Hagendaz ice cream store, and decided to splurge on an ice cream hot pot. The experience was so novel yet so appropriate for the occasion that the ice cream hot pot has become a Lin Family Christmas tradition in Beijing.

Another favorite family tradition is serving breakfast in bed for Mommy or Daddy on Mother's Day and Father's Day. It began simply enough when my kids were small and only able to make toast with jam and cut it into the shape of a heart with the help of Daddy, decorating a tray with beautiful flowers and paper cuttings, and delivering it to Mommy's bedside with a home made card and a wake up kiss. Not to be outdone, I helped the kids cut out a heart shape from a slice of bread and cracked an egg inside to cook it for Daddy on Father's Day. As time went on, the tray decoration got more elaborate and customized by each child, and various elements were added or varied. So another tradition was birthed which allowed Mommy or Daddy to sleep in and get pampered with breakfast in bed and a message on the morning of Mother's and Father's Day.

Other China traditions are more fun and took advantage of long holidays. During the October Holidays we always went camping with other families by the Water Great Wall (where the Great Wall dips into the water). Park personnel would help us build a fire and roast a whole lamb for dinner. The kids played many fun games in the dark with light sticks and flash lights, and stayed up late by the fire to roast marshmallows, eat instant noodles, and sing. Some older kids would go down to the water and tell scary stories. The next morning, we would go hiking and exploring around the area, always discovering a new trail or encountering interesting things along the trail.

Every New Year's Day we would take a long drive to Hebei to spend 2-3 solid days to ski. Besides the beauty of the outdoors being invigorating and inspiring, we always have fun exploring new trails and learning new tricks on our skis or snowboards. The fun part is always planning the activities we would do in the evenings in the hotel room, whether it's watching a fun movie, playing board games, inventing ways to cook food over the little stove in the hotel room, messaging each other's tired legs, or plotting out the next day's trails.

When the May Holidays were still week long, we would teach English together. Now that the week-long holiday has been shortened, we will find other ways to serve, as we look for creative ways to use one of our holidays through the year to serve together, whether it's teaching English or helping out at an orphanage or migrant school.

Finally, we all agree that the word that most aptly describes our family is "adventure". Our love of travel takes us to many cities and countries. Everywhere we go, we always make sure to collect a refrigerator magnet to put on our fridge to remind us of our time there. When time or budget does not permit travel outside of the city, we would play tourist and look for new ways to discover our city. In this way we have discovered new favorite activities such as horseback riding up to the Great Wall, explored many roadside stalls and new restaurants, gone on endless hikes and bike rides around the suburbs, and visited many museum exhibits.

The possibilities to create new and treasured family traditions are endless. What are you waiting for?

Creating Moments of Beauty

One of the amazing qualities about childhood is the ability to marvel and wonder. A story that brings about amazement or laughter can be repeated a hundred times to a child and he will not get bored with it. I remember a story my nanny used to tell us when we were little girls. We would ask her to tell the same funny story every night before we went to bed. Each night she would tell the same story with the same words in the same way and it would never fail to make us laugh until we were crying. Even if we could repeat all her words and tell the story to each other, we would still ask her to tell that story to us night after night.

One of the missions of motherhood is to bring forth that sense of wonder in our children through creating those memorable moments. In our household of boys, that sense of wonder is stirred up very differently from a household of girls. However, I would like to share with you some of the ways we have created those special moments of beauty and wonder in our household through various project ideas that are very simple to do. My hope is that it will stir your own imagination to create those moments of wonder with your own child.

As a trained engineer, I grew up elevating form and function and felt that I had no use for art or anything related to beauty. Everything I did was with an emphasis on efficiency, simplicity, elegance, and minimalism. It wasn't until I became a mother that I learned to appreciate my role in bringing beauty into my home, as I began to relive everything anew through the wonder filled eyes of my children.

Starting from the time they started to bring home artwork from school, the pictures and photos that hung on our walls began to be replaced by our children's work. Each semester, my children and I would select some of their best works to be framed and put up. Some of those works went to my husband's office. The other pieces of paper were taped on the walls of various rooms for a time and then taken down and put away in each child's own "treasure box" to be stored in our garage. Our home came alive with our children's art, whether it's just colorful tracing of hands or scribbles or colored pencil drawings. We marveled at the world through their eyes, and were amazed at how beautiful our home had become.

Later, when their interest in art outgrew my ability to teach them, I hired a friend who worked in the cartoon industry, who would teach my sons various ways of drawing. Sometimes he would take them into his studio to explain to them the process of how cartoons were made. He specialized in drawing the backgrounds for each scene, and my boys were fascinated by the huge number of details that needed to be tracked, in addition to the skills needed to draw an object accurately and three dimensionally. Our home became filled with cartoon slides from the studio, comic books, and simple little cartoons that my boys made. I remember one time when their art teacher was working on the movie "Tarzan" at Disney Studios, and how excited my boys were to watch the cartoon, especially through the eyes of someone who has seen the backgrounds planned and painted by our friend. Art lessons came alive, and our elder son Caleb always had a pencil and paper with him to sketch interesting things that he would see and want to sketch. To them, art was no longer a skill to be learned, but a passion to be cultivated.

One of the first large projects that brought a long period of delight to our children was our space capsule. When our neighbor bought a refrigerator, they threw away the packing box and left it on the sidewalk for the garbage collectors. We went and asked for their permission to give us the box so that we can do a craft project with it on rainy days when we can't go outdoors. After tilting the long box sideways, it was still tall enough for our boys to sit inside. That week, my husband and I bought some picture books for our boys on space and talked to them about the space shuttle. Because my husband studied aerospace engineering in college, he was able to explain the different parts of the space shuttle, what they were used for, as well as the whole process of launching a rocket into orbit. Our boys were fascinated with the idea of flying into space and orbiting the earth, and asked me to help them paint the refrigerator box into a space capsule. It took us weeks of time to slowly paint both the outside and the inside of the box, as we took our time to think through how we wanted our space capsule to look, with all kinds of buttons, knobs, and meters inside. We even cut out little cardboard knobs and pinned them in different places on the inside top of the box above the pilot's seats, so that they can pretend to be flying it. During that whole period of time, we bought videos that talked about space flight, made puzzles of space shuttles, read books on space, and made all kinds of drawings and plans of our space shuttle before painting or making the parts to be fixed on. Sometimes we would paint something on, only to decide to put something else in its place and cover it with another piece of paper. Because it was a space capsule, we used many rolls of aluminum paper to cover various parts, and cut out holes, or "windows", to cover them with Ceran wrap to imitate the insulated windows in a space capsule. We forgot to watch television because we were so busy learning about space and putting together our space capsule. Even though our living room was cluttered with this big box and all kinds of craft items for many days, everyone looked forward to working on our space capsule together. It was even more fun after we finished it to play inside it, imagining that we were astronauts on a mission to explore unknown territories. We even made food like the MREs (Meals Ready to Eat) that the astronauts would eat in space, as we spent time inside our capsule and tried to live life like the astronauts would. To us, the space capsule project was a thing of immense beauty, as it involved all our skills and senses, and was something that brought our whole family together.

When the boys were a little older, my husband, who liked to work with tools, decided to build a play house in our backyard for our boys. What was originally a simple two week project turned into a two month long construction project over the summer as the play house became fancier and fancier. The original design was that our play house was a square board with simple wooden posts that would sit flat on the ground, but the boys suggested that we take out the vegetable patch that was high up on a platform about 1.5 meters up from the ground in the very back of our yard, so that the playhouse became a real "Tree House" that required climbing to reach up to it. The simple square frame soon gained posts with real holes that our boys can nail their toy nails into while my husband and I worked on nailing the wooden frame together. Soon, we added a drawbridge that can be lowered to the ground to let friends in and lifted up shut to keep enemies out. We added benches to the interior, and I bought some scraps of old carpet to lay on the ground. We covered the frame that was originally intended for the vines in the vegetable patch with real roofing material, and I hung rolls of bamboo matt off the sides for walls that doubled as floor to ceiling windows. At the time, our children's pre-school was renovating, and were looking to throw away their old children's furniture. My kids and I picked out some small cabinets that they were throwing away and remade them into a small refrigerator, kitchen sink, and kitchen pantry. We put the finishing touches on everything by choosing a paint color and painting everything in our Tree House that color of blue and beige. Soon we were able to put plastic dishes and toy food into our blue fridge and pantry, as well as a big collection of toy weapons in the corner. The boys proudly named their Tree House "Warrior's Hideaway", and the boys painted and hung up their sign. This Tree House became a focal point of joy and delight to my boys, as they spent endless hours staging battle scenes and living as freedom fighters, making up new scenarios with their friends and neighbors who came to join their ranks. Sometimes I would see teams of boys laying siege to their fort and advancing up the drawbridge, while other times I would see them all enjoying a meal together with their plastic hamburgers and tea sets. My occasional interruptions delivering cold milk and cookies or icy lemonade are always met with wild cheers and grateful "Wow! Thanks Mom! You're the best!" After we moved away from our house to Beijing, they reminisce about the Tree House and talked of going back to visit it during the summer if they have a chance to fly to Los Angeles. This Tree House didn't represent a construction project that my husband assembled from wood and nails purchased from the local hardware store. It represented all the beauty and wonder attached to childhood, and was a source of inspiration that was associated with the best of being a child.

During rainy days, when the boys could not go to our backyard to play in the Tree House, we would set up camp indoors. Our dining room table instantly became our "base camp" when we draped a bedsheet over it. Our couches became forts when they were turned upside down and blankets were taped over them. The couch cushions became the roof, and the pillows were the bricks with which we built the walls of our fort. On dark and rainy days, or in the evenings, we would sit inside our forts and tell stories by the light from our flashlights. We would tell each other stories of being under siege from the enemy and eat snacks in our forts, while some of us would be outside hunting for animals, gathering wood or fighting the enemies.

...e my husband and I are both engineers, we felt that math and science are subjects that are really cool and beautiful. In high schools, I worked at the Vancouver Science Museum putting on science shows and explaining to visitors all the exhibits and what they were trying to teach. I would reproduce some of these shows and exhibits at home, to the amazement of my kids. One experiment we did often was the volcano experiment. By using newspaper and glue to form a shape of a volcano around a small cup, and then painting our "volcano", we had a prop that was reusable many times over. I would put baking soda inside the cup, and color vinegar with all kinds of colors that my kids liked. Then we would pour that colored vinegar slowly into the cup inside the volcano to watch it erupt into all different colors. It never failed to amuse or excite my kids when the bubbles from the volcano spilled over. I'm not sure if my kids ever understood the chemistry involved, but we sure had fun. Another family favorite was the vibrating glass experiment. One Christmas our neighbor gave us a set of 8 wine glasses. Immediately I filled each glass with a different amount of water, and rubbed the rim of each glass to produce different pitches of sound. With the right water levels, we actually had a beautiful musical instrument to play some songs. Throughout the years, every time we did this experiment, they would learn a little bit more about how sound is produced through vibrations, and pitch is determined by the frequency of the vibration, and what dampening an object does to the pitch of a sound, etc. By the time my kids learned about sound in school, it was already a familiar part of their childhood experience rather than a tedious set of facts to remember. Their idea of math and science growing up is always one of fun and delightful new discoveries. Finally, the all time favorite experiment was the corn starch experiment, which every child had at least once in one of his birthday parties. I would fill a low, flat container with two bags of corn starch and a little bit of water. I would invite each kid to slowly stir the mixture with a spoon, and it will be very easy to stir this watery mixture. However, I would take a hammer and quickly, suddenly, and with great force, pound hard on this mixture, only to watch the kids' expressions turn from one of fear from getting splashed to one of puzzlement and then delight as they realized that this watery mixture had now turned as hard as a rock, and that the faster and harder I pounded, the harder the mixture and the louder the sound. No splashes. Throughout our kids' childhoods, we did many fun experiments. Beijing's bookstores have books with suggestions for simple science experiments that you can do with household items with your small children at home. I encourage you to try them often. You will discover that your children will find math and science fun rather than become intimidated by these subjects when they get to higher grades.

Every aspect of life can be experienced with wonder and beauty can be discovered. From film to literature, music to science, when we explore them together through the enchanted eyes of our children, we re-discover the delight that life can be. By paying attention to help your children discover and enjoy whatever your passions and interests are, you will be bringing beauty into your home. Beauty puts us in touch with the transcendent, and gives our existence a greater meaning than mere survival. Without it, we will simply survive. With it, we can truly live.

Mommy's Checklist

This checklist is a great reminder. May Moms use it to remind themselves each day to act on the checklist and appreciate our most precious gift – our children!

Today I want to:
- Hug my child and tell him I love him.
- When my child wants to talk to me, to listen intently to him.
- Read a book to my child.
- Believe that my child can obey me (and not to use anger to get him to listen to me).
- Be patient with my child.
- Sing or listen to music with my child.
- Talk about my spouse to my child with respect
- Not expect my child to do what is beyond his age range (i.e. be quiet and wait patiently for long periods of time while adults are having a long conversation)
- Let my child bear the consequence for his mistakes.
- Help my child to learn something new.
- Encourage my child to do something for someone else.
- Protect my child from being in contact with information that is negative or may cause him harm.

- Challenge and help my child to do something that he has never thought that he could do.
- Discipline my child without being angry.
- Praise my child's good character.
- To model a positive character for my child when I expect him to have that character.
- Laugh with my child, not at him.
- Thank my child for something he did.
- Let my child take responsibility for something.
- Not criticize my child in front of others.
- Apologize to my child and ask for his forgiveness as soon as I've done something wrong.
- Forgive my child.
- Make time to be alone with my child.
- Not promise something that I can't do.

For Your Growth

1. What kinds of traditions did you grow up with? What were your favorite? Have you continued in these traditions in your newly formed family with your children? Why or why not?
2. What other new traditions would you like to start this year on a daily, weekly, monthly, or annual basis?

3.15 HOW TO CULTIVATE AQ?

Adversity Quotient

When my husband and I saw this photo at an airport shop, we immediately purchased it. It's been well over a decade, but no matter where we move, this photo continues to hang on our living room wall. Because my husband David studied aerospace engineering in college, specializing in air dynamics, and I studied fluid dynamics, the moment we saw the picture, we understood its meaning and agreed that we must have it in our home. It's so symbolic! You can say that it represents the family value of the Lin Family. Why? The name of this picture is "Against the Wind". If a bird is flying in front of the wind, the tailwind will push it forward, making it fly faster. We often call this luck. However, if a bird deliberately flies into the wind, it will have a very difficult time flying, but the wind will push it higher, allowing it to see farther. We usually like to avoid the wind and the rain, because it is uncomfortable and difficult to endure. However, this picture is a constant reminder to us that when the wind and the rain comes, to not fear or avoid it, but to fly into it, because even if we can't fly very well, we can be pushed higher and see farther. If we spend our lives avoiding the wind and the rain, we will never be able to see far or develop depth. Instead, we will continue to stay close to the ground with the other little chickens and birds, contending for the limited amount of resources in our very small circles.

ı̈le back, a southern media friend called me and asked to purchase over 100 copies of "The Competitive Edge of Our Next Generation" to give to parent friends around her, because High School Examination results just came out. As a result, she had to report on too many cases of kids that jumped to their deaths because of a few points of difference on their exam scores. She didn't know what she can do to help, but felt that she needed to do something. She felt that these kids' AQ is too low, and asked me when I can go down there to teach parents how to cultivate AQ in their kids. What tricks did I use on my own kids? I was speechless. There are no tricks to teach children AQ, because parents are always treating their children like machines, using this trick and that trick to fix them. I thought for a long time because I really think that my kids have pretty good AQ. They have overcome some very tough circumstances, but we never deliberately did anything to cultivate their AQ!

Then how DO you teach AQ? I feel that is it transmitted. As parents, do we ever fly into the wind, or do we tend to choose to avoid the risk that comes with the wind and try to talk our children out of taking risks? Do we grow through our adverse circumstances, or do we dwell on safe ground, contending for the limited resources in our very small circles? Do we transmit to our kids our confidence and encouragement, or endless anxiety and our own lack of security? If we want to become our children's heroes, what kinds of stories can we tell them to inspire them? I remember that since I met my husband, we have consistently made one risky choice after another that are different from others' around us, and often tell our children many of these stories since we met. Such as during the summer after our college graduation, we decided instead of finding a job or applying to grad school, that we would separate and find a different kind of experience: he to serve for an entire summer in a Palestinian refugee camp in Jordan, learning from them and understanding their history, personal stories, and the challenges that they face; while I went to live in the slum areas of Istanbul with Iranian refugees, befriending them, learning from them, and understanding why they would choose to leave their beloved home and country to drift around in a place that despised and looked down on them. We both felt that the turning point of our lives happened that summer, because it was among the different refugees that our outlooks towards life changed, and we saw clearly what kinds of values we wanted to live by, and what kinds of goals to purse in life. After we got married, we also made a lot of choices to fly into the wind, always against the voices of opposition of well meaning relatives, or listening to the laughter and jeers of others. Some involved less risk, such as when our two older kids were small, we trained for 6 months to go mountain climbing with some friends in the Himalayas. Others involved more risk to our daily lives, such as leaving our comfortable lives in the U.S. right on the heels of SARS to live in China with our children. Or deciding with our children to leave international school and attend local Chinese school, etc. Now that we look back, I can also understand that many of the choices our children made could also possibly have been because they have seen how their parents have acted. Decisions such as choosing military training like local Chinese instead of opting out as a foreigner. Or choosing an international school that is not the best in Beijing, or going to a key high school to challenge oneself instead of staying in the more comfortable international department, or planning to take a year off after graduating high school to spend a gap year to explore his own interests.

Mother Teresa said : "Preach the Good News at all times. Use words only when necessary". Teaching our children is the same: teach our children at all times. Use words only when necessary. Our children don't need our constant nagging, but inspiration from our actions. How is AQ cultivated? Just like all other characters worth cultivating – from the parents' own examples.

For Your Growth

1. Reflect upon your experiences overcoming adversity as you were growing up. Have you had a chance to share them with your child?
2. Currently, in what ways are you taking risks and demonstrating courage to your child?
3. How have you encouraged your child to take risks or confront a fear this past week? Month? Year?
4. What kind of fears does your child have right now? Can you help him to face it a little at a time this upcoming week?

3.16 THE REWARD OF LETTING GO

Letting go is a lesson that every mother must learn. It is also the most challenging lesson for a mother who by natural instinct would be willing to sacrifice everything to protect her beloved baby. Letting go is not something you experience when your child is ready to leave home. In reality, it is something that we mothers must begin to learn as soon as our child is born, and will continue to learn even after our children have left home to build their own homes. In the beginning, letting go is a strange, uncomfortable, and anxiety-producing feeling, but after practice, makes us grow and mature. At the same time, I am amazed to discover that as I let go, my children often turn around and choose to befriend and trust me and seek out my opinions. In our relationship with our loved ones, we all hope that the other party can love us back, but the feeling and degree of satisfaction is greatly diminished when they are pressured or forced to express this love rather than be given the freedom to choose to express this out of their own free will. To gain this kind of love in return, we must experience this highly anxiety producing and risky process of letting go.

I remember that the first time that experienced letting go was when Caleb was still a tiny infant. In theory, I know that the marriage relationship takes priority over the parent child relationship, but when a totally helpless baby is put into my arms, the prospect of leaving this helpless little bundle of joy to care for a grown and independent adult seems rather cruel to me. That night, with the help of my husband, I finally overcame my misgivings enough to hire a babysitter to look after a sleeping Caleb so that we can hop next door to a nearby theater to watch "The English Patient". Every time I think of this movie, a wave of feelings would flood over me, as I recall every agonizing second I spent in the theater feeling utterly helpless, guilty, and anxious, which turned into resentment and anger as the movie progressed. I don't recall a single detail of the movie, because the whole time I was imagining what would happen if my baby woke up, got hungry, and started crying for me while I sat here enjoying myself. I can't believe how heartless I was! Before the movie ended, I already couldn't wait to jump out of my chair to rush home, but my husband patiently waited until the last scene ended, and had the gall to ask if I wanted to go for a cup of coffee after the movie! I only remember that the drive home was one of the longest and unhappiest drives of my life. When I got home, Caleb had indeed woken up and begun to cry. David didn't say anything because I was on the verge of a nervous breakdown as I quickly snatched over my baby to hold him tightly. I think that the one that needed comforting the most was not the baby, but me! This is the first chapter in my own growth in letting go. When I reflect on it, I can't help but chuckle at how ridiculous I was, but I knew that this is a necessary step and process. I haven't given up, and continue to move forward and gain ground.

After that evening, I've learned to let go at every stage of life. Each time my children play sports or go out exploring, I need to conquer the fear or worry that something will happen to them to cause them injury. Each time something does happen, I need to throw off all the voices of self-condemnation and guilt to patch up the endless falls, bruises and scratches that ultimately lead to healing. At the end of each incident, they always came back to proudly brag to me: "Look, Mom! I can do this myself!" Each time I grit my teeth to let go, I discover that my children are equipped with endless wells of resilience beyond what I can imagine, and how often I underestimate their ability to handle pain. In the beginning, I deliberately weakened myself to give them the room to grow. However, I don't know at what point it began to happen, but I no longer need to hold myself back, because their abilities have all surpassed mine. Now, Jonathan washes dishes at twice my speed, and meets my standard of cleanliness as well!

When Jonathan first transferred from local school to international high school, he joined the basketball team. Even though he loved basketball, he never played in any games in local school because heavy school work prevented the formation of any teams, making playing in official games impossible. During the first week on the school team, Jonathan told me with sadness that he was the least popular person on the team because he lacked the game playing experience and his skills were far behind the rest of the team members who have had years of experience playing together. By the second week, he told me that none of his teammates want him to get any court time to practice, let alone play in the real games. He was constantly benched, waiting for practices to end. When I heard this, every protective motherly instinct rose up. I suggested that he quit the team and join other activities instead of living with this kind of treatment. However, he said that Junior Varsity Team was very tough to get in, and he didn't want to give up this opportunity. Then I wanted to go talk to his coach or the principal to explain about Jonathan's situation to enlist their help, but Jonathan insisted that it was his own problem, and asked that I not interfere but just give him a chance to work it out for himself. If the problem does not get resolved by next season, then he will quit. It was really hard for me to watch him being rejected by his teammates, but this is not the first time that my children encountered hardship or unfairness, so I realized that once again, I need to just let go and support him through my prayers trusting that he would have the wisdom to resolve this himself.

Two months later, Jonathan excitedly came to tell me that he's already the most popular player on the team, and that all the other players are fighting for coach to give him more play time. As a result, his skills have greatly improved and he is no longer the worst player on the team. In astonishment, I asked how he was able to get to this place. He proudly share with me: "Every basketball player wants to be a star and shoot that hoop. But I don't need to be a star, so my only goal every time I get on that court is to watch for ways to pass the ball to someone that can get a shot at the hoop. Everyone knows that I will never fight with them to get the ball, but that I always pass the ball to the one who has a good chance of scoring, so they will fight for me to be there to increase their chances of scoring. Mom, I don't need to be a star. I'm happy to help others be a star."

Every time I learn to let go, my children inevitably surprise me. It doesn't matter if the incident results in success or failure, but they always grow and mature through the process, whether it takes the form of more self knowledge or increased confidence. One of my kids' favorite phrases that they use to encourage one another is: "If it doesn't kill you, it can only make you stronger." Even more surprising is my own growth: I'm not as anxious as before, and my doubt and lack of confidence in my children have turned into confidence and true admiration. Letting go is never easy, but the results of letting go is truly worth the effort.

For Your Growth

1. Are there areas in parenting that you are having a tough time letting go?
2. How can you find practical ways to let go? Who can you enlist to help you in your efforts?

3.17 I AM NOT YOUR SAVIOR

During my high school years, I had three favorite novels: Forever Amber (an unknown 1000+ page epic novel), Thornbirds, and Gone with the Wind. I read each book at least 7-8 times. Each time I would brood for hours over the way the stories ended. I would stay up even later obsessing over how the story could have ended differently, and attempted in my mind to write another chapter where the main characters would meet a different end. It wasn't until years later that I realized that the common element to all three books is that they all have a tragic endings. I had also read hundreds of other books, but they all had happy endings, and therefore were totally forgettable to me. What hooked me in these books is that two people who loved each other so much could possibly not be able to find a way to live happily together forever. I remember each time after finishing each book, the ending would leave me with two protagonists who loved each other but had to say goodbye, and I would feel that deep sense of sadness.

Now why would that bother me so much? Well, you see, deep down inside, I believe that I'm the savior of the world! Whenever I see people in trouble around me, I believed that I bore the responsibility to "fix" them up. If that person is a really tough case, I believe that as long as I tried hard enough and cared deeply enough, I can fix them. Which is why nothing bothers me as much as an ending that does not resolve happily.

This kind of thinking first got me into trouble when my husband and I ran into a homeless man on the streets of Los Angeles one day. He said that he had a wife and 4 kids at home and needed some money to feed them. We went over to see them, and saw them living in poor condition, and our hearts of compassion were moved. We gave them $50 to help them with living expenses that week (20 years ago, US$ 50 , or RMB 400+ could have gone a long way), and asked him to go buy some diapers for his kids and food for the family. Within two days, he called back asking for more money. We found out that they were not used to seeing so much money, and took the entire family out to eat a steak dinner, blowing off all $50 just like that. The next day, they were hungry again. I was very angry, and refused to give him any more money. You see, when saviors find that the objects of their "saving" does not improve like they want to, or does not

233

appreciate their efforts, they get angry or emotional. My husband disagreed with me, and felt that we should have trained them to budget their money first. Other friends heard about this and encouraged us to take a longer view, and focus on equipping them with life skills rather than creating dependence on our charity. Together with our friends, we helped this man to get a job, buy a used car, and learn to budget money to run a household. Being a savior would have been much easier than being an equipper. Unfortunately, being a savior would also make them dependent on the savior forever instead of become independent and able to help others. This is true especially when it comes to child rearing.

After my children arrived, the need to train them arose every day. From training them to sleep on their own properly, to eating at the right time, to asking for things nicely, etc., etc., etc. Each time, I found it easier and more natural to play the savior and just do things for them, but each time my husband would step in to disagree. This disagreement was the focal point of many of our earlier fights. I wanted the easy way out. I can do everything much quicker and better than my child. Also, when my child cried, it made me feel good to help him, rather than get into an unpleasant conflict over making him help himself. With each succeeding conflict with my husband, I would see how David handled my child over my protests, and see the results of my child's response to this patient training. Each victory enabled me to have more faith in training over rescuing, and gave me strength to conquer the savior within me. I always knew that it's better to teach a child to fish than to give him a fish, but to silence the voice of that savior within me is a lot more difficult than I thought. You see, that's because I have trouble hearing cries of distress from my baby.

The first stage of a baby's life is always most difficult, because his cry of distress so tugs at your heart, and you just want to make the world safe and warm for him, so that he will never be afraid or distressed again. That is a natural instinct that every mother is endowed with. Otherwise, those cries will go attended and a baby's need for sustenance and physical well-being will be superseded by his mother's own need for self-preservation and comfort. However, the problem is that our emotions often overrule our intellect, because most of those cries do not convey distress, but merely an infant's way to communicate a need having to be met. Because of my savior complex, I could not distinguish the difference between various kinds of crying, and treated each cry as a cry of distress.

However, with each small victory, it gets increasingly easier and easier to tell, because I gain more and more confidence in myself to let go, and in my child's ability to learn for himself from his own mistakes. Here are some major milestones marking victory:

Sleeping: That first incident with training Caleb to sleep through the night gave me a first taste that my baby is much tougher than I give him credit for. I began to appreciate that occasionally letting my baby cry will not damage him for life, like I thought it would.

Swimming: When Caleb was almost drowned learning how to swim and cried in deep distress when we asked him to go back into the water, I wanted to relent and just comfort him, but David insisted on putting him back into the pool to help him overcome the fear of water. I hated him for insisting, but had to respect and agree with him that insisting on Caleb going back into the pool right away was the best move, because he has one less fear to overcome now, and gained the ability to swim.

Eating: When the kids are capable of feeding themselves in the high chair, I still wanted to keep feeding them, partly to avoid them making a mess, partly to make sure that they eat what I want them to eat, in the amount I want them to eat, in order to get enough of the right nutrients, and partly because feeding them saved me time. However, by taking the time and energy to train them to eat properly, they take responsibility for their own feeding. In the long run, this frees up more or my time and energy to do other more useful things.

Chores: When we assign each member of the family to be responsible for certain household chores, I am always tempted to "help", especially when they don't do it up to my standard or speed, or if they complain that they are too tired or too busy. Not rushing in to help them ensures that they are the owners of these chores, not mine. If they neglect to fulfill completing their expected chores, they will need to learn by bearing the consequences of failing to fulfill these expectations. I need to resist the urge to rescue them by doing their chores myself or get upset because they don't get it done. Again, taking that initial time and pain to train them ensure that more of my time is freed up for more useful things later, and that I have more quality time to do more fun things with my children, instead of taking time away from them to do their chores.

Homework: Just like chores, the question is ownership. Is homework their responsibility, or mine? If they don't get it done in time, do they take the consequences, or do I rescue them by doing it for them or get mad?

It's much easier to play the savior, but it's a lot more demanding of us to be a trainer and equipper. As mothers, we have to work very hard to resist the voice of the savior within us to take the easy way out, but to do what is the best for our children. In the long run, if we are willing to take the tough path of learning to become a trainer, both we and our children will benefit for a lifetime by gaining healthy habits for life.

☙❧

When I came to Beijing in 2003, I did not know how to read Chinese. I relied on my children, who were in local school, to help me understand everything from menus to road signs and simple flyers in the mailbox. Last year, as was my usual habit, I went up to Jonathan to ask for help. His Chinese proficiency is by far the best in the entire family.

"Jonathan, how to you pronounce this character?"

"Mom, I'm going to tell you today, but I want to walk you through looking up this word in the dictionary. You see, it's actually quite simple! You should really learn to use it for yourself. I mean, what if I'm not here and you have a question? I don't want you to be stuck, OK?"

It looks like Jonathan has learned the benefit of teaching others to fish, and I am the first beneficiary.

For Your Growth

1. In what areas are you acting like your child's savior when you should be training him to take ownership for a particular habit or responsibility?
2. What will you do to avoid saving your child?
3. What concrete steps do you plan to take to train your child to develop this habit and become the owner of this responsibility? What kind of help do you need?

3.18 CHILDREN WHO GROW UP UNDER EXAM-ORIENTED EDUCATION CAN'T BE HAPPY?

A group of parents from our gated community take turns driving our kids to a character school. Last time when it was my turn to drive, I overheard an interesting debate. One child suggested that everyone nominate a teacher in school who is the best teacher who loves the students the most. Every kid eagerly nominated his homeroom teacher and gave a very good set of reasons. I smiled as I listened.

Who says that children who grow up under an exam-oriented education system in China can't have a happy childhood? Who says that kids must have a "Happy Education" or grow up in a school in a foreign school system in order to have a happy childhood? According to my observation, these kids were all very happy, and they all did well in school. The problems that teachers discussed with us parents tended to be about our children's habits such as procrastination, wasting food, picky eating, poor manners, messy dress, etc. When I picked up the kids that day, I found their teachers also to take their photos together, and then asked them why they think that their teacher is the best teacher in the world. Allow me to share with readers what they reported. I can confidently say that their feelings are not unique, because as I come and go around the school, I can always see the smiles of the children and see the teachers loving on their kids.

Two Kids' Reasons

My son Stephen: Teacher Xu is absolutely the world's best teacher! Even though she's very strict with us during class, as soon as class is over she will express a lot of love to each person! She always plays with us, and never shows partiality towards those who have better grades over others. This week I got sick and stayed home, she called me and asked me how I was feeling, and told me not to worry. She said to first get well, and then I can slowly catch up when I get back. For Children's Day this year, she drew a hand made card for every single student in the class, each card is a drawing she made of each classmate's face, inside she wrote a personal letter to each of us on the reason she likes us and what makes us so special to her. I was so touched that I almost cried in front of her! There are so many students in class. She must have spent so much so much time to make them. Teacher Xu is usually very busy, because she has to prepare to teach classes, has to correct all of our homework every day, and has to teach so many math classes. Where does she get the time? Teacher Xu has a magical cabinet. Inside are all kinds of small stationary, toys, and yummy snacks that she bought with her own money. If we did well or made some improvement, she will open her magical cabinet and take out something from inside to encourage us. If we are naughty, she will criticize us, but she will keep caring for us. So, when we do something wrong, we are all very happy to admit it and change ourselves, because we love Teacher Xu so much! Also, because we like her so much, we all want to learn math a little better so that she can be proud of us.

As you can see, a teacher that students like can help students to more proactively learn her subject. My own journey of learning was the same. I loved chemistry because I liked my chemistry teacher, and wanted to do well in it so that she would have a good impression of me.

Freddie: Teacher Zhao is the world's best teacher! She is so nice to every classmate in the class, and often encourages us. It doesn't matter if our studies or our behavior is good, she will give us a star sticker. If we have a whole week without deducting points, we can get three stars. No matter how badly I do in my studies, she will always find a way to praise me and encourage me to keep working hard. Sometimes when I am polite, she will praise me in front of the whole class. Anyways, I just really, really like Teacher Zhao! Sometimes some classmates in our class are naughty, but she rarely gets mad or yells at us. If someone's behavior is especially bad, he will be made to stand beside the garbage can, but after time is up, she will still be very nice to us. Teacher Zhao is really the world's nicest and loving teacher!

Nowadays, every teacher in the school has a very heavy teaching load. Not only that, but kids in elementary school stage, especially boys, are all very energetic, bringing a lot of challenges to teachers in classroom management. However, they still manage to make every child feel loved. This is not easy. The kids like their teacher, feel loved, and don't feel that studying is very difficult, isn't this win-win?

Facing Everything With a Positive Attitude

Once, a mother brought her son to play in our house. Her son wanted to eat the imported Danish cookies that my son was eating. Because they were living on a tight budget, the mother didn't budget money to buy more expensive snacks. However, the mother was not ashamed, didn't apologize or provide any explanations. Instead, she said in an excited tone of voice: "See, we have these special little buns that we made together. How cool is that! You are just the luckiest kid in the whole world!" When the son heard his mother, saw the expression of excitement, gratitude and contentment on her face, he also started jumping up and down with excitement, yelling, "Yay! I'm so lucky! I'm so lucky!"

These days, the complaining attitude that many children have are transmitted from their parents. Of course every system will have its problems and brings us huge challenges. However, the attitude that we parents have in facing these adverse circumstances will also deeply influence our kids. If our first response is complaint, when our kids run into problems, their first response will also be to complain about others, about the system, even about their own parents, etc. If our first response if positive, giving others the benefit of the doubt, to first face the challenge ahead with an attitude of thanksgiving and contentment, I believe that even the worst school will have some bright spots. It's impossible for our education system to change immediately, but we can help our kids learn to adjust their attitudes and habits in school, so that no matter what kind of a system they are in, they can be thankful people and be a blessing to others.

For Your Growth

1. When your kids come home from school to tell you what happened at school, are they mostly things that make him happy or negative things?

2. When we are guiding our kids, do we first listen to the problem or his feelings? If your answer is the problem, then decide to train yourself to first listen for the feeling, to understand and accept the feelings, before even addressing what happened.

3. Have you developed the habit to counting the blessings that the school as brought to your child? Start now. Together with your child, express gratitude for these blessings and for the people who blessed him. Then make it a daily habit.

4. When a problem occurs and needs to be solved, do you try to think of a solution, or will spend time to analyze or complain about a person?

5. Discuss with your child how he can become a blessing to his class, teacher, friend, and school.

3.19 WEAR YOUR OWN CLOTHES

Growing up as a little girl, I remember my mother as being a beautiful and glamorous woman. She always kept up with the latest fashion, and changed her hairstyle frequently. No matter how she changed her hairstyle, she would still look beautiful. She tried to help me experiment with different looks, too, and no matter what the hair stylists did, I always looked funny, not myself, and assumed that it was because I was ugly and mother was beautiful. This culminated in the ultimate disaster: my sister's wedding in Boston. Before going to Boston, my mother and I stopped by New York, where we stayed at the posh Trump Plaza right in the middle of Manhattan. She made an appointment for me with their world famous hair stylist, who gave me a US$400 perm, and I came out looking like a walking exploded beehive. Somehow I fooled myself into believing that such a famous artist would never make me look bad, so I must just be an ugly looking engineer with an expensive haircut. However, the Rossana walking around posing in those photo sessions in my Qi Pao felt awkward and unreal inside. I was not feeling like my real self.

Last night, on the way to eat some pizza, we had a heated discussion in our car. Jonathan was talking about his friend who was a chronic procrastinator and always waited until the night before a test or an assignment was due before studying. Because he was naturally smart, he always got things done and received very good grades. However, Jonathan believed that when this friend gets into higher grades and has more workload to juggle, just smarts alone will not get him good grades, and he will begin to fall behind because of his poor work habits. Caleb chimed in and said that he is like Jonathan's friend, always waiting until it was close to the deadline before getting down to work, and yet getting it done well, because he worked better under pressure. Jonathan asked his elder brother if waiting until so late would not make him anxious? He himself would never wait that long, but preferred to attack his homework the day it was assigned so he can get it out of the way. Procrastination is poor work habit and is to give yourself too much pressure. What if something went wrong last minute? You will have no margin for error. Caleb disagreed. He did always take a look at the work as soon as it was assigned. The difference is that he would space out his work over several days into smaller chunks of manageable work, beginning with reading and researching the material, and then letting it sit in his brain as little bit while he thought about the assignment or new material. Then, when it was time to write out or complete his work, he already had a good idea how much time he would need the night before to complete it. He found that by alternating between work in different subjects, he was more effective and had more inspiration to write insightful essays or thoughts. Somehow weaving between subjects enabled him to let the last chunk of information submerge into his subconscious to create more links in his brain.

They turned to me to ask who is right? Which way is the right way to study? That's when I thought of my mother's attempts to give me beautiful hair. In the end, after experimenting with all these expensive and ridiculous perms and hairstyles, I found that my hairstyle was best short and straight. In fact, this kind of hairstyle can be managed by an average stylist in any salon in China for less than RMB 50. The question was not which hairstyle is superior, but which style works best for you? I asked both brothers if they had tried the other brother's approach before making a judgment? If not, then how do you know that it doesn't work? Caleb said that teachers in school usually praise Jonathan's way of studying, because it seems to be more diligent. However, he tried this method and it just didn't work for him. He felt that there was something wrong with him, but he continued to use his own approach and it always worked well for him. Caleb should know, because he was admitted into MIT this past December with high grades and a lots of original music compositions as well as a 100,000 word novel to his credit. He can't just do one thing. He has to be juggling many things at the same time and switching back and forth between them to be able to focus well. Jonathan won't even try his brother's approach, because he said that he would not be able to sleep well at night knowing that there was unfinished work before him. I shared my story of the hairstyle, and asked for their opinion. They thought it strange for me to just obediently let others dictate my look and style when I should be firmly in control of choosing a look that I like. I asked them back: "Then how about study style? Is there a right or wrong, or should we try various approaches and see what works for us?"

The more we talked, the more we realized how different our study styles were. What worked for one person didn't work for another person. We also realized that when our kids were in local Chinese schools, the teachers generally taught that there was only one right way to study. Growing up, we are used to being compared to others and being told to imitate someone else in order to excel like them. We are not used to thinking of what's best for ourselves. Often the result is what matters, not our styles and preferences. Even more often, when we try someone else's suggestion, and this someone is a very good student, and this method doesn't work for us, we often blame ourselves, thinking that it must be our fault. Either we're using this method incorrectly, or we are just plain dumb.

Caleb seemed to always do things last minute, staying up late at night playing guitar or writing songs, and was usually grumpy in the mornings. When he studied, he had music constantly blasting in his room, and had to work very hard to follow directions well. He was always questioning things and trying to probe at the deeper meaning of things, and did his best thinking walking our dog Nellie late at night. Caleb's room often looks like a hurricane passed through it, with piles of paper and books all over, yet he can find the things that he is looking for at any time.

Jonathan does his best work in the mornings, and goes to bed promptly on time, never missing a minute of sleep. He is ultra organized and has lists on paper all over his walls. He completes all his work ahead of time.

According to study style experts Cynthia Tobias, there are 8 learning styles: concrete, abstract, sequential, random, concrete sequential and abstract sequential, and then concrete random and abstract random. Concrete learners need facts and data that they can be seen and felt through their five senses while abstract learners use more of their intellect and intuition and often miss the obvious but catch the underlying meaning. Sequential learners need everything well planned and in order. They don't like to be surprised but like everything to go off exactly according to plan. Random learners learn by grouping things together. They seem disorganized, but are often much better able to see the whole big picture than be stuck in the details. Mix up the first four styles and you will get the last four. How does this play out for you?

Here are some general polar opposites in learning styles that I have observed in my children. Both do equally well in school, but do it in a radically different way. Take music. Caleb did not have any previous music background until he started learning the guitar in grade 8. What he lacked in skills he made up with passion, as he listened to all kinds of genres of music at all times and quickly picked up on whatever music theory he needed as he composed over 50 songs over the course of 2 years. Some of these songs moved me to tears. This year his teacher asked him to compose a symphony, and with no previous classical music background, he managed to compose one in two months. He managed to make up whatever he lacked in knowledge by listening to hundreds of symphonies with the scores from great masters such as Mozart and Beethoven. He tested above average on music theory tests because he never bothered to study it systematically and thoroughly, but only picked up what he needed from using it in his composition. Jonathan picked up the drums also in grade 8. However, his intense interested music drove him to practice 1-2 hours a day. Starting this past fall, he practiced an hour a day just going along with the metronome so that he is never offbeat. He also started learning the double bass in grade 9 and by self-disciplined practice is now able to carry his own tune in 3 school orchestras. He is an excellent performer in both his instruments despite his short history while he has trouble composing any melodies that sound anything beyond pleasant. One is a composer, the other a performer. Both love music equally, but express their love very differently.

I can go on and on with other subjects such as math, physics, and chemistry, or English, but I'll stop. It is very clear that one is very creative (Caleb) while the other is very analytical (Jonathan). The key is to master the basic strategies of studying, find your strength, and build on that. If your parents are worried, persuade them to let you try studying in your own style and prove that you can do equally well, if not better, than the "right" or traditional concrete sequential way. Here are some stylistic questions to ask yourself:

Are you a morning person or a night owl? If you need adequate sleep, don't struggle into the night trying to finish up something. Your mind will be muddled and your effectiveness will be a fraction of your real self when you're 100% awake and alert in the morning. Keep your bedtime and make sure that you get your full 8-10 hours of sleep. Then be up extra early to get your work done. If you're a night owl, don't try to force yourself to go to bed early, but do make sure that you have plenty of buffer to catch up on sleep. Caleb often stays up late at night when the inspiration strikes and he needs to write down a song or some poems. Then he makes up for his sleep on weekends. On the other hand, Jonathan is in bed at the same time every night no matter if it's a busy weekday or a leisurely weekend.

Are you an early bird or a procrastinator who does better with pressure? Believe it or not, both styles require planning. If you are an early bird, lucky you, because you will not experience panic when things are running late. However, if you are a procrastinator, be sure to build in plenty of buffer and break up your work into manageable chunks that can be done a little bit at a time each day. And be sure to be giving yourself some time to think and digest what you are learning.

Are you better in groups or working alone? Caleb finds that he studies better when he's helping or tutoring friends. By trying to find ways to explain a concept to a friend, or trying to help someone solve a question, he comes to a much more solid grasp of a concept than if he's struggling with an idea or question alone in his room. On the other hand, Jonathan has no patience for friends or interruptions when he's studying. He's much more effective working on questions alone in his room.

Do you need background noise to block out interruptions, or absolute quiet? Caleb has the music blasting loudly in his room to block out noise or distractions from the outside, and we can occasionally hear him singing along with the music. Jonathan's room is quiet so he can concentrate more deeply.

Can you work for long periods of time with intense focus or need to take frequent breaks? Caleb can focus intensely for 1-2 hours, then has to take a break with exercise (sit ups or push-ups, music or snack breaks), and return to re-focus intensely. Jonathan can be lost in his work for hours at a time without needing to take a break. However, because he is a kinetic learner (meaning that he learns best when his body is moving), he is always tapping his fingers, shaking his legs, or stretching his arms. When I was in college, I obsessively spun my pen without being aware of it. Know what your body needs, and nurture your body accordingly. Then it will reward you with increased focus, energy, and efficiency.

Are you goal oriented or checklist driven? Caleb has a list of general goals of what he would like to accomplish this school year, and arranges his activities and schedule around these goals. He will adjust his lifestyle accordingly when he is not on track to achieve his goals (i.e. if his physics is doing well, he will put less time into studying physics but more time into chemistry, and vice versa). Jonathan has a concrete daily list of things he wants to get done, and will check everything off his list each day. Find which style of goal setting works better for you and stick to it.

Is your room clean and neat or an "organized mess?" Jonathan's desk is spotlessly clean. Only what he is currently working on is on his desk. He focuses intensely on each subject at a time. Once he is done with one subject, he cleans it up, puts it away, and takes out another subject to work on. Caleb's room is strewn all over with piles of papers and books. He will work on one subject, take a break, and move on to the next pile, work on it, and then return later to work on the original pile after that, depending on what he feels like. Somehow he still manages to get everything done, but is more effective when he is skipping back and forth between subjects so as not to get bored.

Are you an auditory or visual learner? Caleb can learn better by drawing pictures and making connections. He often needs to consult his textbook or need to look up additional information on the internet to supplement what he's learning in the classroom in order to better understand what the teacher taught. Jonathan learns better when he's sitting in class listening sequentially to the teacher's talking. He also frequently memorizes by repeating things out loud while Caleb memorizes by looking at a list or having to draw a spider diagram of how things are interrelated.

Are you analytical or creative? Even though Jonathan has been in local school longer, he was much better than Caleb at analyzing English literature, while Caleb is much better at creative writing and liked to explore literature without conforming to the rules of analysis. He liked to arrive at insights from a different angle from what is prescribed by the teachers and is perceived as being poor at following directions. Jonathan wrote excellent analytical essays dissecting other people's work, while Caleb wrote his own original works.

Do you learn quickly or on slow simmer? Jonathan processes data at a high clock speed. When he was small, he had trouble pronouncing his words properly because his mouth couldn't keep up with his brain. He whizzes through tests very quickly and seldom finds mistakes when he goes back to check his work. Caleb is a slow cooker. He mulls things over his head over a long period of time and refines his work over time. His process of learning or studying is in small layers on top of small layers, each layer reinforcing the deeper layer, until his grasp of the subject is deep and firm.

So don't be fooled into thinking that there is only one correct way to learn or study, style your hair or wear your clothes. Don't wear other people's clothes, because you will look weird in their skin, not your own. Everyone is different, and everyone should take the time to explore and learn what suits them best. What is your learning style?

For Your Growth

1. According to this chapter, can you find your child's learning style? If not, be patient. You will be able to observe his habits and learning style as he matures.
2. Based upon your child's unique personality and learning style, how will you help your child to study more effectively and raise his level of confidence?

3.20 HELPING OUR CHILDREN MANAGE STRESS

Stress is a normal part of everyday life. An essential part of parenting is to help our child learn to deal with stress on his own. MIT asks applicants to talk about something that they do just for the sheer fun of it. Part of the underlying reason is that they want to understand how the applicant deals with the inevitable stresses that life will bring, whether it's in the form of difficult academic work, a failed experiment, breaking up with a girlfriend, or living with a difficult roommate. A critical component of increasing AQ, or Adversity Quotient, is helping our children develop his resilience in the face of adversity by having his own healthy coping mechanism for stress. Unhealthy forms of stress involve escape or addiction. Escape can be in the form of passive and mind numbing activities such as watching TV (although kids can watch TV and be stimulated and challenged, too, depending on the program and purpose), playing computer games (same case here of there being different types of games, many of which are educational and stimulating to our children), or "spacing out". Addiction can be in the form of seeking pleasure from something harmful. It could be something "good" such as food, but taken to an extreme degree. Other addictions such as smoking, alcohol, drugs, gambling, or having multiple sex partners, can be harmful. Other addictions can be subtle and approved by society but no less harmful. The applause of crowds, accumulation of wealth and awards, and seeking the praise and approval of people, carried to extremes, can be disastrous to a person, as can be seen in the sad case of Li Yang and how fame and wealth served as his escape mechanism from not knowing how to conduct family life, yet entrapping him in a vicious cycle of giving up his relationship with family to serve this insatiable desire for approval from strangers and increasing degrees of wealth and fame.

What are some healthy forms of coping with stress? It's different for everyone, but a key component is that it rejuvenates a person and gives him renewed energy to continue meeting a challenge or adversity. This is a self renewal process that we need to help our children discover. It could be music, painting, taking a walk, sleeping, or talking things out with a parent or friend. It could be retreating into a "cave" to read, quiet down, think, and breathe. Usually, our children will have an easier time finding his own stress coping mechanism if we know ours and can share of our experiences, because they have inherited their personalities from us. I cope with stress by playing my piano and reading. I also mentioned some other means such as taking a nice hot shower, having tea with a friend and even a good round of cleaning the house. My husband copes with stress by taking a walk, exercising, and retreating into his "man cave" (or his study) to think and depressurize.

Author and creativity researcher Mihaly Csikszentmihaly in his book "Flow" talks about how everyone has a different zone for learning that is in the "flow". When the task of learning is too easy, a person becomes bored and turns off to learning. This happens when a child's ability is beyond what is required for that level of activity. In this case, parents and educators need to adjust the difficulty or stress level produced by that learning task to keep the student engaged so that he is sufficiently challenged. This learning can be in math, playing a musical instrument, or mastering a sport such as badminton or basketball. When a task of learning is too difficult, to a point where the student sees that no matter how hard he tries, he will not be able to master it, he becomes discouraged and gives up or becomes angry and rebels, refusing to continue learning. Our job as parents and educators is to help our child find and stay in that zone termed "flow", where there is sufficient challenge (which then will produce some stress) yet is easy enough where the student can see the hope of mastery if he puts in some effort. Every child's "flow" zone is different, and there is no formula. Therefore, we as parents need to study and understand our child so that we can help him to find his "flow" zone and to develop his own healthy mechanisms of dealing with the inevitable stress that will accompany any learning.

How does your child deal with stress? Does he not stress or worry easily and need the consistent prompting and reminder, or does he need to be reminded to calm down and put things in perspective? Each child is different, and I would like you to hear from each of my three boys about their own process of confronting stress.

Caleb

Caleb is an abstract random learner. He's always looking at the big picture of how everything fits as a whole that he often loses sight of that one particular component with the looming deadline. We joke that if a huge earthquake happened, Caleb would continue to sleep – he's never unnerved by anything. Because he changes his "focus of the moment" easily from one thing to the next, he can easily lose focus on the current stress as he moves on to the next thing to do, and forget about that detail. This makes everyone around him nervous. As a mother, I need to remind him to stress a little, to be aware of those deadlines and stay on task a bit longer. Although at first he did not like being reminded, he appreciates me reminding him and helping him to remember, and often tells me afterwards that he needs me to continue doing that. However, Caleb's load is often very large. He took on an academic load that was beyond the requirements for his high school diploma, and juggles many activities and commitments outside of school. This is what he writes about how he copes with stress:

Not only is it something that I do for fun, but music is also an integral part of who I am. It started as an emotional outlet, but quickly evolved into a creative outlet as well, an escape from the rigidity of life in every sense. In my music I have absolute freedom to be and say whatever I want. I compose in different styles depending on my mood, from classical to jazz to rock. Now it has become something more: I want my music to touch others the way music touched me and helped me through my hardest times.

Jonathan

Jonathan is a concrete sequential learner. He is so focused on the task at hand that he often misses the big picture. He needs help to pull him out of that "hole" of focus to gain a long term perspective of life. He is easily stressed, and is not good at being aware that his feelings are out of proportion with the amount of stress. I need to help him to recognize those stress signals and give him sufficient time and space alone to process and analyze the source of his stress. When he is ready, he will come talk to me about his thoughts to process it further. It is then that he finds it helpful for me to share my own experiences of coping with similar feelings and to remind him of his past successes in dealing with similar stresses to see it in proper perspective. I would also sometimes ask him what's the worst thing that could happen and analyze the impact in the long run, and to help him find ways to deal with his stress. Jonathan is not as adept at getting in touch with his feelings and identifying them, so I often need to ask him to describe his feelings with more concrete words. Once he's able to name them, he has an easier time understanding and analyzing them. Once he's able to analyze his feelings, he has an easier time putting it into perspective.

When I am helping Jonathan to manage his stress, I would often share with him stories of my own battles with stress, affirm that it's natural to feel nervous, and assure him that I accept his feelings. Jonathan is still more easily anxious and stressed, but he is getting better and better at naming his feelings and managing them. Here is an essay he wrote describing his feelings when leaving local school for international school. He's done an excellent job getting in touch with his feelings, understanding his weaknesses, analyzing them, finding and describing how he copes with anxiety, and putting it all in perspective.

Beginning a New life and Leaving an old one behind

Just the other day I was in the city with my parents. As we were crossing a sky-bridge (bridges that span over a road), it re-awakened some old memories and triggered some new emotions.

Last year was my last year in local Chinese school; it was also soon to be my first year at international school. I had an emotional attachment to my friends and teachers, but my last year there was pretty strenuous and stressful for me. The end of the year was like my day of freedom and yet, it was also my day of detachment from everything I knew as the present. The entire year was a build-up of pent-up emotion and feelings. But when the day of so-called "freedom" arrived, it felt anti-climatic in some way. It didn't feel as special, as exceptional of a day as I had expected. Even now I still feel a twinge of disappointment. That day was actually just like any other gloomy, ordinary day.

Cloudy, rainy sky hung over me as I woke up and left for school. The whole day at school my mind was scattered and my heart brimming with mixed emotion. There was tension in the air, it felt as if something special was going to happen today. After an uneventful day of school ended, a couple of my friends took me to a local restaurant to say their final good-byes and buy me a last meal. It was a kind gesture, but I just couldn't bring myself to feel any sort of happiness or any gratitude. Not because I didn't appreciate it, but more so because I couldn't focus on our conversations at all because everything felt so surreal. All I could think of was that today is the day that my reality will change so drastically that everything I know as the present will be torn away- like a drowning man's last bit of air.

After I said my final goodbyes - which was not as plaintive as I predicted - I commenced on walking to the Bus Stop to get home (In local school everyday I would ride the public transport home). As I was crossing the sky bridge to get to the opposite side of the street, I had a sudden moment of realization, a moment of clarity. This would be the last time I'd be taking this route home. The last time I'd ride the bus home. The last time for so many daily routine tasks. So I stopped; stopped while I was crossing that towering bridge and looked up at the sky and took one last good look around me. The sky was grey, dismal and so suffocating. I hate this type of weather. Curiously, these observations were the last things on my mind. All I could think of, all I could feel was relief, accomplishment, emptiness and anxiety. Relief - relief that I had finally made it through those 5 arduous years of local school. I felt accomplishment because I not only made it through my 5 years there, but I had also done my best and achieved excellence there. And yet at this point I felt empty. I felt this way only because I slowly began to realize that at this point in time, I don't have any ongoing friends, I have no one to talk to. All I can only hope for is that my situation will change for the better when I arrive at international school.

Anxiety is and has always been my biggest problem. And right now that was the most overshadowing and overpowering emotion. A new school, new people, new teachers and new experiences. So much new information, so much that I don't know how I should cope with it. My coping mechanism was failing me. Usually when something this big happens, I listen to music. Although most of the time it works, this time I doubt that any song can give me inner-peace. But somewhere deep down inside I felt excited. That excitement alone kept me going. Why excitement you might wonder. I'm not so sure myself but I have a feeling that it's because taking risks is always exciting.

It feels so alien to have so many feelings and emotions at once. So many fears, hopes and anticipations for the future.

In the present, all of this passed through my mind in the course of a couple of seconds. My parents prompted me to keep walking forward. The sound of their voices awakened me from my stupor and so I hurried along. As I was walking along I couldn't shake that heavy feeling of melancholy remembrance. My heart felt so heavy because of it. All the memories of my old life, of old friends, old teachers and old experiences kept coming back to me- some vivid, some hazy. Some times old memories can be such a burden, I wish I could just forget them and move on. Alas life doesn't work that way, memories can be a burden and can trouble you, but most memories should also be treasured and cherished. I guess the best remedy for removing bad memories is time. Only time... Until the time comes, reminders of the past will continue to appear around me; memories of a different life-my old life- will continue to trigger unfelt emotions. My new life has begun, I am enjoying it and I hope that when the next segment of my life to comes to an end, that it will have a happier ending than previous times.

Stephen

Stephen's biggest problem is his speed. He is an abstract sequential learner, which means that he likes to take his time to complete his task in as thorough and neat of a manner as possible. We've tried training with the alarm clock at his desk to remind him of his time limitations, and he owns 3 clocks and watches, each with its own alarm, to remind him of how much time he has to complete each task. Even then, whenever we communicate with his teachers at school, they always talk to us about his slowness. We all know that it's not because of his intelligence because he does very well in school. We know that it's not because he has given up because he enjoys doing homework, especially writing, but he takes so long to do thing that he squeezes time out for everything else.

In dealing with Stephen's slowness, I know deeply that I struggled with the same problems growing up. I was always the last one to finish my lunch, and would be asked to stand outside the classroom to finish my lunch before I was allowed back into the classroom to nap with everyone else. I remember many lunch times when I would not nap at all. I also remembered missing chunks of exams not because I didn't know the material, but because I took my time to write out previous answers slowly and neatly. I shared with Stephen that I accept his speed, because that's how I was growing up, and understood his frustration at being the last one to finish, and the anxiety that it brings. However, I also understand that I have learned to cope with it, and have used it to my advantage, because I am very thorough and detail oriented when it comes to my work, completing each project with the highest standards of excellence. Despite my very slow speed in high school, I was able to manage to achieve top scores in physics, chemistry, and math, learn 4 languages (French, Spanish, German, and Latin), and participate in a number of activities and clubs outside of school, including working at the science museum, helping my parents launch a wholesale import business, being part of a choir that came first in the country in a national competition, and working on a research project that earned me the second prize in the province. I know that Stephen is capable of getting there, too, as long as he does not give up and continues to work on speeding up a little bit more each day. However, the first thing that needs to happen for him is that he needs to accept that he will always be a little slower, so that he does not give up or rebel, but will find ways to cope with his stress and anxiety so that he wants to keep learning and improving. In his compositions, he has found humor to put his slowness into perspective, and has used it to is advantage to write a composition that touched those who read it and earned him a high grade in class. I'm confident that, with continued monitoring, acceptance, and encouragement for him to stay in the "flow", he will improve a little bit every day and find healthy ways to deal with his stress. Here is his composition :

The Slow Fox

Once upon a time, there was a very slow fox. He always took several hours to finish doing his homework.

One day, when the little fox came home from school, his mother told him: "We are going out today to eat yummy food such as BBQ meat, hamburgers, and ice cream." Little fox's mouth began to water and he hurried into the house to finish writing his homework. It took only a few minutes. He excitedly went to his mother and said: "I finished my homework! Let's go eat!" However, his mother said: "The traffic is horrible today, let's go another day!"

The next day, when little fox came home from school, mother again told little fox: "Hurry up! We will go out to eat today!" Little fox did not pay attention, and took his time to go into his room to write his homework. When little fox was barely even halfway through, his mother came into his room and said: "You are too slow! We are going to eat without you!"

Little fox said regretfully: "Aya! I shouldn't have taken so long, I wasted all the time away!"

I'm happy to see that he is aware that this is his problem and that he recognizes and owns the consequences of his problem. When ownership of this problem shifts from parents to child, we are well on our way to helping him find ways to cope with the stresses that come as a result of "his" problem, not "ours".

For Your Growth

1. Reflect on the last few times your child has experienced stress , and how you have tried to help him cope. Has this been effective? Why or why not?

2. Discuss the various ways that your child desires for you to help cope with stress, and ask for his help and input to help you be a parent in times of stress.

3. Write out what you would like to do next time he experiences stress, and follow the plan. As you do, adjust and make changes to be a more effective helper in equipping him to cope with his stress.

3.21 THE 4-T FAITHFUL MANAGER

There is a story in the Bible that talks about a master who goes away and leaves his three servants to manage his resources while he is gone. The first servant invests the ten talents that he's been entrusted with and produces ten more talents. The second invests the five and produces five more. Both get commended by their master with the words: "Well done, good and faithful servant!". Notice that he did not comment on the servants' intelligence, shrewdness, or results, but only on the character of faithfulness as "good". However, the third servant took the one talent that he's been entrusted with, buried it in the ground instead of investing it, out of fear that the master will punish him for bad results from his taking of risks, and upon the master's return, digs it back up from under the ground to return it safe and unused to his master. He told his master that the reason for the inaction is that he is afraid of him because he is a harsh and demanding master. His master's response is also indicative: "You wicked and lazy servant!" and even that one talent that he was given was taken away and given to the servant with the ten talents. Note that the character being labeled as "wicked" is being chastised not due to his lack of intelligence, but to his laziness! If that master were a parent today, would he do the same to his child, praising his diligence and punishing his laziness, or would he praise the resulting profit and punish the lack of results at least in keeping with inflation?

Often, when people talk about the point of the story, they focus on not being lazy, or investing money wisely. However, what is often neglected is the motivation behind the three servants. We see here that fear is ultimately a very poor motivator, because fear of failure will paralyze our children and prevent them from taking the risks that are necessary to personal growth in life. Yet we often use fear, guilt, or other negative emotions to drive our children to study or work hard. I believe that desire to please someone you respect and other positive motivators will outperform fear any day. This is because fear ceases to work when the person causing the fear is not ever present with a threat while an innate desire to excel or do well will drive a person regardless of whether or not someone is watching.

The favorite phrased used inside our family is: "With great power comes responsibility", derived from the movie "Spiderman". During Bill Gate's wedding, his mother Mary Gates used the same sentiment to remind him of his great responsibility that comes with his incredible wealth, because "to whom much is given, much is required also". This is one of the two pillar values of the Bill and Melinda Gates Foundation today. Our exhortation to our children has never been on producing the results to show us how capable or intelligent they are, but to be faithful to invest what talents they have been entrusted with rather than "bury it in the ground" out of fear of failure. The greatest failure in life is not producing bad results as a result of taking risks, or having low IQ and scoring low in your exams in school, but the greatest failure is a failure to be faithful and diligent to develop and wisely steward the gifts, talents, and opportunities that they've been given in life. Undeveloped human potential is a terrible waste, a squandering of resources.

Philanthropy in America has been changing and evolving. Old style philanthropists such as Carnegie would use their money to set up foundations to disburse their money to people or organizations that need the money. New style philanthropists manage the money they give away like they manage a business, demanding efficiency in operations, excellence in management, and effectiveness in the work carried out to help the people who need the help. People like Bill Gates manages his philanthropy like Microsoft, demanding accountability from people who receive his aid money and giving practical help and advice to the people he helps to improve the way their organizations are run. Not only that, he uses his personal contacts and his influence as a rich and famous person to leverage other people's money in collaborating on a philanthropy of a larger scale so that more people can be helped. His visit to China with Warren Buffet to invite Chinese billionaires to a banquet to encourage more philanthropy in China has sparked a wave of debates and action for the wealthy in China to share their wealth with their less fortunate countrymen. Bill has now resigned his day job running Microsoft to devote 100% of his time to managing the money that he's giving away, changing the landscape of philanthropy forever. He has fully utilized his treasure (100% of his money, leaving nothing for his children), his talent from running one the world's most profitable businesses, his time, and his relationships and influence for the betterment of humanity. We aspire for our family to do the same. Perhaps we haven't been given as much resources as Bill Gates to manage and leverage, but what we have, we want to be diligent to do a good job in managing so that more people's lives can be improved as a result of our being here on earth.

In our family, we consider every major part of our lives as something to be intentionally managed. We call this the 4T personal management principal: Treasure (money), Talent, Time, and Touch (meaning our relationships, or the people we touch). Each of these areas is equally important.

Treasure

Teaching our children to manage money is only the beginning. There are currently books such as "Rich Dad, Poor Dad" on the market that teach children some of the skills of money management. Many parents mistaken teaching investment skills as money management with the primary goal of maximizing return on investment. These ideas actually inculcate the value of greed in a child. We feel that teaching children to manage money is an excellent way to instill positive character in them. An ancient proverb says that "Where our treasure is, there our hearts are also." If I tell you that I like fashion, but never purchase any books or magazines on fashion or take the time to shop for new clothes or look at stores, but instead spend all my time on the golf course, then you will know that despite all that I say about my love of fashion, my real love is golf. In the same way, teaching our children to manage money is a concrete way to pass onto them our values on wealth.

There are two parts to managing money: income and expense. For younger children, income entails allowance while older children can find creative ways to generate income. Our two older kids generate their own income through tutoring and helping neighbors do chores or babysit. Therefore they require no allowance from us. Working has given our kids real world experience and helps them to appreciate the value of hard work as well as getting a concept of money. Their character is also shaped through having to work for their expense. Starting from age 10-12, when our kids have independent access to stores located next to their schools and are confronted with all kinds of temptations to spend money on snacks and toys, we begin to give them a small allowance to teach them to manage their income.

Money management training is done by helping them to make wise decisions through fixed savings plan, charitable giving, budgeting, and spending. We teach our children to save up 10% of their income for a larger desired item, and 10% of that income for charitable giving. The remaining disposable income is theirs to allocate and spend, but we give them a lot of guidance and explanation in the beginning to help them understand their reasoning for their spending decisions. In the area of spending, we take the time to help them plan a budget and spending goals. For example, they will allocate money to buy snacks at the store once a week. I offer to pay for their friends that one time if they should invite friends to go to the store with them. However, they are not allowed to go during other times of the week, as I will prepare healthier snacks for them. Therefore, they have little need to spend money but have more disposable income for stationary and small toys. When our children were small, we did not give them allowance until they have proven their ability to be responsible. This occurred around the time they finish elementary school.

Chores are the responsibility of every member of the house. Therefore, we do not reward the completion of chores with money. However, if our children have special savings goals, we will negotiate with them to give them additional chores in exchange for a "bonus". On the other hand, if the children neglect their chores, we reserve the right to deduct their allowance. Allowance, bonuses, and deduction amounts are all set according to the needs of the children, the budget of the parents, and the agreement reached after communication and negotiation. These amounts are adjusted according to changing circumstances. Industry works the same way. Many companies have bonus schemes for rewarding extraordinary performance or contribution, and the awarding of the bonus is dependent on how well certain pre-set goals are achieved. We will save up the children's Red Envelope money from Chinese New Year to save up towards their college tuition. Our children all know how costly it is to go to college, and understand our financial burdens, so they have never objected to our co-opting their sizable Red Envelope money.

Charitable giving is a non-negotiable in our family. Even though the bottom line is 10% of our income, we are constantly challenging ourselves and our children to give above that percentage. One respected friend has done the same of himself and is now living on 10% of his income while giving the rest of the 90% away. He is a source of inspiration to our family. We make

260

our giving decisions together, and often dip into our savings to give to a friend in need instead of loaning him the money. Seeing how borrowing and lending money between friends have ruined friendships, we have decided not to lend money to friends. If they have a real need, and we are able, we prefer to give them a smaller amount rather than lend them a bigger amount. This is the one area in our family life that has experienced a number of miracles and blessings, and we have discovered that the habit of giving and parting with our things enables us to be free from any addiction to materialism or money, but gives us the freedom to use our money to bless people.

We teach our children to forecast, budget, and bookkeeping. As a result, they all became familiar with the use of Excel. They will allocate their income into savings, giving, and spending. We often help them to set up savings goals to help them to enjoy the process of saving first before spending and ability to delay gratifying their desires and increase self-control. In our home, giving is a non-negotiable because it is the basic responsibility of a citizen. We parents have always had this habit and expect the same of our children. Keeping accounts help our children to understand where their money went. After some analysis, they will be able to adjust their behavior accordingly. For example, they love to drink milk shakes at restaurants, but because they have to pay for their own drinks, and milkshakes are rather expensive, they all decided to change their habits and drink water or juice instead. If they want to purchase a higher priced item such as a tennis racket, they can then map out a savings plan and timetable towards purchasing this item.

If our children should compare us with other parents, we usually tell them that different families have different values. If they don't like us to compare them with other children, then they should not compare us against other parents. At the same time, we need to teach our children to be grateful and content, to know the strengths of our family and appreciate family members, especially when their parents are the family's biggest fans.

Talent

Every child is talented is some way. While one may be a good test taker or have excellent memory, another one could be very outgoing and sociable, collecting many friends along the way in life. The quiet and shy child may

good in social situations, but may be very observant of people
keeping track of their needs. She may be a loyal friend, never
leave behind her old friend for a new one. Another one may be
very considerate of others and willing to serve. One child may be a very fast
runner or speak and think quickly, but may be careless and messy in his
hurry, while another may be very slow, making people wait on him, but be
very meticulous and tidy. The best time to praise and train a child is to
intentionally look for and catch him doing something good. What we
choose to praise shows a lot about our values. When we praise him for his
results, he may become performance oriented, thinking that he must
produce tangible results in order to earn our love. When we praise him for
his intelligence, his music sense, or some other innate ability, he may think
that he's entitled to the best scores and best positions just because he's born
with a big brain. However, when we praise our child because of a particular
positive character, it encourages him to continue to live out the positive
values embodied by these traits, whether it be loyalty, consideration,
diligence, honesty, efficiency, or compassion. When my son comes home
with a 100% on his math test, I praise him for his faithfulness, and ask him:
"You've been given such a talent for math, I wonder how you will help
mankind with it some day?" This kind of praise and questioning helps him
to not only be grateful for what abilities he's been born with, but also
stimulates him to consider what he will do to develop it and use it to help
others in the process. There's a long running commercial in the U.S. whose
catch phrase is "A Mind Is A Terrible Thing to Waste". We teach our
children not to waste food, water, energy, or electricity, but what about
their talents, gifts, and abilities?

Equipping our children with the skills to recognize their talents and using
them to bless others begins as soon as they are able to understand what we
are saying to them. When we all went to Gansu to teach English together as
a family, Stephen was only 3 years old. He didn't have any skills or
knowledge to teach others, but blessed others with his exuberant love,
expressed through his freely dispensed hugs and kisses. While the rest of
our family stood in front to teach English, Stephen took turns sitting in the
laps of different students, keeping them engaged and interested. He became
an agent of love and opened the hearts of our students to us as a family.
Each of our children learned at an early age that blessing people is not
reserved for adults, but is within the power of even the smallest of children.

At the very least, because all three of our kids grew up in a family that speaks English and go to Chinese speaking schools, all act as translators on an almost daily basis to help tear down communication barriers and misunderstandings.

Time

The most fair thing about life is that everyone is given 24 hours in a day. No one can exceed that boundary. However, people who manage their time wisely will accomplish a lot more than people who just let time slip by without any awareness or consideration. MIT's informal school motto is "Work hard, play hard". Implied in that motto is that there is a time for everything. No one can work hard all the time, because the body is not designed to keep going without any breaks before breaking down. In the marathon of life, the runner who knows how to pace himself to finish the race is a lot wiser than the runner who uses up all his strength in the first 100 meters and collapses of sheer exhaustion before the race is half over. One of the key tools we must equip our children with is the skill to manage time, and the wisdom to prioritize rightly. When it's time to work hard, do it with gusto and stop procrastinating. When it's time to play, do it with abandon, without feeling any guilt for not working. When it's time to rest, turn off the computer, TV, phone, email, weibo, and all other distractions and allow yourself to truly quiet down and rejuvenate/recharge. In the daily rhythm of life, we need to know when to use time for what. In different seasons of our lives, we need to know when to rest, when to laugh, when to mourn, when to heal, when to charge ahead in battle.

Ever since we discovered Franklin Covey's "Seven Habits of Highly Effective People" years ago, we have benefitted tremendously from his tools, including "Seven Habits of Highly Effective Teens", "Seven Habits of Highly Effective Families", and "Seven Habits of Happy Kids".

When I see Stephen watching TV, I usually ask him if it's time to relax and rest. If he shows me his daily checklist with all the items checked off, I can relax, sit down, and enjoy the program with him. If not, then he will need to live with the consequences of violating our previously agreed on rule to take care of "first things first". Don't let guilt be your child's companion. Give him clear boundaries to live every moment with all his energy, without any room for regrets.

Touch

We don't believe in accidents. We believe that every person we come into contact with in this world is intended to bless us and make us better people, and we to bless them. Therefore, we manage our relationships with intentionality and care, asking ourselves the question: "How can I build this person up today?" It doesn't matter if this person is our ayi or her family, a neighbor in need of a cup of sugar, or a friend in need of a job, we believe that we are to utilize our resources, including our treasure, talent, time, and other relationships, to bless others. We believe that the only things that last beyond time are people and their souls. This means that of all the resources we have, relationships with the people in our lives are the most important and take top priority. This also means that when we prioritize our time, we want to make sure that we first make deposits into the emotional banks of our closest family members before using them to touch others. Only when we are able to truly love ourselves can we truly love and serve others.

For Your Growth

1. Sit down and take inventory of how you and your spouse have been using your 4Ts. What are some areas that need adjustment?
2. Write down 3 new action items of change you desire to make this upcoming week to better manage one of your 4Ts.

3.22 WHY DO WE LOVE YOU, MOM AND DAD?

As parents, we are busy running around every day for our kids. Through this process, we will often doubt ourselves and what we do. When our children don't develop as we had expected, when they can't overcome their weaknesses, we will feel disappointment, be at a loss for what to do, asking ourselves what we can do to help our kids be excellent and different from others?

I often wonder why kids are often on such special behavior on special occasions such as our birthdays, Father's or Mother's Days. During those days, under the encouragement of elders or teachers, they are able to express to us their genuine gratitude. Each year, my husband David and I will receive cards and gifts from our kids during those special days, and they would surprise us with what they would say! These gifts serve to remind us and encourage us why we are parents. Even though we feel lost or disappointed as parents because our children did not meet our expectations, we will still work hard at parenting because our kids love us and need us. Every time we receive these precious gifts from our kids, we are reminded once again that parenting is the greatest calling in the world! Please allow me to share with you the card that our kids wrote to David on his birthday. Each child wrote a card, but I will share this one from Jonathan because he so aptly expresses his love and admiration for his Dad with his own unique brand of humor.

Why the guy upstairs is the...¡Greatest Dad Ever!
1. You're technologically adept. **+1** coolness point
2. You make wise decisions on behalf of the family that always ends up bringing us the most happiness. **+2** coolness points
3. You are the one that actively brings are family together. **+1** coolness point
4. When everyone else is acting rashly you still (99% of the time) manage to keep a level head and think rationally, helping our family to make it to where we are today! **+2** coolness points.
5. You're the parent that still remembers useful academic knowledge. **+1**

6. You're immensely patient with us kids when it comes to teaching us things! **+1**
7. You're brave enough to admit your weaknesses to the family. **+2**
8. You sacrifice without immediate thanks, having the foresight to know that your investments will pay off. **+3**
9. You can make the unpopular choices that we initially resist, but come to respect as we grow up. **+2**
10. You give us the freedom to make our own choices, you're confident that your hand in our lives is sufficient to set us on a healthy path, and you know that we'll all be men that you can be proud of. **+4!**

Yup this guy sure is the greatest dad ever! Holy moly, he has 20! (god forbid) **20! COOLNESS POINTS.** I mean I'm pretty cool and I only have 19... Yup that guy sure is an awesome dad.

We're so happy you're that guy! Caleb, Stephen and I are all so lucky to have you as our dad. Certainly, Caleb and I both aspire to be as good of a dad as you are when we grow up, I just hope you know that! Happy 46th Birthday!!!!!! You've still got a lot of the race left to run, I hope you run it with the same passion that you've run the first half of your life with! I just want you to know that the family supports you in whatever you do, enjoy today, it's special!

Love,
--------> Jonathan

My party hat is on <:-)
woohoooo. Happy birthday!

This is what the kids wrote to me:
- We can honestly talk to you about our lives, fears and anxieties.
- You're the one we go to when we need emotional input.
- You understand our problems and sympathize with us, you don't judge us or tell us we're doing something wrong.
- You always end up keeping the family together when we go through rough patches.

- You care about our future even though it isn't your burden.
- You sacrifice your own time to convenience the rest of the family, even with minute tasks.
- You provide us with opportunities that make our lives better.
- You show us unconditional love even when we're sometimes unlovable.
- You bear the brunt of all of our emotional garbage.
- You continue to do everything for us despite our inability to be grateful.
- You care for every single one of us when we're putting each other down.
- You help motivate us/keep us accountable and on track
- You open unique opportunities for us with your connections
- You have a unique insight into the college acceptance process
- You always listen to our new ideas or creations and provide positive support
- You believe in us
- You are always trying to maintain balance in the family and make sure everyone is feeling secure and loved.

For these things, we love you!
From your sons

From these two letters, you can tell that David and I play different roles in the home.

Our three boys aspire to be a Dad like David some day. Their affirmation is the biggest motivation for David to work hard at being a good Dad. We also need to trust our kids that even though they don't like us when we discipline them, they might even throw a fit, but after the issue is resolved, they will understand, affirm, and respect us for it.

SECTION IV

DON'T FIGHT ALONE:

PROACTIVELY BUILD YOUR TEAM!

4.1 MENTORING

Before my first child was born, I prepared by reading a lot of books on how to be a good mother. However, after my eldest son Caleb was born, I discovered that he usually did not respond the way a typical book would describe. I thought that I was probably not following the book correctly, or that my child required a different method, and would consult yet another book. It wasn't until I started talking to other mothers whose children were older than my son that they were able to tell me about their own experiences and help me to realize that books are typically descriptions of the experiences of the author accumulated over a period of time, and what gets recorded is typically the end result, not the detailed process of implementing the methods. Also, human beings are vastly different. Therefore, it's difficult for an author to discuss and cover all the possibilities of raising children that are so different from one to another. In the process of learning to be a mother, as in all of the important processes in life, I have discovered that book learning is a mere beginning. Being able to ask an experienced teacher in a classroom setting is slightly better. However, the best is being able to learn by observing at close range how someone who is farther along a particular learning process deal with each situation as it comes up.

Mentors fills in that critical missing link in the growth process. Having a mentor who has gone before you will save you from wading through a lot of information to get to the particular life experience you need help with. I have benefited throughout my life from mentors in just about every area of my life: from wrestling with career decisions to marriage questions to learning about balancing work and family obligations. I highly recommend for every new mother to seek out a mentor who would be willing to help you in your journey of learning by sharing from her own life her lessons learned, as well as to help you diagnose a situation correctly by asking the right questions.

There are six general criteria that I recommend you consider as you go about finding a mentor, because finding the right mentor could make the critical difference in your success as a mother and in mentoring other mothers:

1. She is a practitioner, on a theorist. I once heard from a friend who was a student in a Tsinghua EMBA program discuss the difference between two classes. In one class, the professor was a theorist, meaning that he has never worked as a manager in real industry before. Rather, he had studied from books all his life and understood the theories very well, but had never lived to observe the messy application of such theories. So after each lecture, when my friend, who was a manager in a multinational firm, would ask him a question related to what he is facing at work, the professor can only quote from the textbook how he thinks the situation should be dealt with. Any further deviation from the textbook case was met with a blank face because he could not be adaptable with his answers. My friend just ended up skipping all the classes taught by this professor, because he could just as well learn the information from the textbook himself. However, he eagerly looked forward to another class taught by a professor who would fly in from overseas, because this person had many years of experience working successfully in industry himself. When my friend asked him a question about a decision or a situation he was facing at work, this professor would be able to ask him penetrating questions that would help him gain insight in ways he had never considered before, and arrive at an answer that would sometimes surprise, and usually delight himself. Of course, his own unique case is usually not covered in the textbook, but someone who has had many years of dealing with people in his position of management would be able to help him. In my own journey of learning about mothering, I have found experienced mentors to be like that professor from overseas.

   When I first arrived in Beijing, I was a typical "trailing spouse" who left behind my own world and work to follow my spouse who was relocating here because of a work opportunity. My marriage went from a very American model of 50-50 split, where my husband and I divided up the household and parenting tasks equally, to one where I had to manage everything myself with the help of a maid because he was frequently traveling for work or busy with work related social engagements in the evenings and weekends. I remember our first Thanksgiving in Beijing, when he was traveling, how depressed and alone I felt, because Thanksgiving was the biggest family holiday in America, even more so than Christmas. When I called a mentor from Los Angeles and told her how I felt, she was upset at my husband for being a workaholic, not understanding the nature of his job here in Beijing and the different sets of expectations here. She felt that he was not being a good husband and father, which made me feel even worse, because then I started to regret supporting the decisions to move our entire family over. This mentor suggested that I talk to my husband about moving back to America. The next day, I talked to another friend who had moved to Beijing several years earlier from Los Angeles, and complained about how I felt, blaming my husband for my misery. She was sympathetic to how I felt, because she had gone through the same situation when she first came. However, she told me to consider the situation from my husband's angle, having to adjust to a different work culture, work in a different language that he was still learning, in addition to facing a lot of pressures and handling different sets of expectations at work. She painted a picture of our husbands as soldiers who have to go out there to the fierce battlefield everyday and come home all exhausted. What they need are not angry and miserable wives who are not able to help them deal with the new challenges they are facing alone, but a place to heal your wounds. She suggested that rather than expecting him to revert back to the husband I knew back home, that I change myself to be his helper and nurse. Instead of demanding that he come home and help me take care of everything, just to make it my mission in the next little while to take care of everything myself with the help of some fellow mother friends around me, and focus on making the home a warm and inviting place for him to come home and recover in. Not only did she describe to me what she did, but she also invited me over to experience what life is like when her husband came home. While she also grew up in America, where mothers usually dressed very casually at home to facilitate moving around with active children and doing a lot of household chores, she took care to dress up nicely and put on make up and perfume right before her husband came home. She would prepare her children and help them to get into an appreciative and thankful frame of mind by telling them how grateful she is that their father is such a wonderful provider and father. Then she would put on soothing music and light lots of candles around the house as she got dinner set up before his estimated arrival time. She and the kids would be ready to greet him at the door with a smile and a hug, welcoming him home after a long and tiring day. I was there one evening as he came home, and I could see the obvious eagerness on his face as he came home, how delighted he was to see his family, despite the tired lines on his face. My friend told me that her husband has always tried to be home when he could and pushed away unnecessary work related social obligations because he really wanted to be home.

271

My friend's advice would not be found in a textbook on what makes a marriage work in a move from West to East. However, her mentoring during this critical transition period in my life not only saved my marriage from heading towards a dangerous cliff, but also helped me to fall in love with living in Beijing instead of hating it here. After observing how she lived out her own advice, I focused not on copying her form and doing everything exactly alike, but on following her advice to put the focus on serving my husband and helping him make this transition. For example, lighting candles in a house full of active boys would have been dangerous, and putting on perfume and make up would be out of character for someone who's more comfortable being "one of the guys". However, I made sure that I dressed in clothes that my husband liked, tidying up the house before he came home, and putting in effort to have the whole family focused on welcoming him and serving him when he got home rather then demanding this or that from him. By the time he arrived home, the children would have been too hungry, so they ate dinner and waited to eat fruit with him. We kept the dinnertime conversation light and humorous, as the children would share jokes, funny anecdotes from the day, or ask him about his day. The humor always energized the entire family and made some of our difficult adjustments much more bearable, especially when we can make fun of ourselves instead of feeling embarrassed or inadequate.

While both friends I consulted were equally eager to help me, one was a theorist while the other was a practitioner. Choosing the follow the right friend's advice made a whole world of difference in my marriage.

2. She is a learner, not an expert. In the April, 2009 edition of FORTUNE magazine, Bill Gates was asked what was the most valuable lesson he learned from his mentor Warren Buffet, and Gates responded with the following:

"His grace in talking to people where he's always saying, "You know, you probably understand this better than I do, but here's how I messed it up when I first got involved in this." You know, that's a special talent. . . There was a case at the annual meeting where somebody asked a question about should you sell the stocks that have gone up and keep the ones that have not? And he sort of said, "No, you look at the value of the business." And then Charlie [Munger] added, "He's telling you your conceptual framework is all wrong." Which is in fact what the answer had been, but there wasn't one element of, "Hey dummy . . .""

A great mentor is like that. When my second son was a newborn baby, he would have a lot of gas in his stomach every evening, causing him to cry from his great discomfort. Many friends at the time gave me their "expert advice", telling me that I was just not tough enough as a mother and that I just needed to let him learn not to manipulate me with his crying. One mentor who was much older than we were told me that she was no expert, but that her daughter had this particular condition that was greatly helped when she put this liquid in his milk, but that just because it worked for her, it might not work for me. Her reassurance helped me not to feel like a failure should the recommendation not work, and the tentative way she said it showed her humility and willingness to be wrong. In this case, the liquid helped a great deal and my son Jonathan was saved from many evenings of crying and discomfort, if I had followed my other friends' advice to let him learn to cry it out.

There were also other instances when my friend made a recommendation that wouldn't work with me, and I would let her know. She always thanked me and appreciated my feedback, saying that it would help her in the future as she gave similar advice to others, knowing how things didn't turn out in my case. As a result, I trusted her enough to share with her my own failures and weaknesses, knowing that she wouldn't judge me or belittle me even when she was correcting me.

3. She is vulnerable, not perfect. When I lived in Los Angeles, I often went to an older auntie in my church for advice on mothering, because she had successfully raised two wonderful sons who were now adults. What I loved about her was that she was so down to earth, always sharing her from own weaknesses and lessons learned from her own mistakes, rather than lecture at me about the "right" way to be a mother, like some other older aunties that came across so righteous and perfect that they scared and intimidated me. Whenever I complimented her on how well her kids turned out, she would usually tell me how lucky she felt, and that God was so gracious to her to give her a wonderful husband and in-laws, rather than try to take all the credit for herself. She showed me her real self and allowed me the freedom to be real with her.

4. She is an encourager, not taskmaster.

    Miss Elizabeth was my son Caleb's first pre-school teacher. She is short and chubby and is always ready to crinkle up her eyes in a twinkling and gracious smile that radiates joy and sweetness from inside. She is my first mentor in the area of being my child's teacher. Being a first time mother with no mothering skills or inner desire to be "motherly", Miss Elizabeth modeled for me the ideal mother/teacher. It was obvious that she loved her job and had a huge capacity to love every child that comes into her orbit, and her arms are always ready to give a big hug to anyone that needed it. As a first time mother, I was nervous and anxious as I was touring different pre-schools, looking for the "right one" for my first born son. The overachiever inside of me wanted to make sure that I learned all the skills I can from the teachers at pre-school so that I can reinforce their ideas at home and raise my child the "right" way. I have no idea what to expect for children in pre-school, so I would stay after school to ask Miss Elizabeth questions on how to best teach my child to develop in various skills. She invited me to be a helper in her class so that I can observe first hand how she teaches her class. I would be in for a real treat.

It wasn't any one specific thing Miss Elizabeth did that stood out in my mind. Rather, it was who she was that permeated the entire classroom. Miss Elizabeth taught me that all of life was education. She merely brought this larger world into her little classroom for this group of 8 children in this class that she called "Bear Cubs". Miss Elizabeth's classroom was full of life in its varying stages: from little plants that each child was in charge of watering and pruning, to the silk worms in the box that were in varying stages of metamorphosis, to the classroom pet ferret that everyone took turns petting, feeding, and cleaning its cage. Everyone had a job assigned in the class, from the weather monitor who was responsible for putting the pointer to the right weather condition that day on the weather picture chart, to the blackboard person who had to make sure there was fresh chalk and clean board after each class. Every child had an opportunity to express himself by bringing in something from home each week to talk to his friends in class about. Every moment was a teaching moment, and Miss Elizabeth always made sure there were plenty of opportunities for the little hands to be busy. I learned from her that engaging the hands was the best form of learning for little children. There were always things to occupy those little hands: from making delicious chocolate oatmeal balls to collecting leaves from outside to dry and compress into a bookmark, to rolling a marble dipped in paint inside a box to make artwork. Miss Elizabeth was a fountain of new ideas on how to teach children through creative play, and of new ways to make learning an endlessly fun adventure.

I saw Miss Elizabeth first as that source of information, which I eagerly soaked up like a thirsty sponge. Then I would discover that the things I saw her do in class, when I tried to copy them exactly at home, wasn't received as well by my child. When I went back to share with her my puzzlement or frustration, she would always smile at my confessions of failure, and provide ideas to do things my own way. When I would complain that I just wasn't as creative or patient as she was with children, she would be gracious and compliment me on something else she observed me trying to do with the other kids in her classroom that she thinks would work in my own home. For example, when I complained that I was too easily distracted by all the housework I had to complete at home instead of focusing on a particular activity with my child, she encouraged me to brainstorm ways that I can effectively spend time with Caleb. She suggested various museums in Los Angeles that I can visit with him instead of trying to always teach him things from home. That was how we discovered the airplane museum, where we purchased a membership and returned to again and again for repeat visits. When I asked how I could possibly cook a meal with such an active boy, she suggested that I overcome my perfectionism and allow my son to bang on the pots and pans with a wooden spoon on the floor while I cooked. She never tired of my confessions of failure or frustration, but always found new ways to encourage me to try new things, find a new solution, or do it in a way that fits me, allowing me to enjoy the process of mothering. It was her encouragement that freed me from the fear of failure, and allowed me to become like a little child, playing and discovering and learning alongside my child.

5. She gives life, not advice.
I first met Anne when I checked my sons into Sunday School. Half of her face was paralyzed from a childhood disease, giving her a permanent smirk, and one of her legs was crooked, making her walk with an exaggerated limp. While my friend, who was a gifted

musician who graduated from Harvard, was confidently leading the children singing up front, Anne and her husband made fruit drinks and prepared snacks in the back. She rarely spoke, so I never noticed her, until one day, when the children's toilets were stopped up and overflowing. In my state of irritation and impatience, I asked for the Superintendent to complain to him about the poor condition of the toilets. The superintendent turned out to be Anne. As soon as she saw what happened, she apologized and knelt down to clean up while her husband got tools to unstop the toilet. Two other boys that looked just like her husband came along and cleaned up alongside Anne. I was embarrassed for my demanding and critical attitude as they set about the repairs without any words or explanation to defend themselves. After that I started noticing that all along, it was not just Anne, but Anne and her entire family serving together in Sunday School. Each Sunday Anne and her husband Gary would bring in boxes of supplies and snacks that she lovingly prepared from home. Our kids enjoyed homemade play dough made from pure flour and natural food dye so that the children who are allergic to chemicals can also enjoy playing with play dough. The children also enjoyed delicious homemade cookies, sandwiches, and healthy snacks that Anne brought in. After the children finished their Sunday School and left behind messy classrooms, it was her family that stayed behind week after week to clean up, disinfect all the toys and utensils, and take out the trash. Inspired by her life, I volunteered to lead the children in singing and to learn to teach Sunday School, just so I can learn from her example. Anne rarely spoke or gave advice, but she lived her life of humble service before me, and modeled for me what it was to love and serve alongside her family. It was from Anne's example that I learned that a family can serve others together. Even after Anne's children had long outgrown the age to be in Sunday School, they continued to serve together for years. Two years ago when I went back to Los Angeles to visit, Anne and Gary were still cleaning classrooms and taking out the trash after over twenty years of service. It wasn't until after I had known Anne for many years that I learned that she was a high level manager working for a big software company. She never talked about herself, but always sought to serve others and meet their needs. You will never hear Anne teach a class or give a talk on how to be a mother to her own children and how to love so many children, but you can sure learn a lot more from her than from other "experts" about this topic by just watching her live her life quietly without any words.

6. She is wise, not smart.

Michael and Alice were a couple that were mentors and examples to our family. Although Michael was a famous oncologist (cancer doctor), their influence upon our family had nothing to do with how educated they were or how smart they were. Michael and Alice purchased a house and renovated it just for the purpose of helping young families with active children to learn about marriage and parenting. They filled their backyard with a large yard and many little plastic bikes for the little kids who would visit their home every Saturday. They also had a jungle gym (play set) built for kids to climb all over, under, and around it. My kids still remember climbing the monkey bars with the other boys, riding those bikes, and throwing things into their little fish pond. Every Saturday morning, Alice and her three girls, the youngest of whom was in grade 3 at the time, helped to take care of all the little kids in another section of their house which was connected to their backyard, while Michael and the adults had a tranquil few hours of quiet to study about how to manage a marriage and busy family. I remember as a tired and desperate mother of two young and mischievous boys how this was too good to be true, that there must be some catch. But the studies continued year after year for at least the 4-5 years I was there until we left for Beijing. During that time, I saw Michael and Alice attend numerous of our group's birthday parties, soccer games, graduation ceremonies and other important events. Alice was unassuming, gentle, and quiet. Nothing seemed to disturb her. When my boys broke some toys and threw them into her fish pond, I was upset and afraid that we would not be welcomed back into her home next time. In my embarrassment, I was very stern with them, asking them to apologize and offering to replace the damaged items. She smiled and reassured me that boys are just being boys, and that broken things are much easier to repair than broken people, and that in her eyes, things just don't even compare with how important people are. She declined our offer to replace those toys, and sent them back out to play. A few weeks ago, my boys were complaining to me about having to help take care of very young kids who came to our house to play when the adults studied marriage in a different room, because one of the kids broke a toy. I asked them if they remembered that backyard incident in Michael and Alice's house. Their eyes lit up. "Yeah, I loved climbing that jungle gym! And Oh, auntie Alice's cakes and cookies are so yummy! Yeah, and remember us racing on those little pink and blue bikes? I can't believe how naughty we were back then and how nice they were to us. We made a mess of their house every week!" They have such fond memories of childhood spent with their friends in that house. After reminiscing, they had a totally different perspective about their impatience with the kids in our house. "We're really not that patient, are we, Mom? I guess broken things are easier to fix than broken people, huh? I'm glad that it was the toy that broke back then, not me!" Michael and Alice mentored us with a life of wisdom for us to follow. They only used words when necessary, yet when they spoke, we remembered. To this day I never did find out Alice's education background or how smart she was, and it doesn't matter to either of us if I knew. To me, she is one of the wisest women I know, and that was what really mattered.

Today my husband and I find ourselves mentoring others as we've been mentored, not because we are naturally such wonderful people, but because we have received so much, it would be impossible not to give it away. I find that good mentors have usually been mentored by others, whether it's by their natural parents or other older and wiser friends. So for the cycle to be complete, find a good mentor and later pass on the blessing by mentoring others. You will discover the truth that it is indeed more blessed to give than to receive.

7. These first three criteria show that a good mentor has the qualities of being a doer rather than a speaker, and that she is humble and authentic. Just these qualities alone would be good enough to imitate. We will discuss the other three criteria next month.

For Your Growth

1. What kind of a community do you have? Is your community supportive of your values? Your marriage as a top priority? If so, is there an intentional part to this community? Are you learning new things together in support of this priority?
2. If not, how can you and your spouse seek out or build such a community? Through common interests? Parenting clubs? School? Church or other religions communities?

4.2 ASSEMBLING YOUR TEAM: MOTHERHOOD IS NOT A SOLITARY SPORT

Human beings are not designed to be lone creatures, but are designed for relationship. Mark Twain says that "Happiness is best when shared". When we see a beautiful sunset, we want someone else who is there simply to share that moment with us, not necessarily make any comments on its artistic value. Deep within each of us is an innate need for belonging, connectedness, and a need to be accepted. When we are sad and cry, we want someone to be there with us, not necessarily to solve our problems. Solitary confinement is the worst form of punishment in prison not because the conditions in the cell are any worse off than other cells, but because there is no one there for the prisoner to connect to. Loneliness is the worst human condition.

One of the greatest destructive effects of modernization to mankind is the isolation of individuals into small discreet units, where it's "each man for himself" , "dog eat dog", and a "survival of the fittest" kind of a cruel Darwinian jungle. The result is increasing sense of alienation and disconnectedness, causing skyrocketing rates of depression and suicide in cities. Even children are not immune to this kind of malaise inflicting this world, as suicides occur at alarmingly younger and younger ages. Gone are the days of the small village, where there are no locks and where village women gather to cook together, look after each other's kids, and the children roam the streets in safety while playing in the fields and woods. Nowadays, it's fairly common for people who live and work in the big cities to go for weeks, months, and even years without knowing or interacting with their neighbors. I realize that oversimplifying the past with nostalgic portrayals is not helpful, as villages are often rife with their own stifling internal illnesses as closed social systems. The Cultural Revolution rooted out all these symptoms, but also ripped apart the fabric of society so that we need to re-start and attempt to recover some of the good elements of being in relationship with one another. The sad fact is that many of us never recovered community, and are suffering in lonely silence.

The modern marriage and family is no more immune to these social ills or ravages of isolation and alienation. Human relations is so broken at the most basic levels that marriage to many is no longer a commitment of a lifetime but rather just another social contract where there is no basis of mutual trust, and self-protection is more esteemed than self-denial or duty and sacrifice. Many of us enter into marriage with a desire that our mate will meet those needs for intimacy, friendship, acceptance, and unconditional love. However, because we are both imperfect human beings, we often find disappointment; disappointment with ourselves, and with our spouse. No human being can ever meet another human being's needs fully and completely. We are all broken and imperfect people, and selfishness is at the root of our condition.

For those of us lucky enough to have grown up in a healthy family system, we can often fall back on our families of origin for support. However, even healthy families find themselves separated by distance and time as more and more family members move to other parts of the country, or even world, because of job opportunities. Sometimes two spouses might even be forced to live in separate cities for a time for various financial and circumstantial reasons. If we continue to remain isolated, putting our jobs first at the cost of our need for intimacy, friendship, and relationship, we will suffer devastating psychological consequences later in life in the form of broken marriages and family disharmony.

My husband and I learned in pre-marital counseling class the need to have healthy community outside of the marriage relationship to sustain a healthy marriage. This is why at the outset, we started assembling our own "support teams" to help us remain in a larger community. This support team includes our natural families who all live in other cities in North America, but also includes mentors and friends. The easiest first step is to find a group of people who have the same values and worldview, and come together to support one another. So my husband has his "guy friends", I have my "girl friends", and together, we also have our "couple friends".

It used to be that people aspired to be mothers as a noble profession. The movie "Mona Lisa's Smile" depicts a female professor who was fighting against the restrictions that society placed upon women to put marriage and having children above getting a serious education. In one poignant scene, this professor, played by Julia Roberts, expends a lot of energy to help one of her very talented students apply to and get accepted into the prestigious Yale Law School. When she discovered that her student had gotten married and will not be attending, she got frantic and tried to find alternatives to help her student continue getting her law degree. Her student asked her a question that since she fought so hard for a woman's right to choose, why is it so hard to accept that a women would desire and choose marriage and family over a professional career? The women in her generation were beginning to face that choice. Now, many years later, the tide has reversed. Instead of fighting for women's choice, many assume that only people who can't make it professionally would choose to stay at home to be a full time mother.

No matter what the prevailing sentiment in society is, motherhood will always be the toughest and most challenging career. There will be many societal trends are at war with the true desires of your heart, and in those times, it will be hard to go it alone on this path. Motherhood is not a lone sport. You will need to assemble your team to be your companions when you need to buck popular trends or swim against the tide of mainstream thinking.

In my example of trying to not take or borrow money from my mother, go into debt, or generate extra income to enroll in Gymboree classes, my ability to take a stand to not give in to those voices of temptation was not my strong will, extraordinary ability, or amazing wisdom, but was knowing that I am too weak to do this alone, and to enlist the help and support of friends when I need it. These other mothers had the same struggles as me, and were seeking to hold onto the values that they hold dear and stand by the choices they made. This common values bound us together quickly and deepened our friendship with one another. We sympathized with each other's struggles and feelings and supported and cheered one another's decisions. Our friendship enabled our kids to also socialize with one another, and we gave one another the permission to discipline and correct our kids' naughty behavior. We cried with each other and prayed with each when a child had health problems, and helped babysit each other's kids when we needed a break or go on a date with our husbands. We shared money saving tips with one another, and alerted each other to special sales so that we can live within our means financially while living out our ideals to stay home with our babies, deeply believing that the best gift we can give to our children is the gift of our presence. We all faced questions from our family and friends about why we were wasting our talent and education to stay home to do mind-numbingly boring and repetitive work. We also faced tight budgets and the reality of having to depend on our husbands for a living. At the same time, we were the first generation of mothers who were totally untrained for our jobs. We grew up only knowing how to study, which we excelled at, but had no child rearing experience. Some of us didn't even know how to fry an egg when we started out in our marriage. However, through our weekly meetings, I learned to deal with my anxiety and conquer my fears, while at the same time helping others deal with their own post-partum depression or financial worries.

I had the fortune to belong to several critical communities of friends that helped me and shaped me into who I am today. One was the mother's group that I formed. Another was another small group of friends around the same age as me that continues to meet to this day. We called ourselves the "Princess Group", but informally, we jokingly called ourselves the "recovering Asian Overachieving Women's Group". Just like the organization "Alcoholics Anonymous" has members who recognize that their addiction to alcohol is a lifelong weakness, and that they need companions along the way to help each other in their struggle to face this weakness, so we were a group of female Asian high achievers who recognized in ourselves our addiction to the praise and recognition of others to feed our sense of self-worth . We all have in common our desire to please our parents or bosses because we have been labeled as the "good kid" by our elders and are expected to perform to expectations. We called ourselves the "Princess Group" because of our common faith in our real identities, as the beloved Princess of the Heavenly King, who is the Creator of the universe. As that, we remind ourselves daily that we need no other identity or achievement to affirm our worth as human beings, and help each other to keep away from performance orientation or pursuing achievement as a means of winning or earning the love and affirmation of others that we love. We banded together, drawn by our natural affinity and need for each other, and supported one another in this social experiment. In our group was a sales engineer (me), a doctor, an accountant, a college professor, a lawyer, a pharmacist, and a business owner. This group continues to meet monthly after so many years together, and even though I've moved away from Southern California, my Princess friends continue to be a source of encouragement and strength for me today.

Another group that played a key role in my own personal growth has been a group of married couples that David and I belonged to. When we first moved from Boston to Los Angeles, we joined a group of young professionals that was learning about inner healing. Together, we took some graduate level classes related to inner healing, psychology, and families of origin. We practiced what we learned on one another, and through sharing our deepest pains and joys together, became lifelong friends. Eventually, all the singles got married and brought in their spouses to join the group, and we all became fully committed to help one another's marriage not only survive, but to thrive. As such, it was really helpful whenever any of the couples had fights. I still vividly remember one particular incident when David and I had a bad fight. I don't remember what it was about, but only that we were both upset, and I was thinking about leaving again. I called one of my friends in this group, and within an hour, everyone came to our doors. The guys took David into one room while the girls remained with me in the living room while we both complained bitterly about the other person. While each group of friends listened and accepted our negative feelings, some hugged me and even cried with me, but no one uttered a word of condemnation against my husband. Everyone in the group was FOR our marriage, not AGAINST any person who did wrong. My girl friends asked me to reflect upon my own contribution to the fight, and to see if there was anything about how I reacted that needed to change. They encouraged me to take ownership and responsibility for my part and to seek to change what I could about my part. I assume that the guys did the same thing in the other room, because after the group of friends left, it was as if the wind had been taken out of each of our sails, and the anger and finger pointing was gone. In its place was a humility to admit our own responsibility and a desire for change and reconciliation. In this way, we in the group helped each other through many tough times of bitter, almost unresolvable conflict, and all couples remain our closest friends to this day. Now, we are scattered all over various parts of the world, but continue to remain in touch with each other, and whenever we see each other, no matter how successful, how many outward achievements and titles have been accumulated, the first words out of our mouths for one another is always : "How's your marriage doing?" Only when there is praise from the spouse is there an acknowledgement of "success" and a pat on the back of congratulations.

Is it time for you to assemble your team?

For Your Growth

1. What kind of a community do you have? Is your community supportive of your values? Your marriage as a top priority? If so, is there an intentional part to this community? Are you learning new things together in support of this priority?
2. If not, how can you and your spouse seek out or build such a community? Through common interests? Parenting clubs? School? Church or other religions communities?

4.2 WHICH RELATIONSHIP COMES FIRST?

I've always thought that people are responsible for their own choices and sins, and was rather surprised one day during an inner healing class that I was taking to hear about the concept of generational sins, and the concept of soul ties. A group of us were taking the class together, and as we shared about our family backgrounds, it was clear that some incorrect behavior patterns do indeed get passed down from one generation to another. And it has to do with the incorrect prioritizing of good relationships within the family.

The Story of Two Factories
My grandfather was a rags to riches self-made millionaire who built a successful pharmaceutical empire from literally nothing. Unfortunately, he died at the tender young age of 38 from overwork and exhaustion, leaving my grandmother with 5 children and a busy pharmaceutical empire to run. A couple of years after my grandfather died, my father decided to drop out of medical school to return home to help my grandmother run the factory. As the eldest son in the family and a newly married husband, he was needed at home to help my grandmother raise his 4 younger siblings. My mother would treat my aunt (Dad's younger sister) as her first daughter. My grandmother, being a widow long before her husband passed away (her husband was rarely home because of trying to build a business), relied heavily on my father for emotional support. When my father got married, she immediately took a disliking to my mother, who was from a poor but educated family. The birth of three daughters did not help the relationship between mother and daughter-in-law, but only served to give my grandmother a more concrete reason to reject my mother. The ensuing years would see repeated efforts on my grandmother's part to replace my mother with another daughter in law who was more obedient, more moldable, and more able to give birth to boys.

My parents went to the same elementary school, and my mother was always the top student in her school. My father could only admire her from afar, but when he arrived in medical school and saw her again when he visited the bookstore where she worked, immediately decided that he wanted to marry her. He was not alone, however, as there were two other medical school classmates there who also became his prime competitors. In the he won and managed to marry her. This hard won victory was not about to be easily relinquished just because my mother produced a daughter (me). However, an opening came up for my grandmother when my mother agreed to her father's request to convince my father to invest money to open up a factory, but instead the factory never opened and the money disappeared. This act of betrayal ripped away the trust in the marriage. He consented to his mother's request to find another woman who can produce a son for him. Obviously, this effort did not succeed, because my parents are still married and two more sisters were born to them, but my father still mentions this disappearing factory to this day as the day his marriage fell apart. Growing up, I have no memories of my grandmother, who refused to look at or hold me or any of my sisters. I admire and subscribe to a lot of Confucian values, but stop at what he says about the value of women and the priority of the familial relationship. What my parents were unable to do was put their marriage relationship at the top of their priority list, and by trying to honor their parents before loving their spouses, ended up not being able to sever the emotional soul tie that exists between parent and child and to build a brand new soul tie to their mates. Years later, history would repeat itself when my mother rejects my choice of a husband because he is from a poor and educated family.

Reversing the Curse: A Jar of Spaghetti Sauce

My husband and I had purchased our first home, and my mother-in-law came to stay with us. She was a very frugal woman whose husband had died shortly after my husband graduated from college. She was shocked to find me making spaghetti sauce one day using a bottle of expensive Gourmet sauce bottle instead of making it from scratch with fresh tomatoes, and came to tell me that this is too wasteful. She turned around to ask my husband for his support, because he is also very frugal. He put his arm around her and said: "Mom, Rossana is just starting to learn how to cook. She's my wife and I love her very much. I didn't marry her because of her cooking skills, but have committed to love her with all her imperfections. You are our respected guest, but she is the hostess of this house, so I ask that you please respect and support her instead of criticize her when you come." My mother-in-law looked hurt, and went away with an expression of sadness on her face, saying that she should just go home now. Her son is grown up and gone, and she's not welcome anymore. I went over to take her hand and say: "Mom, I'm a part of your family now. Please forgive me for being so ignorant about so many things, but please give me a chance to learn to be a good wife and a daughter in law. You are right! This bottle is very expensive, and I will look for ways to learn to make food from fresh ingredients to save money and be more healthy. You are always welcome in this house." She went back into the kitchen. "Tell me about this sauce. Why did you buy it? There must be a reason that it's so much more expensive than other brands. I'd like to learn more." This was the beginning of a beautiful friendship between me and my mother-in-law.

It took more than a jar of spaghetti with my mother to communicate the priority I put on my marriage, despite my desire to be a daughter in law who is the most filial. I know how much my mother had suffered because of her mother in law, and I wanted to make her happy to ease her suffering. I wanted to stand up for her when her husband couldn't. However, these desires came to a collision very quickly. It was not long after I got married, and I was working in my office when the phone call came. Something came up with the business at home, and I need to take a week's vacation to go help my parents resolve the situation. My husband and I had made another commitment to a group of people that week, and I could not walk away. When I insisted to my mother that I needed to check with my husband to discuss the situation first before giving her an answer, she got upset. Being one of the most intelligent women I've ever known, my mother used that intelligence to come up with ways to insult and scold me. All the old familiar sayings came out: "You just married him, not sell yourself to him", "who raised you up all these years, him?" , "you only have one set of parents, but you can change as many husbands as you want", etc. When I told her that I was my own person, not my parents', not my husband's, she replied that of course parents owned their children. That's the Chinese way. I disagreed, but after an hour of this conversation, I was in despair, because she issued an ultimatum. If I insist on putting David first, it means that I am choosing him over them, and that means that I will cut off parent-child relationship with them. Then she hung up. I didn't call back. An excruciatingly painful day passed by, and my father called me the next evening. "Your mother is getting sick from such disrespectful behavior from you. Just go apologize and she'll forgive you." Both David and I decided to go back together to see how we can help.

Impact: Love and Respect Across the Generations

These incidents are not isolated events, but our attempts to reverse that generational curse began with these little actions at putting the marital relationship above the parental filial relationship. However, it does not mean that we neglect to take advantage of every available opportunity to reach out to our parents to express our continued and unwavering love, while allowing the new son in law and daughter in law more opportunities to love the in-laws. Being the caretaker of remembering everyone's birthdays and special holidays, I am often in touch with my in laws to express these birthday and holiday wishes, and my mother-in-law usually calls me up first to enlist my help before asking my husband.

Last summer, my father had an operation to remove a cancer that was discovered in his colon. After the operation, David and I flew home to Vancouver to be with him. As the three sisters got ready to fly in from various parts of the world to see my father, my mother asked David to take charge of the schedule. In front of everyone, she said that she respects his wisdom the most, and trusts him to make the best decisions and arrangements for the family. 20+ years later, after all the opposition, line drawing, doubts, and tears, I cherished those words in my heart and whispered a prayer of thanks. Those words are my graduation speech.

For Your Growth

1. In your household, when there is a difference of opinion, who has the last word, the parents or your husband?

2. In what ways has the marriage relationship been subjected to other relationships such as honoring the parents relationship or the parenting relationship (raising your child)? How can you elevate it to the highest priority again?

4.3 MANAGING HOURHOLD STAFF

When my son Stephen was 5 years old, he had a classmate named Freddy in kindergarten. He was a rather fat little boy who always arrived in school on the back of his nanny with his beautiful and thin mother at his side. His nanny also came to pick him up at school every day, always carrying big Freddy on her back to and from the car. He cried easily and always got his way when he cried. He did not eat very well because he was always fed by his nanny, whose sole objective in life is to make sure that Freddy was safe, ate everything fed to him, and had every desire catered to. Freddy could not run around with the other kids very well because he was so overweight, and because the teachers at school didn't want him to get hurt and for them to get the blame, he just stayed in the classroom when the other children played in the playground. Freddy seemed to have the perfect comfortable childhood except that he was under so much constraint under his nanny's watch that he missed his childhood.

At the same school, my son Jonathan had a classmate Jason, a Korean American, who was living in Beijing by himself with his nanny and driver. His parents work in Korea but want him to go to school in China to learn Chinese. Jason was being raised by his nanny and driver. He was an angry young man and was always getting into trouble. Therefore Jason's nanny and driver were always getting fired and changing faces. Jonathan became his best friend because he was able to communicate to him in English. Jason skipped classes often and dared his teachers to punish him, because he would just defy them and continue to do whatever he wanted. He often told my son how angry he was that no one cared about him and how much he wanted to kill himself.

I have many friends from Ivy League schools who grew up in boarding schools in the U.S. while their parents lived and worked in Asia. Their common experience has been that once they graduate and started working, they have no desire to move to the same city as their parents because they have different worldviews and values than their parents. Even when many of them are offered houses and cars as a bribe to move home, they do not want to go, because they have grown used to a different lifestyle. Many of these parents wonder why after they work so hard to send their kids to the best schools overseas why their kids won't listen to them anymore. In the process of pursuing the best education for their kids, they have lost that relationship with their kids.

What is the common element in all of the three stories? It is that when parents do not spend the time to develop a relationship with their kids when they are young and leave the mundane tasks of parenting to others, their children have no desire to be with them when they are grown, because they have never developed a close relationship in the early years. In today's China the prospect of having a maid or nanny is a given for most white collar families. There is great danger in leaving the raising of young children to other caretakers while the mother enjoys a life of comfort and ease and continues to develop her fast track career. I sometimes hear of new mothers brag to their friends that their children love living at boarding school, even requesting to go to school when they return on the weekends, or that their nanny manages the household so well that she can go to the spa on her day off, or that their parents back home take care of their child so that they won't need to waste all the years of hard work, education, and training. These are often the same mothers who years later cry for help when their children have developed problems focusing at school, lacking the desire to study or obey their words of instructions, or later in the teen years develop addiction to internet games, online chat, or have huge cell phone bills. They often wonder why their kids won't listen to them, or why they have such poor study habits when they themselves have been such independent and self disciplined students growing up. One of the greatest culprits in this is the inappropriate use or abuse of the nanny.

An analogy with the corporate world might be helpful here. A CFO of a company would never dream of letting the bookkeeper, or the person who enters numbers in the accounting books, come up with and approve a multi-million dollar budget for the new year. This is because all important financial decisions are made and executed by the CFO while the other less significant tasks such as keeping the books balanced are left up to the CFO's helpers. The same goes for mothers and maids. The important mission of raising and training a child belongs with the mother, not the maid. While it is very convenient to have your maid, or your mother in law toilet train your child because you are busy at work, it will be just as easy and tempting to continue that pattern of behavior and leave the other sacred training tasks to them as well. Slowly, you will realize that for your life of ease and expediency you have forfeited your role to be the primary source of influence on your child's life because you have given up the tough tasks of training and spending time with your kids to others. When you want to use your authority as mother to tell your child to obey you, he will look at you like a stranger and wonder what gave you the right to tell him what to do when you were never around for him, and have put other priorities above him?

So does this mean that you fire your nanny and do everything yourself? No. I suggest that you can develop a very healthy relationship with your nanny and your child, if you manage the boundaries well. Here are some suggestions:

1. Your maid is an employee with a job description. Define that clearly. I have a work chart which outlines a list of my maid's responsibilities by day, by week, and by month. Manage your nanny or driver as if you were their boss in a real company, with career development goals and regular performance reviews. Employees are also humans who need your guidance, care, and understanding, just like you need guidance, care, and understanding from your manager. Build in incentives for a job well done, or for ideas and improvements that she suggests and implements on her own initiative.

2. Keep and protect boundaries in terms of work scope, time, and decision making. Just as you have needs to spend time with your family, so your maid needs time for herself and her family, as well as regular breaks in between the hard physical labor of cleaning, cooking, and caring for your children. Happy employees keep turnover low and saves you trouble in the long run. Nannies are different from other employees in that our children become emotionally attached to them. When they leave, our children lose a close relationship and go through a period of grieving the departure of someone in his small circle of close relations. Expectations for her job scope and work hours should be clearly laid out, and then there should be plenty of give and take on both sides from there. For example, if she is experiencing problems at home and needs some time off to take care of it, work out your schedule to accommodate that, and next time you need her to come in to help you during her time off, she would be a lot more willing to help you.

I have a friend who has a hard time trusting her nanny, yet relies on her nanny too much because of the heavy demands on her work. She often surprise checks on or tries ways of surveillance on her nanny, who will inevitably not measure up to her high standards. Nannies and drivers come and go, and she is always asking her friends for good referrals. Her children are confused and withdrawn from the constant parade of strange faces in the home, and have a fear and distrust of people. At first we would feel sorry for her as a friend when we hear about all these bad nannies that are lazy or are irresponsible or too demanding. Finally, after introducing several nannies to her that we felt were pretty good, and then having her tell us surprising or shocking things that she discovered about these nannies, we her friends realized that the problem was my friend, and not the nannies. She has a knack for getting too busy and forgetting to return home from work in time to let her nanny go home, and is shocked when they would not help her out on Sundays or ask for overtime pay. After awhile, we stopped referring nannies and drivers to her, and she ended up being disappointed with her friends who wouldn't help her.

3. Training: I adhere to the principle that I don't expect my employee to do something that I haven't done or cannot do myself. That way I have an idea of what I can reasonably expect from someone in terms of how much workload she can handle. The most effective way to train a nanny is the following three step process:
    a. She watch, I do.
    b. We do together.
    c. She does, I watch.

After the last step where I watch her doing something I've trained her to do, then I can safely walk away, knowing that I've seen her perform a task the way I would like her to do it. Friends who visit my home are always envious of my maid, and wonder how I was so lucky to find someone like her, who keeps my house so clean with minimal supervision and cooks delicious Western dishes that you find only in expensive Western restaurants. Little do they know about the initial training period when I allocated time to spend with her to teach her how to do things to my specifications and show her how I like to keep my house. Now that I have gotten very busy during the day with many projects, she is an invaluable source of help because I know that I can trust her to manage my household for me and even make good decisions in my absence. My maid has been with our family since we arrived in Beijing, and is an indispensable member of our family.

4. Our kids are expected to respect our maid and listen to her instructions. Because we love and care for my maid's son like one of our own sons, she also treats my sons the same way. This means that I have given her permission to discipline my children if they violate any family rules, or to pull me in in more serious situations. Similarly, she has given me permission to discipline her son. This relationship of mutual trust and respect has resulted in kids who are raised by adults with the same and consistent standards and expectations of behavior. Kids feel safe in a consistent world where the adults agree with each other. Sometimes I would see a mother with a nanny walking with her child on the street, and when the child is disrespectful to the nanny, the mother would be silent or would even scold the nanny. This means that in the mother's absence, the nanny has no authority to discipline the child and he becomes a tyrant, with no respect for adults or authority figures. Worse still, he learns to treat people according to their class, and becomes a person with a divided heart, with multiple faces presented to multiple people. In our family, if any of my kids are disrespectful towards the nanny in any way, he will be disciplined because that is a serious offense. Fortunately, this has not yet happened because we try to model that respect towards our nanny for our kids to follow.

5. Do not allow your maid to do everything. Reserve some chores for yourself, your family members, and your child. In our household, our nanny leaves right after she cooks dinner and our children are expected to take turns washing dishes. Each child is expected to make his own bed and clean his own room. On the weekends, we enjoy cooking and cleaning together while our maid takes the weekends off.

In an interview for the March 9 issue of People Magazine in the U.S., First Lady Michelle Obama said that her daughters Malia and Sasha must still do their chores – make their beds, clean their rooms, and clear the dishes from the dinner table. She said that people around the White House wanted to make their lives easy, but that the kids don't need their lives to be easy. They need to be normal kids.

This Chinese New Year when my maid took 10 days off to return to her home town, we continued to function normally without her, with each of us taking on a part of the daily chores. If we were used to being served all the time, we would be flustered when that help is not available for a time. When our maid returned from home, she did not have piles of backlog work or laundry waiting for her to catch up on, but was able to work normally like any other day.

6. Monitor the time you spend with your kids. Don't let a competent maid make you too complacent to parent. Be intentional and proactive in your mothering. Allocate time, sweat, and money to parent your child. Schedule time with your child and block it out of your calendar. Proactively developing your relationship with your child and setting aside the time to be with him ensures that you will not need to deal with future communication problems or rebellious teenagers. By having a maid help you offload household chores, you will have time to develop hobbies or pursue interests together as a family.

7. Help your maid to improve herself. Just as good companies provide perks where employees have opportunities to pursue training opportunities and improve their job skills, we can encourage our maids to pursue learning new skills such as driving, cake decorating/baking, computer, or English. Having opportunities to learn new things or for self improvement ensures that she less likely to be bored with her job and leave.

When employees are well cared for, respected, and treated fairly, they will reciprocate and become trustworthy, diligent, and capable. White collar workers in China have the luxury of being able to afford helpers. We are grateful for this luxury, and are so blessed by our maid, who is a trusted household manager and a valued member of our family. This relationship, after intentional and thoughtful investment of time and training to develop on both sides, has become a tremendous source of blessing for both our family and hers.

For Your Growth

1. If you have household employees, what would you like to stop doing? Start doing?

EPILOGUE I

A Quiver Full of Arrows

A group of us friends were sitting around the dining table chatting animatedly about all kinds of topics. We talked about the financial crisis and speculated on whether the riots on Wall Streets would eventually restore the economy to normal. We talked about the latest environmental disasters, oil spills, and water problems around the world. As everyone's expressions grew more and more grim, I turned to face Caleb sitting beside me, patted him on the back, and said: "Sorry we'll be gone soon and will leave these problems for you and your peers to solve!" At which point, everyone broke into nervous laughter.

An ancient Jewish song likens children to arrows, and proclaims that the man whose quiver is full of them is indeed blessed. I've heard of many analogies made about children (such as a gift, a treasure) which immediately produced a resonance in me, but I never related much to this analogy of the arrow. It sounded as if we were fighting a war and our children are to be used as weapons. How can the soft and cuddly little bundle in my arms be a weapon? As my children grow older, I am increasingly appreciative of this analogy.

It doesn't take a genius to look around the world we live in today to know that mankind is in deep trouble. We are in a battle zone and a race against time as climate changes continue to deteriorate, environmental pollution results when companies and governments choose rapid economic development, expedience, and profit over long term sustainability; earth's resources are rapidly depleted in our insatiable appetite for consumption; and greed, selfishness, and cold hearts invade every corner of society in the form of fake milk powder, shoddy construction, and exploitation of the poor as the gap between the rich and the poor increase at alarming rates. Soon we will run out of places on earth to run to for safety. Our children's generation are born into a war zone. The battle has never been more fierce to beat back human shortsightedness at the expense of our children and their children. It will take some courageous souls who are willing to lay aside their petty self-interests to rescue the human race from self-extinction.

How we parent our children matters deeply. If these arrows are shaped crooked, they will be of no use, and can sometimes harm our own ranks rather than destroy the enemy. Each arrow will be of a different shape, length, and material, but they all need to be shaped in the environment of our home. Our goal is not to keep them as pretty decorations on a shelf, but to shoot them off one day into the world. Would we shape and equip them with the right "backbone" to deal with the grave problems facing mankind? This backbone will consist of their character and values, not their IQ or EQ or other neutral knowledge or skills. Will our children be a positive force to help clean up our messy world, will they get bent and destroyed in the process, or will they leave a path of destruction and heartache behind for others to clean up long after they are gone? When our kids reach the age when they need to be launched forth from our homes, will they be ready and equipped? Will we shoot clear and straight with all our might and blessings, or hold on and not be willing to let go? This is a question we must be prepared to answer, because that day will surely come, and it will come quicker than you think.

Our children are little arrow gifts entrusted to us to shape and mold for a time, but they will need to be launched someday. Are you ready?

Time For Letting Go

"How do you like it, Mom?"

There Caleb stood in front of me, with the help of his Dad to tie his bow tie, he is dressed in a black tuxedo, holding the flowers that he purchased for his date, getting ready to leave for the prom. In typical fashion, David's first response was to grab the camera to commemorate this momentous occasion. This scene brought me back to a time over a decade ago, when Caleb asked me the exact same question. That time, 4 year old Caleb flipped open a can of red enamel paint onto the ground in the backyard, stripped himself naked, danced in the red pool, finger painted himself all over, and walked through the house admiring his handiwork in front of the mirror closets in every room of the house, leaving red footprints all over my beautiful white carpet. At that moment, I wanted to roll on the floor laughing, but also wanted to give him a good spanking. David's response at that time was the same – he asked me to be sure to take a picture to remember.

Caleb is now all grown up, and all kinds of mixed feelings arose within. On the one hand, I am so very proud of this handsome and mature young man, because I genuinely admire him. He often shares such mature and deep reflections that astound me with their wisdom. On the other hand, I know that my child is grown up and it's almost time for him to leave my side. I remember that when I was leaving high school to go to MIT, Mom cried at the airport saying goodbye to me. I didn't understand why she was so sad then, but now I understand. I am about to release this little eagle who has only been at my side for a short ten some years, and let him fly. It's so hard for me to let go, because time had flown by too fast. I thought of a movie I had seen, "Fiddler on the Roof". Inside was a scene when the father sings a song at his daughter's wedding. The lyrics reflect how I was feeling inside exactly:

Is this the little girl I carried?
Is this the little boy at play?

I don't remember growing older
When did they?

When did she get to be a beauty?
When did he grow to be so tall?

Wasn't it yesterday
When they were small?

Sunrise, sunset
Sunrise, sunset
Swiftly flow the days
Seedlings turn overnight to sunflowers
Blossoming even as we gaze

Sunrise, sunset
Sunrise, sunset
Swiftly fly the years
One season following another
Laden with happiness and tears

I asked Caleb if there are any girls that he likes right now. He said that although there are lots of beautiful girls around him, David and I have set the bar high for him. "Mom, I don't want to settle for just any pretty face, hot body, or smart brain, but I want someone who 'gets' me and complements me the way you & Daddy complement each other." I guess the effort we put into our marriage is the best kind of instruction and preparation for our children.

The time that we have our children under our care is so short. It's not until it's almost over that we begin to treasure them. I believe that he will fly well, and hope that he will come home often to visit us two old goats.

When The Nest Is Empty

I was having tea with a dear friend whose daughter will be leaving for college in the U.S. soon. She told me that she was scared to death. I was rather surprised to hear this from her, because from my observation, she seemed to have a very successful career and have an excellent relationship with her son. She confided in me that she was scared to death of facing the stranger in her house who is her husband. Long years of conflict avoidance has guaranteed seeming harmony in the home, but in actuality just meant that the marriage was devoid of intimacy until they were just each other's cordial house guests. She found safety and shelter in her workplace, but shared nothing in common with her husband other than their daughter. After she leaves, there would be nothing left, and the thought of having nowhere else to run after her own retirement and having to rebuild her marriage with someone she has grown to dislike and avoid terrified her to the core.

Since the laws made divorce easier, a large group of the people getting their divorce papers turned out to be older couples whose kids have grown and left the home. When we take a look at the older folks around us, we will discover two surprising extremes. Some are sour and bitter, having nothing positive to say about anything or anyone, but reserve the most stinging comments for their own spouse. Others are resigned to a life of stagnation, waiting for their time to die. However, I find another kind around me as well: the parks are filled with happy old people dancing, playing chess, flying kites, or chatting happily with each other. I see old couples holding hands going to see the movies, as if they were teenagers falling in love for the first time. When all the noise of life is over, the applause has died down after everyone has gone home from the award ceremonies, and there is only one person left staring you in the face, what will you find? What will you do? What kinds of regrets will you have that you can avoid, or choose to live with? What kind of person will you be, before you leave this world?

According to Erikson's Theory of Socioemotional Development, I am at the tail end of "Middle Adulthood", where the main developmental issue facing me is "generativity vs. stagnation", and my main interest is in guiding the next generation, starting from my own children, and on to the next generation of women and mothers. As my children leave my nest one by one in the next two years in rapid succession, I am preparing to face my next developmental stage of "Older Adulthood", where my main developmental issue will be "Ego Integrity vs. Despair", I will need to decide whether my significant relationships will be "mankind or 'my kind'", my psychological mode will be "to be, through having been, to face not being", and my main work is to "Develop a sense of acceptance of life as it was lived and the importance of the people and relationships that (I) developed over (my) lifespan". What my husband and I are finding increasingly important to us is the desire to leave a positive legacy for those who come behind us, to leave the world a better place than when we arrived. This kind of legacy has nothing to do with awards, recognition, money, fame, or tangible achievement, but has more to do with meaning, significance, and impact through the relationships that we developed over our lifetime. Have I played the role of daughter, self, wife, mother, friend, neighbor, citizen, mentee, and mentor well? In light of what others have invested in me to help me become the person I am today, how do I use my life experiences to help the younger wives and mothers become even better wives and mothers than me? There is a time to mourn and feel the sadness of our nest emptying, but I firmly believe that the best years of our lives are yet to come when the nest is empty. So many other women have done it, and so can we. In the words of St. Paul:

"Therefore, since we are surrounded by such a great cloud of witnesses, let us throw off everything that hinders and the sin that so easily entangles, and let us run with perseverance the race marked out for us"!

May we all keep our eyes on the end line, and finish well!

EPILOGUE II

Releasing The Arrow

This June I sent my eldest son Caleb out of our home to begin his adult life. This is the first time I am empty nesting, and as the old saying goes, "The first one's the hardest". I had been preparing myself to face this moment, and both my husband and I wrote letters of encouragement and blessing to send him off. Both our letters were written with tears dripping onto our computer keyboards, but then again, I also believe that tears are nature's agents for healing. This is part of what I wrote to Caleb:

"As I reflect on what to write to you to send you off to explore the big wide world, I am filled with gratitude because you have truly been a wonderful gift to me. I am so blessed to have you as my son. Not only that, if you were a stranger on the street, I would naturally want to be your friend because you are a truly great kid! Although raising you has not been without its headaches, with regular trips to the Emergency Room and lots of stories of your childhood escapades to write in my current and future novels, and my furniture has rarely been turned rightside up, the joys of raising you and watching you grow far outweigh those moments of distress. You have always been full of curiosity and wild ideas, but I know that your greatest asset will always be your heart for people.

My "Motherhood" book ends with this analogy of children being like arrows, which are the weapons that I will use to fight this dark and fallen world. I know in the depths of my heart that you were put on this earth for more than just to make money to support a nice lifestyle, but that you have a mission and destiny waiting for you to fulfill. Do not shortchange your inheritance for a bowl of soup! Aim high, keep your ideals, and you know that Daddy and I support you all the way no matter what you choose to do with your life. There is only one life, so make it count, and give the devil a bad headache!

I love you so much, my son! Letting you go is so hard, but I know that you are going to do extremely well. Don't forget to stay in touch and let us know what you are up to. Your home and our hearts will always be open to you, so come home often, even as you go out to conquer the world!"

This is part of what my husband wrote to Caleb:

"I am confident that you are ready for the rigor and challenge of the college life. MIT is a competitive place but you will do well. You have been well equipped and prepared for

academics, social, physical, spiritual, and emotional aspects of life. You are up to the task of any challenge MIT can throw at you and find it within you to excel. Discover your passion and pursue them relentlessly. I know you will make us all proud. I love you for who you are, not because what you do or will do. You will always be special as my first child.

As you stretch out your wings and take flight, as you run into trials and stumbles remember you are loved, and that God is watching over you, and that He who begins the good work in you will carry it on to completion. Run the race marked out for you. Run, persevere, focus on the goal and finish well. Whatever you start, finish well. Choose well, befriend well, and learn well. You will always be in our hearts and our prayers. I confer God's abundant blessings upon you as your father."

When I talk with others about our experience of empty nesting, many would quote to me what celebrated culture critic and Taiwanese essayist Lung Ying-tai wrote in her book "Watching You Go" :

"I slowly, slowly realized that the parent child relationship just means that your predestined affinity in this life is to continually watch the shadow from his back fading farther and farther away. You are standing on one end of this small road, watching him slowly disappear around the bend in the road, and he is silently telling you with his shadow: No need to follow."

This quote produces sadness and a sense of helplessness in parents. I don't feel the same way. Yes, I will miss my first child. Yes, my husband and I held each other and had a good cry before we sent him off to the airport. But the shadow ends there. Lung Ying-tai left her child in Germany to pursue a career. Her son was a stranger to her, so she had to reach out when he became an adult to get to know him and make up for missed time together. She did not share a common history with her son, and he did not grow up sharing her values. She and her husband were divorced, and she was alone. There's a vast difference between that kind of feeling of emptiness and the kind of empty nest when you've had your time with your child and he's ready to be launched from your home, that sense of anticipation and excitement, because your child, the product of your upbringing and hard work, is ready to take on the world! My husband and I still lead full and busy lives, and most important of all, we had our best friends intact – each other. While the configuration of our families has changed, and Caleb's relationship with us has moved online to regular skype chats and exchanges of photos, our lives continue to include one another, and continue to be full. During our last skype session, when we discussed where we want to go for vacation, Caleb would chime in and ask us to reserve that next location for when he's back with us. He uploaded photos of his European trip to Facebook to share with us, we shared with him what we were learning, and we continued to trade jokes and funny YouTube Video links with each other. Our past histories included each other, and our future histories continue to include each other, because we like each other, and like to be with each other, and therefore in the future will choose to be with each other in our plans, even if the frequency of our being physically together will decrease.

Stephen, who worships Caleb as a hero, had the hardest time with Caleb's departure. However, he said that he continued to chat with Caleb regularly via skype, and it didn't feel as if Caleb was gone from our home forever.

Lest you think that coping with the emptying nest is a walk in the park, let me assure you that those feelings of sadness and loss will still overtake you. The family system is like a mobile, with each piece of the mobile being a member of the family. When one leaves, it takes the entire mobile system out of balance, and we all have to adjust ourselves to reach a new balance and equilibrium. The loss of Caleb from our family system in daily living brought about feelings of loss. Here were some things we did to deal with our loss:

1. The evening before Caleb's departure, we all sat together to look through our old photo albums, laughing over all the great and silly memories we were able to share together, giving thanks for one another.

2. After Caleb's departure, we thoroughly cleaned the house, throwing out old unused things and adding new decorative touches.

3. Each of our children took a whole day to clean out their own rooms and rearrange the furniture in their rooms. Having things rearranged in the house reflects the change in our system. It helps not to have to keep looking at the same backdrop scenery to remind us that one of our members is missing.

4.   With Caleb gone and Jonathan getting busying with college applications, we made a decision to look for another family to adopt our dog Nellie. After a 6 month long search, we found a loving family with small children who would have the time for our Nellie. This freed up more of our time and made us more mobile to go on outings and leave the house for the entire day.

5.   With the Lin Family Band missing a member, we had to find new ways to play. Instead of a rock band, we are incorporating our smallest member Stephen, a violin player, and shifting to playing classical music instead. Now Jonathan plays the double bass instead of drums while my husband plays the violin instead of guitar. With a different configuration, it's not as easy to miss our guitar and bass player Caleb.

6.   During this time, my husband and I are finding more time for each other, entering into a new season of renewed romance. Old irritations seem easier to live with, and with a slower pace of life at home, we are finding more contentment in just being with each other.

7.   We are taking time and expressing appreciation for the other two remaining children. They continue to be a blessing and source of companionship for us.

Some parents, especially mothers, fall into depression after their child leaves home for college. While their children are off to a bigger world with exciting new experiences ahead of them, mothers whose lives have revolved around the child only feel the emptiness of the bare room. If the marriage was child-centric, there are also some new bonds to re-establish instead of facing a stranger. Here are some suggestions for empty nesters:

1.   Don't stalk your kids. The first few days Caleb was gone, I checked FaceBook constantly and looked for his email or postings. When I do see a picture or two, my heart would jump with joy and I would leave a comment to encourage him. His friend in Europe apparently played a trick and typed in an update while he wasn't looking. I mistook it for him and commented back, not

understanding that it was a prank and a joke. This greatly embarrassed him, but it was Jonathan who saw the comment and came running out to tell me that parents posting comments on their kids' Facebook pages was bad etiquette. It was called Facebook Stalking! It was a warning for me to let go. I need to move on with my life here. I need to start living with him being preoccupied with building a new life. It's healthy that he doesn't miss us as much as we miss him. I need to stop checking very other hour for news of him.

2. Communicate positively. Try to avoid saying things to make your child feel guilty. Instead of crying over the phone or telling him about how sad you are or how bad things are at home, let him know the new things that are going on in your life, what you're looking forward to (things that don't include him), and how you and your spouse are rediscovering each other.

3. Invest in your marriage, again. After a couple of days of sulking around, my husband started dragging me out again for our nightly walks. It was time for us to find comfort in our friendship, talk about the life we still have together, and plan for our immediate future.

4. Make changes and set new goals. Instead of facing the same house and feeling sad that Caleb is not here, we rearranged the furniture, tried out a new diet, and set some new goals. I'm sure that with each new configuration of the family after each child's departure, we will continue these changes and adjustments. The Lin Family Band evolved from rock to classical. After everyone leaves, it will be back to our original two. When we started dating, my husband was my guitar teacher, and we often played together, him on the guitar, me on the piano. Then we picked up other instruments along the way. I learned the drums while pregnant with Caleb, and the saxophone when pregnant with Stephen. I would love to take the time to get better in both instruments. Who knows, we might try being a Jazz duo when the kids leave! The possibilities are

endless and a little exciting!

5. Pursue new hobbies, find new friends, and build a new and richer life without your child. My husband promised that after the kids leave, he will learn ballroom dancing for me. I promised that I will learn tennis. We are both excited that we will finally have time to enjoy each other's hobbies. In the meantime, we will continue to serve others, whether it's the friends that need help with their marriage, children, work, or just life in general, or the poor, who need the extra financial help to have an opportunity to help themselves, or the broken who need a friend and mentor. Helping others will help ourselves to feel useful and needed, and will make empty nest more fulfilling. Even though are physical children are out of the house, there are plenty of spiritual children around us in need of nurturing.

6. Give thanks for what you've had. There are always things we will regret, whether it's what we said that hurt them, what we didn't say, what we failed to do, or what we did. Take stock, perhaps write it down, and rip up the list and throw it away forever. Instead, write down what you did right, the good times you've had together, how you've grown, how you've seen your child grow, and the common history and values that you share.

Empty nest is a difficult process to go through, but if you proactively work on ensuring a positive transition, empty nest can be one of the most fulfilling times of your life. You have done well, your child is now out of your home and on his own, and now, you can truly begin to live for yourself. The best is yet to come. Enjoy!

ABOUT THE AUTHOR

Both Rossana and her husband grew up bi-cultural in North America and raised their North American born children in China as bi-cultural kids. Rossana's familiarity with both Chinese and Western education systems, both from a student's perspective and a parent's perspective, has enabled her to gain valuable insight on how to combine the best of Chinese and Western practices in parenting and education. She and her husband have raised their three boys in the U.S., Canada, and China, where they have gone to American, local Chinese, and international schools. During their 10 years living, working, and raising 3 school aged boys in Beijing, Rossana developed a career as an author and speaker on marriage, family, and education. She is often interviewed on various national print, radio, and internet media in China.

Made in the USA
Middletown, DE
16 December 2020